HOPE
AND A WHOLE LOTTA
PRAYER

Daily Devotions for Parents of Teenagers

Barbara Canale

Liguori

Imprimi Potest:
Stephen T. Rehrauer, CSsR, Provincial
Denver Province, the Redemptorists

Published by Liguori Publications
Liguori, Missouri 63057

To order, call 800-325-9521 or visit Liguori.org.

Library of Congress Cataloging-in-Publication Data

Canale, Barbara S.
Hope and a whole lotta prayer : daily devotions for parents of teenagers / Barbara Canale.
pages cm

p ISBN 978-0-7648-2582-8
e ISBN 978-0-7648-7034-7

1. Parenting—Religious aspects—Christianity. 2. Child rearing—Religious aspects—Christianity. 3. Parent and teenager—Religious aspects—Christianity. 4. Parents—Prayers and devotions. 5. Devotional calendars. I. Title.
BV4529.C367 2015
242'.645—dc23

2015020531

Liguori Publications, a nonprofit corporation, is an apostolate of the Redemptorists.
To learn more about the Redemptorists, visit Redemptorists.com.

Printed in the United States of America
19 18 17 16 15 / 5 4 3 2 1
First Edition

CONTENTS

DEDICATION

This book is dedicated to Joseph and Barbara Casper, my selfless and generous parents, for having raised me and my siblings with an infinite stream of love, commitment, and encouragement.

INTRODUCTION

Lord, make me an instrument of thy peace.
Where there is hatred, let me sow love;
Where there is injury, pardon;
Where there is doubt, faith;
Where there is despair, hope;
Where there is darkness, light;
And where there is sadness, joy.

O divine Master, grant that I may not so much seek
To be consoled as to console,
To be understood as to understand,
To be loved as to love;
For it is in giving that we receive;
It is in pardoning that we are pardoned;
It is in dying to self that we are born to eternal life.

Prayer of St. Francis of Assisi, circa 1100s

Parenting teenagers isn't easy. Teens deal with everything from hormonal surges to peer pressure. Some become sexually promiscuous or hang with the wrong crowd, possibly experimenting with alcohol and drugs. Some kids lead lives complicated by a medical illnesses or sport injuries. Some may have emotional difficulties, or personality or attachment disorders. It isn't uncommon for teens to be bullied, perform poorly in school, have weight issues, or struggle to make friends. Being a teenager is tough; parenting a teenager is tougher.

Parents of teens face myriad problems each day. The bad news: God never said it would be easy. The good news: Even with problems, life can still be good. I know because I have experienced much of it raising my two daughters. I did it by turning to God in my turmoil and trusting in his miraculous ways. This devotional is specifically for parents to help them cope, to buoy them through turbulent times, and remind them they are not alone. God is there through it all. When parents are faced with hardships, it's essential to cling to something constructive. Prayer is the answer. Not just any prayer, but God's words reminding us that everything happens for a reason. Constant prayer—with repeated and reinforced messages of trust, hope, and love—is woven into this daily devotional. It's a spiritual parenting tool to help manage daily struggles.

Each generation has had to face its own unique set of challenges. However, today's technological advances confront parents with many uncharted trials. It's easy to get discouraged when problems surface. It's understandable to get angry with God when our kids misbehave or become ill. It's reasonable to ask, "Why me, Lord?" Seek comfort in God's words and stories from the Bible. God says he never gives more than we can carry, and as my back was breaking raising teenagers God's soothing words reenergized me and enabled me to move beyond my worries, dilemmas, and sufferings. This uplifting devotional offers relief to Catholic parents carrying the weight of the world on their shoulders.

The daily devotions—which begin with the traditional start of school in September—consist of a Scripture passage, a brief reflection, and a prayer. Take a few minutes as the day begins, before you go to sleep, or any time you're able to make time to read this daily devotional. It's a vitamin to boost the soul. Remember, there isn't anything you and God can't do together—including raise a teenager.

✠ DAILY DEVOTIONS ✠

september 1

STEP OUT

But when he saw how strong the wind was he became frightened; and, beginning to sink, he cried out, "Lord, save me!" Immediately Jesus stretched out his hand and caught him, and said to him, "O you of little faith, why did you doubt?" (Matthew 14:30–31).

When my husband and I offered to teach a confirmation class, we had no idea what was involved. We thought the hard part was agreeing to it. We hoped God would work through us, and he did. However, on one occasion we felt overwhelmed when we took twenty teenagers to a university campus ministry workshop. The kids were rowdy, and it was difficult to keep them together and focused on the topics they were supposed to be learning. In that situation, I, like Peter, felt my faith waver.

An accurate measure of someone's faith isn't the first step of their journey, but the subsequent steps that follow. Have you started something with enthusiasm but become consumed with self-doubt halfway through? Perhaps a family event is not going as planned as reality fails to live up to your high expectations. Something similar occurs when we believe Jesus wants us to do something. We begin enthusiastically, but then it doesn't start unfolding in the way we imagined; we begin to sink with quivering faith, and Jesus appears blurry. If God calls us to take a step toward him, he will provide a way for each step that follows.

REFLECT

Consider where Christ is asking you to walk in faith. Maybe you have been considering involvement in a youth program at church, volunteering more at your parish, or something altogether different. Maybe you have contemplated changing careers, which will impact the time you are able to spend with your kids. Pray on it. God is with you.

✠ PRAY ✠

Dear Heavenly Father,

Calm the rough waters in my life. I know you are there and won't let me drown. In the storm I cannot hear you or see you. Help me, Lord, through these times of torment. I need you, Lord. Don't abandon me. I ask this of you in Jesus' name. Amen.

september 2

BE VIGILANT

Be vigilant at all times and pray that you have the strength to escape the tribulations that are imminent and to stand before the Son of Man (Luke 21:36).

News outlets report school shootings, where innocent students are gunned down in their own classrooms. These are not isolated incidents and are becoming more common than many parents want to admit. While administrators try to keep students safe by implementing safety precautions, rogue shooters still manage to infiltrate security barriers and create havoc in schools. It's no wonder parents teach their kids to be vigilant when they leave home. We live in a scary world, and all we can do is trust in God's plan—whatever it is.

God's plan is for a community concerned about each other and providing help in a variety of forms. God's plan is centered on peace, love, and forgiveness. God's plan is to provide a safe place for us and our families to grow and learn. At the first sign of danger, call out to the Holy Spirit to empower you to escape the evils that surround you. Maybe it's not a gun you are worried about. Maybe it's your teen's exposure to drugs or alcohol. Maybe it's an apathetic attitude toward faith and religion. Whatever your fear, ask the Holy Spirit to help you handle it in a way that's best for your teen and builds up your family community.

REFLECT

Start with prayer in your home. Use holy water to make a Sign of the Cross on your teen's forehead each day before school. Ask God to keep your son safe and to be vigilant against the evil forces of the world. Remember that with God, anything is possible.

✠ PRAY ✠

Dear Heavenly Father,

Keep (name) safe in school today. Don't let harm fall upon him. Shine your love down upon us today as we strive to make this world a better place. I ask this in Jesus' name. Amen.

september 3

RELEASE

For freedom Christ set us free; so stand firm and do not submit again to the yoke of slavery (Galatians 5:1).

Most of us cannot know what it's like to be freed from slavery or prison. In watching Victor Hugo's 1862 novel-turned-movie *Les Misérables,* I sensed a sliver of the freedom Jean Valjean felt after being released from prison for stealing bread to feed his family. I could almost feel the weight of his ball and chain being removed.

Today's Bible passage is a declaration of our freedom—Christ has freed us! That freedom was given to us through Jesus' death and resurrection. Holy Scripture declares that the whole world has been a prisoner of "sin, that through faith in Jesus Christ the promise might be given to those who believe" (3:22). Freedom is a gift from the Lord, given and received by faith. But that kind of freedom comes with a price. We have to obey God. And obeying God means we sometimes don't get what we want.

Some teens do whatever they desire, believing it isn't fair to deny themselves anything. Think for a moment what your teenager might be in constant pursuit of: more money, better technology, fame. As parents, we sometimes have to say "no," and it's hard for our teen to see that "no" as a way to freedom. Remember: When you say "no," say it with love.

REFLECT

Focus on the freedom from oppression that comes from making your way to God; the freedom from sin, guilt, and condemnation. God beseeches us to take his strength and walk in that freedom and not be tangled again with a burden of bondage.

✠ PRAY ✠

Dear Heavenly Father,

Thank you for the gift of freedom and for clearing a path for me to you. Thank you for your guidance when I wander off. Let me lean into your strength and love every day of my life. I truly love you, Lord. Amen.

september 4

ONE BODY

As a body is one though it has many parts, and all the parts of the body, though many, are one body, so also Christ (1 Corinthians 12:12).

When my daughters played in the pit band for their high school musical, I was able to appreciate all the parts that made the show happen: actors, costume designers, backdrop builders, and stage crew. Without the parts coming together as one, the show can't happen. The Corinthians passage reminded me of the school performances. Each student brought a different skill or talent to the performance and, working as one, put on the show.

We all come from vast walks of life, are baptized, and celebrate the Lord's Supper without consideration to differences. Saint Paul implies that all body parts are essential and no one part is better than the other. He also states we honor "our less presentable parts " (1 Corinthians 12:23) by clothing them with greater care.

God constructed the body to give greater honor to the lowly members; there is no dissension in the body. All members are concerned for one another. When peer pressure is so thick you can cut it with a knife, it's challenging to teach our kids to embrace everyone, be kind, gentle, and loving, especially if classmates ostracize our kids. Sometimes it's difficult for teens to find their place in life when they don't fit the mold of their classmates or neighbors.

REFLECT

Whatever your teen's difference is, celebrate that uniqueness as a gift from God and encourage your child to embrace and celebrate the uniqueness in their peers.

✠ PRAY ✠

Dear Heavenly Father,

Bless my family with the ability to overlook faults and focus on the attributes that make them outstanding. Help me to look at the bigger picture and stop dwelling on (name)'s problems. Enable me to find the gifts in my teenager so I can help her to be a caring and responsible adult. Amen.

september 5

FORGIVENESS RULES

All bitterness, fury, anger, shouting, and reviling must be removed from you, along with all malice. And be kind to one another, compassionate, forgiving one another as God has forgiven you in Christ (Ephesians 4:31–32).

Whenever I feel angry, I take a walk. I begin with fast strides, having considerable energy to burn, but then I slow down as I listen to the birds singing in the trees. Sometimes I get lost looking at nature, the beauty of the changing foliage, the way the leaves rustle as a gentle breeze blows through them. Then I thank God for allowing me to step away and enjoy all he created. Before I know it, my anger has dissipated and I can think logically about what upset me.

Sometimes I am unable to solve my dilemmas, but I trust in God's plan. I give my problems to God and continue living. It sounds lovely, doesn't it? But it isn't easy to do when you feel your blood boiling and you want to wring someone's neck. Forgiveness isn't easy, but Christ wants us to be compassionate and loving creatures. It's a choice: Hold on to anger or let it go. Holding on to rage gnaws at you, creating bitterness and resentment. It prevents you from learning, growing, and moving forward. Forgiveness doesn't mean you weren't hurt but that you care more about your relationship than "getting even" or being vindicated.

Has your teenager hurt you recently? What have you done about it?

Let go of your teen's problems without letting go of the kid. You can never stop loving your teen, no matter how deep the pain is.

REFLECT

The willingness to accept an offense and move on is liberating. Forgiveness keeps disappointments from clouding our view of life. It allows us to see someone's faults and help. It also warns us to avoid similar situations in the future. Forgiveness draws us closer to God because when we forgive we are living the life he intended for us.

✠ PRAY ✠

Dear Heavenly Father,

Touch my aching heart with your mercy and love. Fill me up with goodness so I can be more forgiving to (name). Let me rise above it, learn, and grow in the joy you put into my world. I love you. Amen.

september 6

FORGIVENESS HAS ETERNAL SIGNIFICANCE

If you forgive others their transgressions, your heavenly Father will forgive you. But if you do not forgive others, neither will your Father forgive your transgressions (Matthew 6:14–15).

Have you ever wondered why it's so hard to forgive? Perhaps our brains are hard-wired to retaliate when someone hurts us. But what if our kids upset us through disappointment? Consider how you've become disillusioned. Does your child act careless or unappreciative? As parents we want to teach our kids and help them learn from their mistakes, which usually entails some form of punishment. We justify it by saying, "It's our job to teach them right from wrong."

Remember that our kids' brains are still developing. They're still learning coping skills. Teenagers will become infuriated or frustrated by outside circumstances with friends, teachers, teammates, bosses, or coworkers. Because you are a "safe" person, they will take their exasperations out on you. Recognize misdirected anger when you see it. Then, relay to your teens how their comments made you feel without degrading them. Remind them that you will always love them and help them through any situation, especially difficult ones that weigh on their heart.

REFLECT

Teach your teen how to learn from a problem and move on. Don't keep reliving it or bringing it up. Focus on forgiveness, teaching your kid that sometimes we need to forgive ourselves, too. Forgiveness has eternal significance because if you are unwilling to forgive others, God will not forgive you. Forgive as you have been forgiven.

✠ PRAY ✠

Dear Heavenly Father,

Sometimes (name) knows exactly what buttons to push to annoy me. Give me the patience to get to the bottom of the teen's insecurities and troubles. Grant me the wisdom to react to situations as you would and not out of anger. I trust in your plan. Guide us, Lord, to the place you mean for us to be. I ask this in Jesus' name. Amen.

september 7

TRIALS

My child, when you come to serve the Lord, prepare yourself for trials. Be sincere of heart and steadfast, and do not be impetuous in time of adversity. Cling to him, do not leave him, that you may prosper in your last days (Sirach 2:1–3).

When you agree to do God's work, don't expect smooth sailing. If you encounter spurts of calmness, celebrate it. Consider the rest a reward for a job well done. If you question your worthiness, ask for God's blessing. If you believe you're unsuccessful, God might be glad for your enthusiasm, your commitment, and perseverance despite the hardships you encounter. Trials are not supposed to be easy or pleasant.

What trial have you been struggling with? Has your daughter shown signs of an eating disorder or other dangerous behavior? Are you concerned for her future? Worried about the influence of her friends? Trust that God will not leave you in your time of need. He has the answers to everything. But don't expect the solutions to be easy.

REFLECT

Consider talking to an expert in the field to gain more wisdom about the issues that are troubling you or your teen. Ask God to bring the perfect person into your life for help. Discuss with your spouse the best methods to overcome your teenager's problems or your concerns. It's OK to cry and grieve. Having an outlet for your stress will serve you well. Get involved in a craft or project where you can be creative. Could you learn how to build a birdhouse or paint your living room a new color? Perhaps it would be helpful to write about your feelings. This might be a good time to exercise your stress away. Consider using a treadmill or take a long walk with your spouse, a good friend, or confidant. Whatever you choose, incorporate prayer, too.

✠ PRAY ✠

Dear Heavenly Father,

Help me through this difficulty as I flail in a sea of misery. Enable me to stay focused and be helpful to (name) as we work through these issues with your loving guidance. Amen.

september 8

STOP, PRAY, MOVE ON

Then the Lord *said to Moses: Why are you crying out to me? Tell the Israelites to set out* (Exodus 14:15).

When Moses was leading the people out of Egypt, Pharaoh's army was catching up to them as they approached the Red Sea. Moses had to decide whether to go on or stop and pray. In our own lives we face myriad tough choices and must make that decision for ourselves.

What recent decisions have you struggled to make? Perhaps you encouraged your teenager to enroll in a school program that you now question or you prompted your son to drop a class or sport that could have repercussions. You might be questioning every decision you've made!

We all run into barriers just as Moses did with the Red Sea. When this happens we can question what God called us to do. Moses had no way of knowing that the roadblock he encountered would actually end up saving the Israelites. When we are faced with opposition, let's stop to rethink it, pray on it, and reevaluate it. God calls us, guides us, and protects us. God has no boundaries and no limits or restrictions. We have to trust in God even when we don't understand.

REFLECT

What obstacle in your path has stymied or altered your decisions? Maybe God wants you to stop questioning and move forward with confidence that he has your back and knows exactly what he is doing, even though you don't know. You are not supposed to know everything.

✠ PRAY ✠

Dear Heavenly Father,

Guide me as I walk the path you have established for me. Give me the confidence to move on knowing you are watching over me, directing every step I take, every move I make. Help me to see around the barricades; enable me to navigate them on my journey. Let me choose to see obstacles as gifts that you have positioned for my benefit. You are my loving Lord; thank you for having mercy on my soul. Amen.

september 9

BE PART OF THE SOLUTION

A mild answer turns back wrath, but a harsh word stirs up anger (Proverbs 15:1).

Throughout my childhood, whenever I became angry, my mom would say, "Bite your tongue." Back then, hearing those words infuriated me; now, I appreciate the pearls of wisdom. As a teenager, I remember wanting to give people a piece of my mind, but Mom's advice was to mull it over and pray on it. A friend of mine says, "Do you want to be part of the problem or part of the solution?"

Think about being a spectator at your teen's sporting events. It's one thing to cheer for our kids; however, it's unacceptable when parents heckle other players, parents, coaches, or the referee. Poor sportsmanship and acts of aggression have become common in youth sports and anywhere else our teens may be competing. Don't get caught up in that atmosphere. Instead, remember that Jesus would be kind and lead through example.

Proverbs reminds us a mild response turns back anger. Imagine whacking a hornet's nest. What good comes out of that? It's easy to fight back instinctively, especially if we feel our child has been wronged. That's why we have to ask the Holy Spirit to fill us with right words and actions—before we react.

REFLECT

It's important to speak nicely to other people, to be sympathetic, and considerate to others regardless of the situation you find yourself in. It's essential to think before you speak to set aside hostilities, exasperations, or complaints that can possibly create tension. Teach your daughter to focus on perfecting her own personal growth in a sport while being challenged by the efforts of her team.

✠ PRAY ✠

Dear Heavenly Father,

Wash away the bitterness that lingers from ill feelings. Replace it with loving thoughts and desires to spread your indelible joy, infectious kindheartedness, and divine mercy to people I meet today. Even if I feel they don't deserve it. Teach me, Lord, to be more like you. Amen.

september 10

CENTER ON GOD

Arise and go down to the potter's house; there you will hear my word. I went down to the potter's house and there he was, working at the wheel. Whenever the vessel of clay he was making turned out badly in his hand, he tried again, making another vessel of whatever sort he pleased (Jeremiah 18:2–4).

A potter can transform a lump of mud on a spinning wheel into art. The clay must be centered correctly or it will be off-balance, forcing the potter to struggle with it the entire time. Potters smack the clay down, knowing the success of the pot depends on the centering.

In today's passage from Jeremiah, the potter made pots that turned out badly. Some might have been off-center or had flaws making them weak or lopsided. We are all imperfect earthen vessels, and our families can easily get off-center. When we're off-center it's easy to see things aren't right and focus on the flaws. But like the potter we also have to see the potential for good. If you have been noticing your teenager's faults more than usual, remember that even flawed pots can be treasures.

All families are centered on different things: education, travel, spending time in nature, sports, or friends. What is your family centered on? Refocus more on God and everything else will fall into place.

REFLECT

Make time to attend Mass as a family, even if you have to miss a football game or school function. Make an effort to eat together as a family, giving thanks to God for the food you eat. Make God a priority in your life.

✠ PRAY ✠

Dear Heavenly Father,

Thank you for loving me despite my flaws. Teach me how to be more loving toward (name) and overlook his mistakes. I love you, Lord and want to be more Christlike. Help me, Lord. Amen.

september 11

REBUILD

Afterward I said to them: "You see the trouble we are in: how Jerusalem lies in ruins and its gates have been gutted by fire. Come, let us rebuild the wall of Jerusalem, so that we may no longer be a reproach!" Then I explained to them how God had shown his gracious favor to me, and what the king had said to me. They replied, "Let us begin building!" And they undertook the work with vigor (Nehemiah 2:17–18).

We will remember for years to come what we were doing when the planes hit the World Trade Center in New York. We will remember the decimation of Ground Zero with profound sadness: the lives lost, the injured, the responders, the bystanders, and the construction workers. A recent visit to the new memorial and museum demonstrates that we can rebuild and keep going. Remembering the tragedy of 9/11 reminded me of Nehemiah's story about the annihilation of Jerusalem, his home. It was rubble, but he acquired money to rebuild, so they began working vigorously.

Disastrous times unite people, as in New York City and Jerusalem. People rolled up their sleeves and got to work doing whatever they could to help, whether it was offering a hug, a plate of food, or a needed skill. You may feel that your relationship with your teen is beyond repair, but there is always a chance to rebuild and allow it to become something new.

REFLECT

Has there been damage to your relationship with your teenager? How can you start to rebuild it today? Maybe you could offer a smile when you really feel like crying, or you could offer financial assistance, or a morale boost. Perhaps there has been spiritual ruin. Call out to God right now for help with this. He will hold you in the palm of his hand. With whatever devastation you are grappling with, remember to act on it as Nehemiah did. Let God's love cement your brokenness back together.

✠ PRAY ✠

Dear Heavenly Father,

Save me, Lord! I cannot bear the pain that engulfs me. Shield me from the anguish that surrounds me. Invigorate me with your bounty and endless stream of affection. Help me rebuild my relationship with (name). Teach me how, Lord. I ask this in Jesus' name. Amen.

september 12

FOLLOW GOD

It is he whom we proclaim, admonishing everyone and teaching everyone with all wisdom, that we may present everyone perfect in Christ. For this I labor and struggle, in accord with the exercise of his power working within me (Colossians 1:28–29).

It's not good enough to send your kids to school. Teens also need proper nutrition, exercise, rest, and spiritual nurturing. If one element is lacking, everything is out of whack. If your kids don't eat right, they can become ill. The same thing holds true for not maintaining a deep and interpersonal relationship with God.

Teach your kids to pray constantly in the silence of their heart. God hears everyone's prayers and he'll answer them on his terms. This might mean that you or your teen will have to wait and trust in God's plan. Waiting can be the hard part. Teach your son to surrender entirely to God, because our Lord will never abandon him. God will shower his followers with an infinite stream of love and abundant blessings. God has something wonderful in store for those who love him!

You might feel it's necessary to give your teenager everything he wants and not just what he needs. The best phone or laptop won't make him better or smarter. Those gadgets might make him more popular, but where will that status take him? Eventually, a newer model will hit store shelves and he'll want that. Perhaps what your teenager needs the most is hope. Hope gives your teenager a reason to live and something to strive for. That kind of hope comes from Jesus Christ.

REFLECT

Jesus calls us to serve, so we obey. Christ loves us, therefore we love others. Sometimes, expressing that love calls us to do extraordinary things, like take a mission trip, lead a youth group, or teach religion. Jesus calls us each day to make the most of it. What will you do with this day?

✠ PRAY ✠

Dear Heavenly Father,

I exalt you, Lord and adore having you in my life to guide my footsteps. Teach me how to influence (name) to pray and develop a relationship with you. I want to serve you every day of my life. Amen.

september 13

TRUST IN TINY STEPS

[Then, Jesus said,] the one who had received two talents also came forward and said, "Master, you gave me two talents. See, I have made two more." His master said to him, "Well done, my good and faithful servant. Since you were faithful in small matters, I will give you great responsibilities. Come, share your master's joy" (Matthew 25:22–23).

Some teenagers get overwhelmed trying to decide what they want to be when they grow up. Will they learn a trade, enter the armed forces, or go to college? How many kids wonder what God's plan is for them and how that will impact their dreams for their own life? I taught my daughters that it's similar to braiding someone's hair: It's a slow process with many steps that looks messy and confusing. You have to incorporate stray hair that falls out and smooth down clumps along the way. But before you know it, the braid is complete and it looks beautiful.

Like the completed braid, teenagers want to see the "big picture" of their life, not the little steps here, there, and everywhere. That's too confusing. They want to know what God's plan is for them so they can approve or decline it. If people told me in high school that I would adopt two orphans from Romania, I would've said they were nuts. But God led me there by taking minuscule steps here and there. If God had shown me the big picture in high school, I would have been shocked and might not have believed it.

REFLECT

God will take your teen to where she needs to be on a slow and steady journey. We begin to see the big picture become a reality when we're faithful to the relationships, opportunities, and needs God has already put in front of us. Lead your teen by example, and be OK with starting small.

✠ PRAY ✠

Dear Heavenly Father,

Grant me an opportunity to serve within my home and community. Thank you for only giving me what I can handle right now and being satisfied with small stages. Since they are from you, they are significant. I will follow you, Lord, one tiny step at a time. Amen.

september 14

TRADITIONS

[Jesus] responded, "Well did Isaiah prophesy about you hypocrites, as it is written: 'This people honors me with their lips, but their hearts are far from me; In vain do they worship me, teaching as doctrines human precepts.' You disregard God's commandment but cling to human tradition" (Mark 7:6–8).

As a teenager, my parents bought me new shoes at the beginning of each new school year. It was a family tradition I anticipated with much enthusiasm. A tradition I anticipated with less enthusiasm was covering my head with a lace scarf, called a chapel veil, each time I entered church.

In today's Scripture, Jesus reacts to how the Pharisees judged him because he broke their hand-washing tradition, which was initially meant to honor God. However, we are not always honoring God when we uphold cultural rituals or force others to do things the exact same way we do.

Are you judgmental about something that isn't one of God's commandments? Maybe it's the way your teen dresses to attend Mass, his aloofness during Mass, or his lack of participation that bothers you. Don't be like the Pharisees and let your teen's church-time behavior irk you. Remember the most important part: Your kid is attending Mass! Many teens reject their parents' way of doing things, but that doesn't mean they aren't open to God's commandments.

REFLECT

Emphasize what Jesus calls you to do instead of what a tradition requires you to do. Help your teens find something in the faith that resonates with them, even if it's not the way you'd do it.

✠ PRAY ✠

Dear Heavenly Father,

Teach me how to overlook the irritations (names) express before they go to church. Let me focus on the fact that we are together, praying as a family, honoring you, sweet Lord. Help me to put everything into proper perspective. You are vital to my well-being. Without you, I am nothing. Amen.

september 15

RAINY DAYS

For a persistent leak on a rainy day the match is a quarrelsome wife; Whoever would hide her hides a stormwind and cannot tell north from south (Proverbs 27:15–16).

Imagine a rainy day living in a house with a shoddy roof that leaks. You want to go out but because of the downpour, you stay put. At home you're uncomfortable because of the dripping inside. Have you ever been bothered by a dripping faucet? Today's passage suggests that irksome noise is like a quarrelsome woman. The dripping is maddening! Likewise, the sounds of nagging, constant arguing, and jabbing with barbs are similarly annoying.

A long soaking rain isn't necessarily a bad thing. In fact, it makes the flowers and gardens grow. Rain on a secure house makes a pleasant sound. On rainy days, I bake cookies, watch old movies, or read a good book. Rain in and of itself is good. It's the constant dripping noise inside that destroys peace.

Who is destroying the peace in your home? Is your teenager constantly questioning you? Is she debating, disputing, or disagreeing with you? A continual drip is exasperating and destructive. You might want to escape the noise, but where can you go? Why are some teenagers so obnoxious?

Do you frequently argue with your teen? Are you continuously nagging with phrases like, "Pick up your stuff," "Clean your room," or, "Is your homework done?" When you begin to feel this way, call out to God to rescue you from this downward spiral.

REFLECT

This could be a chance to set new guidelines for the start of a new school year. Create a routine that works well for everyone. Maybe, when she gets home she can have a snack and then do homework until dinnertime. Devise a realistic plan that will be easy to adhere to. The more complicated it is, the more likely you will find holes in it that will let "rain" drip through.

✠ PRAY ✠

Dear Heavenly Father,

Save me, Lord, from the bickering in our home.
Wash away the soot of disparity that crept into our home
and replace it with the bright sunshine of your love. Amen.

september 16

OVERCOMING TEMPTATIONS

Now the snake was the most cunning of all the wild animals that the LORD God had made. He asked the woman, "Did God really say, 'You shall not eat from any of the trees in the garden'?" (Genesis 3:1).

I created an oasis in the back yard for birds, attracting a motley assortment of delightful creatures. A hawk uses this sanctuary as a hunting ground. The hawk is like the evil lurking in our world seeking easy prey. There are many temptations waiting for us the way Satan tricked Eve.

Ever since Eve ate the forbidden fruit, our hearts have been tormented with a struggle between good and sin. Satan constantly exploits our physical and emotional desires to sever our relationship with God. While God calls us to holiness, it's difficult to resist desires of the carnal heart. Remember that God is always with us and can help us through any difficulty, especially temptations. God can provide everything necessary to resist evil and keep us strong against all wicked enticements.

Are you tired of another routine to adjust to as your kids brace for another year of classes, sports, and activities? Are you tempted to skip parent-teacher orientations this year? Are you tempted not to volunteer this year? Is your teenager being tempted to do something harmful? Maybe your teen is hanging out with the wrong crowd, skipping classes, getting poor grades, or dressing inappropriately for school. It's not easy for kids to say no to peer pressure. Whatever our temptations are, God will help us through them. Use the best protection we have against temptation: Pray—often! Jesus turned to prayer to resist temptation. Therefore, we should, too.

REFLECT

Encourage your teen to pay attention to her own beliefs about what is right and wrong. That will help her determine the right thing to do.

✠ PRAY ✠

Dear Heavenly Father,

Help (name) to develop the confidence to walk away
from the evils lurking at school.
Give me the courage to be supportive
and loving even when I'm tempted not to. Amen.

september 17

LOST SOUL

What man among you having a hundred sheep and losing one of them would not leave the ninety-nine in the desert and go after the lost one until he finds it? And when he does find it, he sets it on his shoulders with great joy and, upon his arrival home, he calls together his friends and neighbors and says to them, "Rejoice with me because I have found my lost sheep." I tell you, in just the same way there will be more joy in heaven over one sinner who repents than over ninety-nine righteous people who have no need of repentance (Luke 15:4–7).

This passage gives great hope to those who have sinned and seek forgiveness. In different situations, there are times when we are all three characters. Sometimes we're the ninety-nine faithful who stay because we're good. Sometimes we're the lost sheep who has gone astray. Sometimes we're the shepherd. Which character are you today?

My daughter had a texting problem: She didn't know when to stop. She texted throughout the night, during classes, while she did homework, constantly. There was no end to it. When she lived at home and I paid the phone bill, it was easier to control. I set the rules, and if she wanted the phone, she had to obey them. After her first year of college, she was the lost lamb who wandered off course. Even though I brought my lost sheep home, I had to stay vigilant to ensure she didn't drift away again.

REFLECT

Consider ways you can prevent your teenagers from wandering. Try spending more quality time with them. Go for a walk with them. If there is a particular sport they enjoy, participate in it with them, even if it's something you normally wouldn't do. Go on an outing, just you and your teens. Look for ways to let your kids know that you appreciate their uniqueness.

✠ PRAY ✠

Dear Heavenly Father,

Thank you for the ability to embrace (name) and keep him from going astray. Amen.

september 18

ATTEND MASS

We should not stay away from our assembly, as is the custom of some, but encourage one another, and this all the more as you see the day drawing near (Hebrews 10:25).

What teenager doesn't like to sleep in? Maybe he stayed out late the night before hanging with friends. For some parents it's difficult to get their teen up and ready for Sunday Mass. Has your child fallen away from God or is he indifferent to going to church? When it comes to faith, most teens are "cradle Catholics," riding their parent's coattails to church. If you want your teenager to value his religion, teach him how to have a relationship with Jesus. Help your son to strengthen his faith through daily prayer.

Before my daughters ran out of the house each morning, I blessed them with holy water, making a Sign of the Cross on their foreheads and saying a quick prayer to help them face difficulties they might encounter throughout their day. Riding the school bus, classmates, exams, difficult lab partners, cranky teachers, appointments with guidance counselors, gym class, and lunchroom activities created tension in their school day. When kids are reminded that they don't have to face these difficulties alone because the Holy Spirit is with them, they are more at peace with themselves. Our mealtime conversations were opportunities to share moments when we experienced God's love throughout the day.

REFLECT

Teach your teenager to notice God's gifts, to recognize him in other people, to hear his voice, and to thank him for his blessings. Cultivate a friendship with God at home by saying nightly prayers, perhaps after dinner, before homework, or at bedtime. Kids are never too old to share bedtime prayers. The better job we've done fostering our kids' personal spirituality at home, the less we have to force them to go to church.

✠ PRAY ✠

Dear Heavenly Father,

Empower me to enlighten (name) about you and your marvelous ways. Teach me, Lord, what I should say and do to spark a burning curiosity in you and desire to seek you in all things. Amen.

september 19

A PROMISE IS A PROMISE

When a man makes a vow to the LORD or binds himself under oath to a pledge, he shall not violate his word, but must fulfill exactly the promise he has uttered (Numbers 30:3).

An auto parts worker vowed to split any lottery winnings with his restaurant server as her tip. He did win and honored the promise, giving her $92,000. He was a man of his word. Today, it's hard to find people who value keeping promises.

Has your teenager broken a promise he made to you? Maybe he broke his promise to find a job or get good grades. Maybe your kid had honorable intentions and truly wanted to fulfill his vow but wasn't able to for good reasons.

For some people, saying they will do something feels just as good as actually doing it. Their intentions begin genuine and admirable, declaring them publicly makes them feel accountable, but then they are unable to carry it through. Perhaps you could encourage your teen to keep intentions private and speak through actions. Try to understand why your teenager talks a big talk but is unable to go the distance. Let him know that small steps can be better than grand gestures.

REFLECT

Lead through example. If it's hard to do, remember that Jesus led by example. When your adolescent sees you practicing what you preach and following through, he has a model.

✠ PRAY ✠

Dear Heavenly Father,

Keep me strong as I aspire to live a more Christlike life. Enable (name) to grasp all that is necessary to live a life revolving around Jesus. Help me with my vulnerability. I ask this in Jesus' name. Amen.

september 20

INTIMATE RELATIONSHIP WITH GOD

Even all the hairs of your head are counted (Matthew 10:30).

My daughters hated having their hair brushed. Their friends would brush each other's hair, but my girls didn't want any part of it. Recently, one daughter got head lice and needed meticulous combing for several weeks to pick out the myriad nits attached to her hair. By the time we eradicated the lice, I spent so much time examining each hair on her head that I came to know her on a more intimate level. This experience bonded us in a way we weren't expecting. She had to stop working, offering us more time alone; friends and family avoided our home until we were lice-free. The louse episode had benefits that we both embraced and appreciated. I thought of Matthew's words, how God knows each hair on our head, and I gained a better appreciation for it.

Have you had an untimely incident occur that had the potential to take down your entire family, but instead you found the silver lining? It isn't easy to do, especially with a head full of bloodsucking parasites! However, one positive is that you have an opportunity to get to know your teen better, maybe on a level you didn't expect. If something unfortunate strikes, put it into perspective and stay grounded.

REFLECT

God seeks a closer, more intimate relationship with us, too. In order to do that, we have to step away with the Lord and spend quality time getting to know "each hair on his head," too!

✠ PRAY ✠

Dear Heavenly Father,

Help me to establish a more intimate relationship with you.
I want to rejoice in the splendor that I will find in your
gracious mercy and love. You alone are my God and Savior;
you are all I want and need. Amen.

september 21

GOD IS BESIDE YOU

I command you: be strong and steadfast! Do not fear nor be dismayed, for the LORD, your God, is with you wherever you go (Joshua 1:9).

There have been many mornings that I wanted to pull the bed covers over my head and refuse to get up and face the day. Have you ever felt like that? Sometimes I lack the courage to stand up against the evils of the world because it takes such great effort, but running and hiding isn't an option. When I remember that God is with me, I am filled with joy, because whatever I face, God will face with me.

Contemplate all of the things you have in your life that truly matter to you: God, your spouse, your children, your extended family. Those precious gifts cannot be replaced. Everything else can be reacquired. If your teenager has dented the car fender, remember that it can be fixed. The tragedy would have been an injury—or worse—to your child.

REFLECT

What situation have you been avoiding with your teenager? Maybe you need to talk about a sensitive topic that you fear will escalate into a heated debate. Put each topic you need to discuss in its proper category before you decide how to talk about it with your teen. How important is it? Is it worth creating tension over? Is it something you can let go? Remember that God will help you through it. Keep your rosary beads in your pocket as a reminder that you are not alone. God can help you speak words of wisdom.

✠ PRAY ✠

Dear Heavenly Father,

You are my saving grace and inspiration for everything I think, say, and do. Thank you, Father, for doing everything with me. You strengthen me with your love and devotion. Let me do the same for (name). Amen.

september 22

JOURNEY ONWARD

For if anyone thinks he is something when he is nothing, he is deluding himself. Each one must examine his own work, and then he will have reason to boast with regard to himself alone, and not with regard to someone else; for each will bear his own load
(Galatians 6:3–5).

Sometimes orientation seminars are offered to acclimate parents to the changes they could experience as kids enter middle school. When I attended this seminar, I looked at the other parents wondering if their kids would be my daughter's friend. Would their kid take mine to the school dances? Would they work at the same places, attend the same colleges, or marry? We would travel this span of school highs and lows together. We began the journey as strangers but would eventually come to know and enjoy (or loathe) one another's company.

This passage reminds us that we are all fellow travelers through life. Some people think they are better than others because of their education or profession, others compare children's accomplishments to determine who is the "best" parent. Do you know anyone like this? Today's Bible passage suggests that we all need to do our own work and be honest about our burdens and shortcomings.

REFLECT

The better we understand our own ways and thoughts, the less likely we'll despise the efforts of others. The more we realize our heart's capacity to love and forgive, the more likely it is that we'll be able to support those with weaknesses and shortcomings and teach our teens to do the same.

✠ PRAY ✠

Dear Heavenly Father,

Show me how to transform myself into a better parent, a wiser leader, a nicer friend, a kinder person. Grant me the ability to change gracefully into a more knowledgeable student and to be more mindful of my own actions and how they affect everyone around me. Lord Jesus, I ask this in your sweet and holy name. Amen.

september 23

THE NEWNESS OF AUTUMN

[Jesus said,] "Do you not say, 'In four months the harvest will be here?' I tell you, look up and see the fields ripe for the harvest" (John 4:35).

Each spring I watch my dad plant his garden. While he waits for the plants to grow, he waters, fertilizes, and weeds faithfully. Mom constantly questions his progress with, "What's ready to be eaten?" Dad reassures her that in time she'll have her reward. Waiting isn't easy to do.

Today's Scripture passage reminds me that the amount of time necessary to save souls is comparable to the farmer's wait to harvest his crop. Paul spent much time in Galatia spreading the word of God. He knew he would reap the benefits of his efforts at some point, but he had to be patient as the word took root.

We live in a world of immediate rewards. On Independence Day, a lit sparkler emits an instant burst of brilliant sparks. Imagine lighting a sparkler or firecracker and waiting ten minutes for it to work. Who would want that? We want instant gratification, but sometimes God wants us to wait. We all have to wait to get to heaven, which will be more wonderful than a sky full of fireworks, but eventually we will get there.

REFLECT

Are you the parent of a teenager who has abandoned the faith, morals, or values you instilled over the years? Does your teenager put up a fuss about attending Mass or youth group? Continue loving and caring for your child, even if it's hard to do. Don't allow your teenager to wear you down. When you start to feel discouraged, recharge by praying. God will hear and answer you, but you might have to wait.

✠ PRAY ✠

Dear Heavenly Father,

Help me to be patient while I wait. Enable me to see the fruits of my labor, Lord. I have worked so hard. Please don't let it be in vain. I ask this in Jesus' name. Amen.

september 24

U R GR8

The whole world had the same language and the same words
(Genesis 11:1).

Imagine moving to a remote village in Japan without knowing a word of Japanese. Not knowing the language would make life challenging. Do you speak the same language as your teenager?

Many parents complain they feel distant from their teens. Sometimes "attitude" is the only way kids know how to deal with tense situations at home. They would rather walk away from an unpleasant situation than have it erupt. You might feel like you and your teenager are living in two totally different worlds even though you live in the same house.

Try putting yourself in your teen's situation before you begin a discussion. Put your emotions on hold. It isn't easy to do, especially if you are hurt by your teen's behavior. Remember that teens' brains aren't fully developed and they lack skills. It's your job as the parent to guide your kid toward better choices. Solicit input from your daughter on ways to solve personal dilemmas. When your teen notices that you believe in her ability to work out problems, she might develop more confidence to make wiser choices.

REFLECT

Consider learning how to communicate the way your teen does, through text, email, or social media—even if that means creating your own accounts. Don't make these methods the only way you talk, but make them part of your communications portfolio. Try to send one compliment each day. Perhaps you could send something like, "I am the luckiest parent in the world to have a kid as nice as you. Thank you for taking out the trash!" Teens respond favorably to praise and acknowledgment.

✠ PRAY ✠

Dear Heavenly Father,

Bless the conversations I have with (name). Let my heart drive my words so that I build up my offspring's self-esteem. Show me ways to be inspirational, loving, and kind. I ask this in your sweet name, Jesus. Amen.

september 25

SEEK AND YOU WILL FIND

And [Jesus said] I tell you, ask and you will receive; seek and you will find; knock and the door will be opened to you. For everyone who asks, receives; and the one who seeks, finds; and to the one who knocks,the door will be opened (Luke 11:9–10).

Christ inspires us to pray intensely and constantly. He wants us to ask him for what we need. God might not answer right away, but he will respond. Sometimes the reply is not what we want, but God wants us to be open to accept it. Maybe God wants us to look deeper into a particular situation to find the answer concealed in it or to discover something to be grateful for while continuing to bombard heaven with persistent prayer.

Try to find the positive hidden inside the negative you are currently dealing with. For example, if your child was arrested, maybe that was necessary in order to get her help with a problem you have been in denial about. Maybe your daughter has just told you she is pregnant. Maybe your teenager is addicted to drugs. Or maybe it is something totally out of anyone's control, like cancer or illness. Celebrate that your child is alive right now. No matter how bad things may seem today, you can give your problems to God and he will give you strength. Keep praying because everyone who asks, receives.

REFLECT

Take time today to consider how God has answered your prayers. Is there an opportunity you need to take? A difficult conversation you need to have?

✠ PRAY ✠

Dear Heavenly Father,

Please, Lord, help me through the difficulty that my family now faces. It is overwhelming and consuming us. Remove it from me, if that is your will. Give me the strength and courage to overcome it and journey on in your grace and love. I ask this in Jesus' name. Amen.

september 26

PRAY EACH DAY

The next day, while they were on their way and nearing the city, Peter went up to the roof terrace to pray at about noontime. He was hungry and wished to eat, and while they were making preparations he fell into a trance (Acts 10:9–10).

This passage describes how Peter received a revelation during his special prayer time. Peter set aside time each day to pray because he knew God speaks to us through times of silence and prayer. Even though we know God does this, it can be hard to break away from chores or our job to listen to God's messages. Peter was busy, too, but he made time every day to pray. When you institute a daily prayer routine, God's voice becomes familiar.

Are you too busy to pray regularly? Look for those times when you might peruse social-networking sites, read magazines, or watch mindless TV shows, and use some of that time to pray. Maybe you could talk to God as you drive to work or to the grocery store. Consider praying as you stand in line at a store to make a purchase. There are many opportunities to reach out to God, even if it's only a few minutes. Could you get up earlier by making an appointment with God to listen to him? If you made an appointment with the dentist, you wouldn't break it. Therefore, don't break your appointment with God, either.

REFLECT

Get in the habit of setting time aside every day to pray, like Paul did. Maybe after dinner, instead of reading the paper or watching the news on TV, give that time to the Lord. Ask him to help you raise your teenager, give you spiritual direction, or ask him to create in you the very best possible version of yourself.

✠ PRAY ✠

Dear Heavenly Father,

Help me to set aside time to be in your presence. Teach me to listen to your messages and transform my heart into one that is generous, loving, and forgiving. I want to be more like you, Lord. Amen.

september 27

SEEK GOD FIRST

Have mercy on me, God, for I am treated harshly; attackers press me all the day. My foes treat me harshly all the day; yes, many are my attackers. O Most High, when I am afraid, in you I place my trust (Psalm 56:2–4).

David cried out to God when he was surrounded by enemies who trapped him. He had confidence that God would send him help from heaven. What troubles face you today?

One of the worst feelings a parent can experience is when his or her child is attacked physically, verbally, or online. No one wants his kid to be picked on by classmates. Is your teen a victim of bullying at school? You can help your kid deal with the problem before it gets out of hand by identifying it. Ask your teen if someone or something is bothering him and listen without bias. Perhaps you could offer guidance about coping with whatever is wrong.

If your child has been depressed or anxious, having difficulty sleeping or eating, or refusing to go to school, don't ignore it. Ask what's wrong, then talk to a teacher or guidance counselor. Encourage your teen to walk away, log off, and block numbers. Most bullies want a reaction, so ignoring them could end the problem. If it doesn't, continue to pray for guidance and actively seek help.

REFLECT

Reaffirm your love and respect for your teen and remind him that if the problem becomes impossible, call out to God. Teach your teen that, just like David, when we are afraid we can place our trust in God. But remind your youth that it's OK to ask for earthly help, too. God wants us to turn to him in silence, not to suffer alone.

✠ PRAY ✠

Dear Heavenly Father,

O God on high, hear my prayer. Save (name) from the bullies who are tormenting him. Instill in him your limitless love and mercy. We place our trust in you. I ask this in Jesus' name. Amen.

september 28

BLESS THE CHILDREN

Then children were brought to him that he might lay his hands on them and pray. The disciples rebuked them, but Jesus said, "Let the children come to me, and do not prevent them; for the kingdom of heaven belongs to such as these." After he placed his hands on them, he went away (Matthew 19:13–15).

The disciples scolded the children, probably because they felt that they would be troublesome to their Master. However, Jesus drew them near. Perhaps the apostles didn't want to bother Jesus or waste his precious time with impish or powerless children who seemingly have nothing to offer. The disciples had an important mission and no time to waste. However, Christ valued the tiny creatures and blessed them regardless of how many came or how noisy they were. There was a Jewish custom to bring people to be blessed by those with superior holiness. It's not unusual for parents to bring their children to Jesus hoping for a blessing even today.

"Childlike" equates to powerlessness, weakness, or sickliness. Do you need God's loving arms wrapped around you? Do you seek his blessing for survival in a sinful and difficult world? We can request a blessing, but we must come to God humble, powerless, weak, and meekly. There is no place for arrogance.

REFLECT

What has caused you to be "incapable" lately? Are you questioning your parenting skills? Has your teenager brought an enormous problem into your life and you are unsure how to deal with it? Or perhaps you are helping your teen through a disappointment: not chosen for the school play, cut from a much loved sport, or maybe your teen didn't get invited to a friend's party. It's tough coping with the daily grind, especially when problems are tossed into the mix. Know that when you or your teen feel deflated, reach out for Jesus.

✠ PRAY ✠

Dear Heavenly Father,

I come to you with empty hands and open arms. Please provide all that I need to serve you, Lord. You gave me everything I have. You are the Alpha and the Omega; the Creator of everything. You deserve praise, glory, and honor. I love you. Amen.

september 29

LONELINESS

Look upon me, have pity on me, for I am alone and afflicted. Relieve the troubles of my heart; bring me out of my distress (Psalm 25:16–17).

Do you feel as though your son is testing you? Maybe he is pushing your buttons more than usual and that's draining your energy and wearing your patience thin. You might wonder if you are the only parent to feel the way you do. Is your child embarrassed by you? Has he said something hurtful to you about the way you dress or the way you act around his friends, teachers, or classmates? Perhaps your child has become disrespectful by rolling his eyes or slamming doors. If your teen screams, "Leave me alone," remember not to take it personally. As unpleasant as it is, your child needs to go through this stage en route to maturity.

Turning to the Lord during these times is crucial. In times of difficulty, some people turn to alcohol, drugs, pornography or other substitutes; but those temporary things won't help you and can make things worse. If you need consoling, don't go looking in the wrong places for it. If you feel emptiness in your life, let God fill it as only he can with grace, love, and mercy. The Lord can give you lasting help. Find hope in God because his compassion is greater than your failure.

REFLECT

Trials tend to make loneliness seem worse. If you're feeling that way, you might sense that nothing is going right or that the whole world is off kilter. If you don't see an end to your pain or problems, call out to God.

✠ PRAY ✠

Dear Heavenly Father,

Help me to find new strength in a deeper and more meaningful way than I have in the past. Heal my pain, Lord and carry me through this difficult stage with (name). Help me to cope with outbursts and be the loving parent you meant for me to be. I truly love you, Lord, and put all of my faith in you. Amen.

september 30

LISTEN INTENTLY

That resourcefulness may be imparted to the naive, knowledge and discretion to the young. The wise by hearing them will advance in learning, the intelligent will gain sound guidance (Proverbs 1:4–5).

When I was a little girl, my father would say, "Children are to be seen and not heard." Often my siblings and I would talk just to make noise, not sense. This passage reminds me that those who are wise don't talk just to make noise. Who makes the most noise in your house? Are you always lecturing your kid? Do you feel as if what you say goes in one ear and out the other? It can be frustrating to talk to your kid and not see any sign of progress or that she is listening or heeding your words of wisdom. Perhaps your teen doesn't think you are wise.

Or maybe it's your teen doing all the talking. Recently psychologists examined how much talking between female adolescents is too much. Some studies concluded that talking about problems excessively can actually contribute to anxiety and depression. Rehashing problems can trap girls in negative thinking patterns. Consider if your teenager overanalyzes situations obsessively. Do friends have negative thoughts that affect your kid's mood?

REFLECT

Sensible people don't think of themselves as wise. They listen more than they speak and have a tendency to learn from those around them. What can you learn from someone you consider to be wise? If you are lacking wisdom, practice listening to those you believe are wise. Wisdom doesn't mean giving your opinion; it's listening and waiting for the right time to speak. If there is too much talking in your house, encourage quiet meditation and try listening to God's voice instead of your own.

✠ PRAY ✠

Dear Heavenly Father,

Open my ears and my heart to your word. Let me hear your message and live by your instruction. I want to focus on listening intently to you, creator of heaven and earth. Guide me with a whisper. Guide me with your light. I love you, Lord. Amen.

october 1

GOD'S PURPOSE

I do not want you to be unaware, brothers, that I often planned to come to you, though I was prevented until now, that I might harvest some fruit among you, too, as among the rest of the Gentiles (Romans 1:13).

Have you ever questioned what God's purpose is for your life? Maybe right now God wants you to be the very best parent you can possibly be. When your teenager leaves home to attend college, begin a job, or join the armed forces, God might have another plan for you.

Are you wondering what God's plan is for your child? Maybe he is trying to decide what college to attend or what field of study or career path to pursue. How are you guiding your teen? How are you teaching him to trust implicitly in the Lord's will? It would be so nice to have God speak directly to us, telling us what we need to do. Often, we must plod along and trust that what we are doing is our purpose. If the doors before us are closed, maybe God wants us to stay where we are for a while—or check the windows.

Paul had a desire to visit and teach; he acted on it but it didn't work. That's when he realized what God's will was. Sometimes it's tough differentiating between what we want and what God's plan for us is. Discovering God's will is more than merely discovering your way. Discovering God's will requires seeking him first, as Paul did, and to dwell solely on Christ. When we do this, our desires will be Godly and Christ-exulting ones.

REFLECT

What is God's will for your life? Instead of allowing this question to create havoc or anguish with your life, allow yourself to be the best at what you are doing right now. Trust that God has a wonderful plan for you and accept the changes that come because it might be God's plan.

✠ PRAY ✠

Dear Heavenly Father,

I trust your will for me. I am putty in your hands. Shape me, I am yours. Amen.

october 2

WHERE IS GOD?

You will show me the path to life, abounding joy in your presence, the delights at your right hand forever (Psalm 16:11).

Do you enjoy spending time with your spouse? Does he or she make you laugh or feel comfortable and safe when you're together? Perhaps you enjoy a friend's company, maybe a coworker or neighbor. This person might allow you to relax and feel at home in his or her presence. This psalm reminds us that there is abounding joy in God's presence, too.

Often people are consumed with the busyness of their day: chores, work, running errands....While those activities aren't very rewarding, in the midst of it all there is an opportunity to find joy. That pleasure can be found when you take a few moments to reach out to God. He is waiting patiently, silently, and steadily, hoping you will set aside time to pray. When you do, he will fill you with elation. Imagine walking down the frozen-food aisle in the grocery store and allowing your heart to dwell on the Lord. You will be filled with joy right there in the store! Imagine waiting for your child after football practice or a play rehearsal and you begin to pray. God's love will fill you up.

REFLECT

When you attend Mass, you know God is there. But church isn't the only place where we sense God's presence. He is everywhere we want him to be. Sometime today, acknowledge God's presence in your life.

✠ PRAY ✠

Dear Heavenly Father,

Allow me to feel your presence in my life today. As the warm autumn sun warms the earth, let your love warm my heart each time I think of you. When I feel jubilation over the motley colored leaves on the trees, I am blessed that you created that spectacle to delight my soul. Thank you, Lord, for reaching into the depths of my longings and touching that place with a special sweetness that only you can provide. You are my loving Lord, and I am privileged to always have you with me, no matter where I am, regardless of what I'm doing. Amen.

october 3

PRAY TOGETHER

Again, [amen,] I say to you, if two of you agree on earth about anything for which they are to pray, it shall be granted to them by my heavenly Father. For where two or three are gathered together in my name, there am I in the midst of them" (Matthew 18:19–20).

Gazing over the parishioner's faces at Sunday morning Mass, it's noticeable that there are fewer teens in the pews. When I was a teenager growing up, attending Mass wasn't an option the way it is today. We often make excuses for why our kids aren't in church: They're tired and want to sleep in, they're at a sleepover, they're at soccer practice, or they're bored during Mass so we leave them home. If the future of our church is in their hands, we are in trouble. There's no time like the present to open their ears, eyes, minds, and hearts to the Lord.

There is value in praying together as a faith community. In today's passage, Jesus tells us that if two or more people pray on something, God the Father will grant it. When two or more are gathered in Jesus' name, he is there. Who wouldn't want to attend Mass knowing God is there? Would your kids want to go to the mall knowing Taylor Swift or another much-loved star was there? Rock stars can't get your kids into heaven. God cares about your kid's eternal salvation. God cares about all aspects of your teenager.

REFLECT

The cliché is true: The family that prays together stays together. Pray for each other's needs and desires each day. This will make your kids feel loved and cherished.

✠ PRAY ✠

Dear Heavenly Father,

Help me, Lord, to keep (name) interested in you, wanting you the way I do. Empower me with the right words to motivate him toward you. I ask this in your name, Lord. Amen.

october 4

REPENTANCE

When all these things, the blessing and the curse which I have set before you, come upon you, and you take them to heart in any of the nations where the Lord, your God, has dispersed you, and return to the Lord, your God, obeying his voice, according to all that I am commanding you today, you and your children, with your whole heart and your whole being, the Lord, your God, will restore your fortunes and will have compassion on you (Deuteronomy 30:1–3).

Have you ever driven somewhere without your GPS and realized you were lost? The first thing you probably did was stop driving and turn your car around. The same thing happens when we have lost our way in life with the Lord: We stop the bad behavior and turn our lives around. We go back to a place of familiarity and try again. It's also essential to repent, seek forgiveness by being truly sorry, and vow not to repeat that wrongdoing.

Has your teenager gone astray by hanging with the wrong crowd, misbehaving, or committing a crime? It's normal to feel disappointment when your child makes a mistake. Remember that we are all human; therefore, everyone has occasional slip-ups. Try to look at blunders as a teaching opportunity and coach your child through it. It's important to stand by our teens when they stumble and fall.

REFLECT

Think about times in the past when you fell and your spouse, parent, or friend was there to help you pick up the pieces and go on. Do not "rescue" your teenager because that enables him to repeat the mistakes. Be there for him the way Jesus is beside you when you experience the difficulties of life.

✠ PRAY ✠

Dear Heavenly Father,

Strengthen me, Lord, and give me the endurance to be kind,
loving, and gentle to (name) when he makes mistakes.
Let me teach him with compassion so he doesn't keep
making the same blunders throughout life.
Fill me with wisdom to guide, coach, and encourage.
Let me lead by example. I ask this in the name of our Lord Jesus.
Amen.

october 5

GOD IS IN YOU

Do you not know that you are the temple of God, and that the Spirit of God dwells in you? (1 Corinthians 3:16).

Imagine your teens want to be the best at golf. What would you suggest they do? They could watch Tiger Woods play, learning from the clubs he favors, his stance, and his swings. Perhaps they could take golf lessons and train using these methods. But no matter how hard your children try, they'll never be like Tiger Woods.

But what if that superstar could actually dwell within your kid; how wonderful would your teenagers' golf games be then? Even though that's not possible, it's important to remember that the Holy Spirit can and does dwell within us. God resides inside our earthly body, guiding our spirit.

Being a good parent is a difficult job, but we can be the best possible parent when we listen to the Holy Spirit guiding us into truth. We don't need to worry about teaching our children when we let the Holy Spirit help us every step of the way. God the Holy Spirit will teach you and remind you of everything he said. The Holy Spirit intercedes on our behalf and provides us with peace and joy, love, kindness, goodness, faithfulness, gentleness, self-control. Whenever you feel so troubled that you are unable to pray, remember the Holy Spirit will intervene in your best interest because he knows your heart and mind.

REFLECT

When you feel tested by your teenager, stop and invoke the Holy Spirit for direction and support. God the Father speaks through the Holy Spirit. Listen within, for you are never truly alone on your parenting journey.

✠ PRAY ✠

Dear Heavenly Father,

Speak to me and tell me what to do with (name).
Help me to be a better parent, one who is more loving and forgiving.
Talk to me, sweet Jesus, and bolster me when I am feeble-minded and weary. I need you, O Lord, and I trust in your ways. Amen.

october 6

BE KIND

Your kindness should be known to all. The Lord is near (Philippians 4:5).

My niece recently began a medical internship at a Catholic hospital founded by St. Marianne Cope. She loves working there because everyone is kind, loving, and patient. Many staff workers are women religious. It reminded me of my mother singing "They'll Know We Are Christians." When we are one in the Spirit, we are one in the Lord, and that love will radiate to everyone around us. When the health-care workers are extra patient, generous with sympathetic words and kind smiles, gentle with touch, compassionate with actions, their Catholic mannerisms surface and spread to everybody.

When teenagers act out or turn moody, it's difficult to be nice to them. When they roll their eyes, it's tough to hug them and say, "I love you," but that's exactly what you need to do. "Kill" them with kindness, remembering how you are called to act toward a total stranger. You might smile and say something pleasant. Therefore, do the same thing to your daughter, even if you don't feel like it. Remember that the Lord is in her and what you do to her, you also do to God. The most important thing you can do is be kind to her—especially if she's not being kind to you. You are setting a good example. You are planting seeds, and at some point they will take root.

REFLECT

Take a walk and enjoy the crispness of the air. Talk to God as you stroll around your neighborhood or a nearby park. Thank God for all of it. Notice the gifts that God gave you and stop dwelling on the negativity of your teenager. Kids go through trying stages and have bad days. Remind your teen that you and Jesus will always love her, no matter what.

✠ PRAY ✠

Dear Heavenly Father,

Thank you for allowing me to enjoy this glorious day.
Thank you for giving me the stamina to endure another difficult day with (name). Help me not to take it all personally.
Let me focus on you, sweet loving Lord. Amen.

october 7

DEPEND ON THE LORD

He called a child over, placed it in their midst, and said, "Amen, I say to you, unless you turn and become like children, you will not enter the kingdom of heaven. Whoever humbles himself like this child is the greatest in the kingdom of heaven. And whoever receives one child such as this in my name receives me (Matthew 18:2–5).

One of my family's favorite things to do when we're all together is watch the movies we took of our children when they were little. Times were tough because they depended on me for everything: meals, medical care, therapies, clothes, entertainment, a safe house, and loving home to live in. They also relied on my ability to teach them about the Lord and instill morals and values in them. Without the movies to remind me of all of that, I don't think about it because now they are independent adults.

I am self-sufficient, too; able to provide for my worldly needs. Today's verse remind me that I need to depend on the Lord or I won't get into heaven. The reality is that God is my provider. I am dependent on God for everything just as my children were dependent on me for clothes, food, and shelter. Consider thanking God for every little thing you have, even if it takes you the entire day to do it. Everything you have is from the Lord.

REFLECT

Ponder all that God has given to you, including your teenagers. Your children are gifts from God. Allow them to remind you to be dependent on the Lord, the way your children depend on you.

✠ PRAY ✠

Dear Heavenly Father,

Thank you for all that you give to me each day; I am truly grateful for it all. You are the reason for everything I have and everything I do. I love you, Lord. Amen.

october 8

REQUEST A SIGN

He answered him, "If you look on me with favor, give me a sign that you are the one speaking with me (Judges 6:17).

Look around to notice the signs God provides each day. The golden and crimson leaves will fly off the trees; a sign that winter is near. When the sun sets, it's a sign to rest. The three Wise Men were given a star to follow, a premonition of the coming of the Son of God. If God provides subtle signs, isn't it plausible that he will give grander indicators if you request one? Perhaps you are second-guessing your parenting techniques or maybe you want to try a different approach to raising your kids.

God can speak to you through the people you know and love. Maybe a friend called you at the perfect moment offering words of encouragement when you needed it most, or your priest spoke to you about a topic you needed to hear. One time I thought I was alone in a struggle and I cried out to God, "Where are you, Lord? I need to know you are with me." When an electric candle beside a picture of Jesus turned on by itself, I knew there could be a scientific explanation for it, but I decided to believe it was God winking at me, reminding me that he would never leave me during my difficult times.

REFLECT

It's important to spend quality time together as a family, even if your teen thinks she would be better off alone or with friends. Expand her horizons prayerfully. Ask God to give you a sign that you are on the right track doing the right thing as a family.

✠ PRAY ✠

Dear Heavenly Father,

Please, give me a sign so I know I'm doing your will. Sometimes (name) acts out and I don't even want to be in the same room with her. Yet I know I need to set a good example and expand her abilities to do something rewarding with her time and talents. Help me, Lord, to do what is good, honest, and just with all you have provided. I adore you. Amen.

october 9

TAKE HEED

The LORD *turned to him and said: Go with the strength you have, and save Israel from the power of Midian. Is it not I who send you? But he answered him, "Please, my Lord, how can I save Israel? My family is the poorest in Manasseh, and I am the most insignificant in my father's house." The* LORD *said to him: I will be with you, and you will cut down Midian to the last man* (Judges 6:14–16).

This passage is about trusting in God to empower you to accomplish a task you don't think you can do. Even if your family is poor and you consider yourself insignificant compared to others, God says he will be with you. Maybe you have to take a stand against your child's attitude or bad behavior. Maybe you have to stand up to a teacher or an entire school board for practices you don't approve of. It can be unnerving to stand up for your beliefs when you must face more than one person on your own.

Whatever scary situation you find yourself in, remember that the Holy Spirit dwells within you. Call upon him to quell your anxieties and enable you to think clearly. Perhaps your teenager has "something important" to discuss with you; don't allow your imagination to run wild. Ask God to keep you strong while you listen with an open heart.

REFLECT

Remember that God is always with you to fortify you. Ask God to put the right words in your head so that you can speak intelligently. Draw the Lord into all of your conversations and see where that takes you.

✠ PRAY ✠

Dear Heavenly Father,

When my heart is quiet, speak to me, sweet Lord. Let me hear your will for me. Guide each step that I take, rule each action that I take. All I say and do is for you. Bless me, Jesus, with your patience and love as I stand up for what is morally right. I love you, Lord. Amen.

october 10

PRAY EVERY DAY

He was praying in a certain place, and when he had finished, one of his disciples said to him, "Lord, teach us to pray just as John taught his disciples" (Luke 11:1).

It may be hard to imagine the Son of God praying, but he did. Knowing that Jesus prayed enables all believers to pray. While Jesus roamed the earth, he prayed quietly to his Father in heaven. Sometimes he withdrew to deserted places to pray (Luke 5:16), or he went up a mountain to pray (Luke 6:12). Perhaps Jesus sought his father's guidance or maybe he merely wanted to feel a special closeness to him.

You can't be too big or small to pray. Jesus taught that setting aside time to pray is wise. If Jesus prays, then we should, too. If I could do a video call with Jesus, I would want to know how to cure cancer and heal broken hearts. I would ask how to evangelize lovingly. I would ask him how to spread peace to end all wars in our families, neighborhoods, and around the world. I would ask him how to feed the hungry.

He would probably tell me to begin with prayer. Prayer is the essential beginning component that every action stems from. Prayer is the necessary element through which God empowers us to do his will, even if we don't know what it is.

REFLECT

Prayer is that integral part of your day that cannot be overlooked or postponed just because you are busy. It's what builds a strong foundation for your day, your week, and your forever journey.

✠ PRAY ✠

Dear Heavenly Father,

Reveal to me how I should be praying to you. Teach me how to focus solely on you. Help me eliminate the worldly distractions and dwell on your divine mercy and love. Teach me so I can teach (name) so that we can all have a resilient, peaceful, and caring life wrapped in your indelible love. Amen.

october 11

FEED YOUR SPIRITUALITY

I am the vine, you are the branches. Whoever remains in me and I in him will bear much fruit, because without me you can do nothing (John 15:5).

When my daughter went to college, my dad gave her an ivy plant to keep in her dorm. She kept it on her desk and watered it faithfully the first month of school. As her course work intensified, the plant was moved, seldom watered, and withered in the clay pot. By the end of her first semester, the plant needed help. I tried to revive it, but it was hopeless.

Something similar happens when we begin a new spiritual program. We decide to pray or read holy Scripture each day. We might be gung ho to start out, but as our responsibilities shift and our interests change, our enthusiasm wanes and our spirituality gets neglected. Today's passage paints an image to remind us not to abandon our faith but to feed it daily so that it bears fruit. Don't skip a few days of prayers, because soon you could become like the withered plant.

What are the things that cause you to disregard your spirituality? Maybe you were dismayed with a situation that your teenager unleashed on your family. Perhaps you became so involved in your teenager's life that you didn't make room for God. It might happen gradually by skipping Mass one Sunday and before you know it, you haven't attended in months. Remember that without God in your life, you won't be successful with anything else. God has to come first.

REFLECT

If your life is out of whack, change it right now with a vow to pray today. In order to have a close relationship with God, you need to spend time with the Lord in prayer. After you read this devotion, close the book, and sit in silence for five minutes meditating on God's love. Open your heart and mind and wait to hear the message God has for you. Only then can you enjoy the fruit.

✠ PRAY ✠

Dear Heavenly Father,

Thank you for waiting patiently for me. I love you, Lord. My heart is open; I am waiting and listening for you to speak. Amen.

october 12

BLESS MY MESS

And the Word became flesh and made his dwelling among us, and we saw his glory, the glory as of the Father's only Son, full of grace and truth (John 1:14).

There have been occasions when my life seemed so chaotic that the only prayer I could muster was, "Dear Lord, bless my mess." I could be distracted by a houseful of people coming and going with too many irons in the fire, or myriad stressors pushing me to the breaking point.

When the Word was made flesh, Jesus dwelled among us by entering our messed-up world. He was born in a foul-smelling animal shelter to impoverished parents who made a bed for him in a feeding trough lined with hay. Lowly shepherds were the first to witness his coming. Jesus wasn't a haughty guy. He was down to earth, shared meals with tax collectors and sinners, and interacted with the most improbable people, even those who denied, betrayed, and crucified him. As difficult as it may be, follow Jesus into the mess of life to make a difference.

REFLECT

Have you felt stretched too thin with countless chores or obligations to tend to? Perhaps your teenager is involved in too many activities requiring you to fund, work at, or attend many functions in addition to your own commitments. Often when you juggle numerous things, something can inadvertently get dropped. Consider if you have forgotten something important in the messiness of your life.

✠ PRAY ✠

Dear Heavenly Father,

Please, Lord, bless my mess. Help me to survive this desperate situation and find a tolerable solution. Help me look past difficult situations, dwell on you and do your will. I trust you, Jesus. Be with me today and every day. I ask this in your name. Amen.

october 13

SLOW TO ANGER

It is good sense to be slow to anger, and an honor to overlook an offense (Proverbs 19:11).

What do you do when you get angry? Maybe your teenager has just told you that he failed an exam, smashed the car, or is involved in some other type of trouble. Do you yell, count to ten, cause an uproar? How do you manage your anger?

One of the best things you can do is take a moment to quiet yourself while trying to be sensible. Search your heart and be silent. Quiet might suppress fuming reactions to help you conquer insults or aggravations. The longer you remain quiet, the more effective your reactions will be. It's an opportunity to evaluate if you have misplaced anger or if the devil is messing with you by creating an imaginary scenario when there is no real reason to be upset. Maybe you're just having a bad day.

If quieting yourself is too difficult, take a break from the situation and go for a walk to meditate. Call out to God for help. Use this time to pray and focus on God. The Lord wants us to have a righteous life; anger can hinder that. Whenever you are angry, nothing seems to go right. Ask yourself, "What would Jesus do in this situation?" As you walk and cogitate, God will reveal his plan for you. Be open to accepting his will even if you do not understand it. Give your anger and negativity to God; he can deal with it better than you can.

REFLECT

Think of a time when you did something wrong. Did you seek forgiveness? How many times have you sought your Savior's mercy? Each time he covered your transgressions and shortcomings with grace. Try to remember this when dealing with your child's inadequacies.

✠ PRAY ✠

Dear Heavenly Father,

Please, Lord, help me to see beyond my anger and to resolve disagreements with (name). Help me to replace harsh and bitter words with those of the same unconditional love that you have for me. I am fragile, Lord. Empower me with your grace so that I can live the righteous life you created me to have. Thank you, dear Lord, for listening to me. Amen.

october 14

CONSTANT LOVE

Then Pilate took Jesus and had him scourged. And the soldiers wove a crown out of thorns and placed it on his head, and clothed him in a purple cloak, and they came to him and said, "Hail, King of the Jews!" And they struck him repeatedly (John 19:1–3).

Imagine what Mary was feeling as she watched Jesus being tortured; how her heart must have ached. Whenever my kids suffer, I writhe in pain with them. If neighborhood kids taunt them, if teachers belittle them, if friends exclude them, if classmates ridicule them, I feel each pang of their injury. Each time something hurtful happens to my kid, I think of Mary and the depth of her suffering as she watched her Son be crucified. How did Mary endure such extreme agony?

The Bible doesn't mention what Mary was feeling; however, as a mother, I imagine the extent of her suffering must have been severe. She could only endure such punishing torment with God's help. God was cradling her broken heart in his tender, caring hands while he empowered her with a prevailing and penetrating force of love. Have you heard dramatic stories about people who lift heavy objects like a car off their child and pull them to safety? God provides such strength.

REFLECT

What dreadful circumstances are you forced to endure with your teenager? Maybe your child is physically or mentally ill and it's strenuous on your entire family. To cope with such a painful condition, invoke the Holy Spirit to keep you strong. Think of Mary as she watched her innocent Son beaten half to death. Ask God to help you hold yourself together physically and mentally while you endure this hardship. God will help you through your suffering with his constant stream of love. Ask and you shall receive.

✠ PRAY ✠

Dear Heavenly Father,

Help me through this adversity with (name). I offer up my suffering to you, sweet and merciful Lord. Let this misery cleanse my soul. You suffered and died for my sins. I thank you for it all. Amen.

october 15

LET PEACE REIGN

You will hear of wars and reports of wars; see that you are not alarmed, for these things must happen, but it will not yet be the end. Nation will rise against nation, and kingdom against kingdom; there will be famines and earthquakes from place to place (Matthew 24:6–7).

Look at the globe to note the countries that have waged war with neighbors: those in the Middle East, Africa, Asia, Russia, and Ukraine. Even the United States experienced a civil war. Our daily news reports political unrest and turmoil all around us. Why must there be so much bloodshed and devastation around the world?

Is your teenager your current enemy? What caused conflict between you? Pray about how God wants you to resolve this situation. Ask the Almighty for enlightenment. With God through his divine mercy you can overcome evil. Sinfulness has a tight grip on our society and easily ensnares people into immoral behaviors. Jesus can help you; he wants to shower you with his grace. All you have to do is ask for it. Give your problems to Jesus and trust in his ways because he is all-knowing, infinitely kind, and merciful. Let go and let God drive your life.

REFLECT

Is there a raging war within your neighborhood, extended family, your home, or your heart? What caused it and is there anything you can do to stop it? Consider handing over an olive branch to pave the way to peace. Pray for your enemies.

✠ PRAY ✠

Dear Heavenly Father,

Take away the pain I have been harboring and free my arms from the heavy burdens I have been dragging. Open my arms to welcome you back into my life. Take my aching heart into your merciful hands and cleanse it with your purity and grace. Allow me to see the way out of my dilemma and teach me how to avoid imminent pitfalls on my journey. Fill me with peacefulness, tranquility, and love, Lord Jesus. I love you today and always. Amen.

october 16

LAZINESS

We earnestly desire each of you to demonstrate the same eagerness for the fulfillment of hope until the end, so that you may not become sluggish, but imitators of those who, through faith and patience, are inheriting the promises (Hebrews 6:11–12).

Have you ever thought your teenagers were lazy? Maybe you assumed your kid would be more enthusiastic about learning, and you're unhappy with her grades, her unwillingness to seek help, or the effort she is putting in. Or perhaps her room is a wreck with clothes strewn across the floor.

Perhaps you fluctuate between reasoning with kindness to threats and punishment. It can be unpleasant watching your child turn into an unruly adolescent. It's especially challenging to tolerate the messiness, strange behaviors, or repetition of annoying mannerisms. How many times do you have to ask your teen to clean her room, and once it's "done" is the room actually clean? Maybe you want your kid to get a part-time job after school but haven't seen any signs of progress on that front. There could be a million reasons why your kid doesn't live up to your expectations. Give her a break and open the lines of communication to discover what's really going on.

REFLECT

Consider if your teenager is easily distracted, unable to focus long enough to accomplish a task. Maybe your daughter has organizational difficulties or lacks the skill set to be successful. Maybe your kid is bored and needs something more challenging or exciting to do. Does your teen get easily discouraged by failure and quit too quickly? Perhaps your child gets confused and can't decide what to do. Help her find a solution instead of just making her cover up the symptoms.

✠ PRAY ✠

Dear Heavenly Father,

Help me to be more tolerant of (name)'s messiness and idiosyncrasies. Teach me to be more respectful of her weaknesses and shortcomings and be more Christlike. Help me, Lord, to be the best parent I can possibly be. I ask this in Jesus' name. Amen.

october 17

END CONFLICT

Where do the wars and where do the conflicts among you come from? Is it not from your passions that make war within your members? You covet but do not possess. You kill and envy but you cannot obtain; you fight and wage war. You do not possess because you do not ask (James 4:1–2).

Being in church doesn't preclude harsh words and angry sentiments, sometimes even while Mass is still happening. Someone is unhappy with something from the homily so she leaves church grumbling under her breath. Perhaps you have encountered a similar person in the parking lot after Sunday service complaining she is unable to get out quickly because of the crowd. Not all Catholics are Christlike. Some debate stupid things. Others pretend to be someone they are not.

What causes the conflicts James describes? Maybe someone put her own desires or agenda above her neighbor's. Possibly she believed having pleasure was more important than doing what was right. Satisfying cravings is not what God wants for us. Arguments stem from corruption rooted in the heart. Sinful desires impede prayer and the working of our desires toward God. Conflicts arise between people because of our own inner conflict between what we want and what is right. When we lack peacefulness, we aren't using Godly wisdom.

REFLECT

No wonder there is discord in our family! We can't get along with our fellow parishioners, we grumble at the checkout lines when someone takes too long, we are annoyed at drivers who go too fast or too slow. Why are we always in fighting mode? We are irritated when the kids run late at football or cheerleading practice. We are cross when our kids let us down. When this happens to you, call on the Holy Spirit to instill a desire to do what is right, honorable, and just.

✠ PRAY ✠

Dear Heavenly Father,

Teach me to look inward at what is driving my motives and actions. If I am the cause of the conflict in my home, help me to change. I want to be a good Christian and a good parent. Shine your sweet mercy and grace on my soul. I love you, Lord. Amen.

october 18

SHARE A MEAL

And it happened that, while he was with them at table, he took bread, said the blessing, broke it, and gave it to them (Luke 24:30).

Imagine taking a two-hour hike with a friend and along the way a stranger joins you. He inquires about your conversation and accepts a dinner invitation to join you later that night. At home you are reminded by a gesture that you know this stranger, perhaps an old classmate or neighbor. Imagine the stranger was Jesus walking beside you and you fail to recognize him.

Recall the last time you were nice to a stranger. Maybe your kid asked if a friend could join you for dinner, but you were reluctant because you were tired or didn't have anything special prepared. We should always be kind to strangers, even if it's your kid's friend, because you never know when you are helping or interacting with God. Add another plate to the table and know that God brought this person to you for a reason.

REFLECT

Catholicism centers on a meal where Jesus breaks the bread, blesses it, and gives it to be eaten as he did thousands of years ago at the Last Supper. As Catholics we are invited to share this glorious event each Sunday, or every day if our schedules permits daily Mass. When we gather our family members around our kitchen table, stop to think of Jesus. He teaches us to crave a blessing on every meal regardless of what it is. Prayer makes every meal special.

✠ PRAY ✠

Dear Heavenly Father,

Thank you for opening the eyes of my mind to allow me to see you in everyone I meet. Remind me, sweet Jesus, to think of you as I break bread, and to share that joy with (name). You are my saving Lord. With you I can do anything. Amen.

october 19

ACT ON IT

Seated in his chariot, he was reading the prophet Isaiah. The Spirit said to Philip, "Go and join up with that chariot." Philip ran up and heard him reading Isaiah the prophet and said, "Do you understand what you are reading?" (Acts 8:28–30).

In this passage, an Ethiopian eunuch went to Jerusalem to worship and was returning home when Phillip leapt into action to explain the reading to him. Sometimes the Bible can be difficult to understand and it was divine intervention that Phillip was in the right place at the right time to help enlighten the eunuch.

Having faith is not enough. You cannot just go to Mass, say prayers, sing hymns, and think you will go to heaven. There is more to the Catholic faith than simply believing; we also must act. How do you know when you are supposed to act and what you are supposed to do? The Holy Spirit causes a stirring within you to cast a smile to a homeless person, offer a granola bar, or share a pleasant conversation. If you notice a young mother struggling with her children, offer a helping hand even if it's just to hold the door open or let her ahead of you in line. Consider adding a treat to your or son's lunch or pray for him throughout the day while he is at school.

REFLECT

Have you felt the Holy Spirit working in you to acknowledge your son for something he did at school? Perhaps you could give your kid a compliment today. Allow God to use you as his special tool to do his work, whatever it is.

✠ PRAY ✠

Dear Heavenly Father,

I hunger and thirst to know you, Lord, Jesus. Direct me to the place you mean for me to be. Guide me into someone's wearisome path who needs my help. Tell me what to do, Lord. Let me be his steppingstone. With you I can do anything. I trust you, Jesus. Amen.

october 20

OVERCOME TRIBULATION

I have told you this so that you might have peace in me. In the world you will have trouble, but take courage, I have conquered the world" (John 16:33).

When you encounter a trial in your life, do you immediately ask God, "Why me, Lord?" or "What have I done to deserve this?" Each time we ask such questions of God, we undermine him. We cannot tell God how to do his job! When we question God's methods, we demonstrate how little faith we have in him.

Jesus reminds us that in the world we will have trouble. He didn't say, "You might have trouble." He said, "You *will* have trouble." It's a fact just as sure as the sun will rise and set each day. Take heed because Jesus has conquered the world, so have courage in all you do. Remember that God is always with you through good times and bad. Through the good times, say, "Thank you, Lord for blessing me," and through bad times say, "Help me, Lord. I don't know what to do." Know that God will never abandon you in your hour of need.

REFLECT

Consider what tribulations you are trying to overcome. Maybe an illness has spread through your house recently, leaving you feeling weak and vulnerable. Or perhaps your daughter has struggled with dental issues like braces, missing teeth, or infections. Perhaps your child is struggling with school. Whatever the trouble, don't doubt God's wisdom or his unconditional love.

✠ PRAY ✠

Dear Heavenly Father,

Thank you, sweet and merciful, Lord, for showering me with blessings to enrich and enhance my life. You have paved each step on my journey with rose petals and honeycomb. Though I didn't see the bees and thorns, they were there. You guide me down the straight and narrow paths. Where you lead, I will go because, sweet Jesus, I trust and love you, Lord. Amen.

october 21

DRY YOUR TEARS

Then David and those who were with him wept aloud until they could weep no more (1 Samuel 30:4).

Has something happened between you and your son to cause you so much grief that you can't stop lamenting over it? Crying can be cathartic; some people actually feel better after a good cry because it reduces emotional stress. Crying can reduce blood pressure and remove toxins from the body. Crying is not necessarily bad.

First and foremost, give your sadness to the Lord. God is so big that he can watch over the whole world, so he can certainly handle whatever is making you sad. God can also be very small and dwell within you; so call out to him when the difficulties of life get you down. No problem is too big or small for God. Just say, "Jesus, I trust in you." Then release your sorrow and anguish to him. God will do the rest by healing your broken heart. Life is full of challenges, disappointments, frustration, and failed expectations, especially with teenagers in your home. Don't try to do everything by yourself; do it with God.

REFLECT

Try to watch funny television programs; something that will make you smile or laugh more, or better yet, watch a movie about a dearly loved saint. Read a religious book or begin a novena. Open the Bible and read passages from Psalms. Go for a long walk and thank God for everything he has given to you or how he has helped you out of a difficulty. God is good and wants you to be filled with joy. Call out to him today; he's only a heartbeat away.

✠ PRAY ✠

Dear Heavenly Father,

Please lift my spirits, Lord, so that I can rise above the problems that engulf me. Teach me how to put them in perspective so I can focus on living totally for you. Bless everything that I do today, Lord; I offer this suffering up to you. With you I can do anything. I love you, Lord. Amen.

october 22

FOSTER A THANKFUL HEART

Offer praise as your sacrifice to God; fulfill your vows to the Most High. Then call on me on the day of distress; I will rescue you, and you shall honor me" (Psalm 50:14–15).

When my daughters were little, I taught them "please" and "thank you." I wanted polite children who would grow into gracious adults. I prayed it would encompass praise and thanksgiving to God for his many blessings. Mealtime became a forum for daily thanksgiving as we took turns recognizing God's blessings throughout the day. We might say, "Praise God for the sunshine. On my walk I saw two bluebirds." One daughter might say, "Praise God that we had a kind substitute teacher who didn't bombard us with homework."

When I take my kids and their friends out, each teenager will thank me for the ride, the movie, or the ice cream; but, sometimes my own kids don't acknowledge the sacrifice I made for them, and it allows resentment to creep in. I don't expect my kids to buy me a gift for my day of service, but I do expect them to show thankfulness. I question if these feelings are similar to what God senses when I don't show appreciation for his daily blessings. God wants us to have thankful hearts, just as we want our kids to be grateful for the things we do for them. God gives us everything we have.

REFLECT

Evaluate your motives as you offer sacrifices to God today.

✠ PRAY ✠

Dear Heavenly Father,

Praise to you, Lord! Thank you for your countless blessings.
You fill me up when I am empty. You lift me when I have fallen.
You put the bounce in my step and the smile on my face.
My heart, as light as air, is filled with your love and compassion.
You are the best, Lord. With you I can do anything. Amen.

october 23

WHAT DOES IT COST?

Which of you wishing to construct a tower does not first sit down and calculate the cost to see if there is enough for its completion? (Luke 14:28).

Both of my daughters looked at expensive colleges, enticed by their exciting programs, intriguing courses, and thrilling opportunities. They didn't worry about the exorbitant price tag because they wanted the best at any cost.

Sometimes, living the American dream can create the attitude that we can do or have anything, accomplish anything, or go anywhere. When it comes to religion we are free to worship however we please: there are Masses on TV and even at some shopping malls. We don't face danger or persecution like the apostles did, but this sometimes cultivates the attitude that if there's nothing to lose there's also nothing to gain.

Christ instructs us not to stockpile treasures on earth but to build up treasure in heaven because your true wealth will reveal your heart. When my husband and I adopted our two daughters from Romania, we arrived home broke, yet we felt rich in our hearts. If you keep this world's riches, you will lose them and your soul. You cannot serve both God and wealth.

REFLECT

When the apostles decided to follow Jesus, do you think they calculated the cost of their choice? Have you considered your cost to follow Jesus? Being a Christian will cost you your sins; you cannot be a Christian if you are unwilling to abandon them. You must repent. Being a Christian will cost you those desires that oppose God's will and his word. God commands us to abstain from every form of evil; to abandon immorality, lust, idolatry, and greed.

✠ PRAY ✠

Dear Heavenly Father,

I give you my life to do as you please. I am yours forever. I am here to do your will, I trust you. If I am to be a parent right now, let me be the very best one I can be. If I am waiting for an assignment from you, bless my wait. Fill me with peace as I fortify my bones to carry the load you place on my shoulders. I am ready to serve you, Lord. Amen.

october 24

STEADY COUNCIL

Even if you should have countless guides to Christ, yet you do not have many fathers, for I became your father in Christ Jesus through the gospel. Therefore, I urge you, be imitators of me
(1 Corinthians 4:15–16).

On a family vacation to Yellowstone National Park, we only ventured into the woods with a guide. We needed someone to lead us, point out interesting features of the landscape, and keep us safe from bears, wolves, and other dangerous animals. When the excursion was over, I wished that ranger could stay with us. He was clever and knowledgeable and we enjoyed our brief time with him. As we drove home, I realized that as a parent I had to teach and lead my daughters, make interesting points, and keep them safe. That's the role of a parent.

There have been times when I wanted a break from parenting, but there really is no good time to stop providing guidance. It's a full-time job that requires more than a park ranger's witty banter and knowledge of trees and animals. As a parent, we must provide in-depth, quality insight to guide our kids along their lifelong journey to make it into heaven. It's no easy task. Are you a lifelong spiritual mentor to your teenager or just an occasional guide?

REFLECT

Perhaps you need a spiritual advisor you can learn from. Consult your parish priest to identify such a person. Seek this individual prayerfully. Maybe you can act as a spiritual mentor to a young person in your parish who thirsts for the wisdom you possess. Have you considered being a religious-education teacher in your home parish? What is God calling you to do?

✠ PRAY ✠

Dear Heavenly Father,

Fill me with the grace I need to do your work. Enlighten me, Lord, so that I am open to receive and give as you deem necessary. Sweet Jesus, I trust in you and your miraculous ways. Amen.

october 25

CHOOSE GOD

A violent squall came up and waves were breaking over the boat, so that it was already filling up (Mark 4:37).

The sea is mentioned frequently in the Bible. If there is one thing I learned from living in the Finger Lakes region of New York state it is that if the waters are tranquil, eventually they will turn choppy. And if the waters are rough, eventually they will calm. The one thing that can withstand any kind of weather is a strong ship. Rickety vessels will get tossed and turned or possibly sink. In the storms of your life, the strong ship you cling to is God. The Lord will calm the rough water in your life. Call out to him; he will toss you a life preserver and pull you to safety in the comfort of his warm embrace.

What is rocking the boat in your home life? Do you feel bullied by other parents who allow their kids to stay out later than you think is reasonable? Are other parents allowing their kids to go places you don't agree with? Are your teenagers pestering you to do things with their friends that you question? When kids are bullied, they run to someone they trust, know, and love. As an adult, make God be the one you turn to. Trust in his miraculous ways.

REFLECT

How well do you know God? How can you get to know him better? Spend time talking to him. Instead of driving in silence, talk to the Lord. He will certainly keep you safe behind the wheel! Find idle moments throughout the day that you can fill with pleasing thoughts of God. Set aside quality time to offer praise and thanksgiving. Remember when God rescued you in the past. Spend a while meditating and reading the Bible. He will empower you to stand up to the bullies of the world. Always choose God.

✠ PRAY ✠

Dear Heavenly Father,

Calm the rough seas that have been tossing me about. Bring tranquility back into my life. Be my beacon of hope and let me fix my gaze on you today and always. Amen.

october 26

OBEY GOD'S COMMAND

Whether we like it or not, we will obey the command of the LORD, our God, to whom we are sending you, so that it may go well with us for obeying the command of the LORD, our God" (Jeremiah 42:6).

When I was a teenager, my mom left a note on the kitchen table with a list of chores for me to do before she got home from work. I dreaded it because I had to get dinner ready. I really wanted to relax after a long day of classes, have a snack, and watch TV. I didn't like the tasks, but I obeyed. It wasn't until years later that I realized I knew how to cook because of Mom's chore list.

We can't always appreciate what God asks of us until some later point in our life. We simply have to act on the faith we have in God. He knows what's best for us. He knows the plan; we don't know much at all. Sometimes God asks us to do things we're afraid to do. In that case, we have to prove to ourselves that we trust God. Ponder what God might be asking you to do. Are you hesitant to do it? When you step on a plane, you trust the pilot to fly you safely to your destination. Face your fears by leaning into your discomfort, knowing God is with you through it all. Throw yourself totally and completely into his pure love, because with him you can do anything.

REFLECT

Take a leap of faith by obeying God's command even if it makes you feel uncomfortable at first. You might not even understand it, but trust that God has a glorious purpose for it all. Let God release the energy within when fears abound. God will never desert us.

✠ PRAY ✠

Dear Heavenly Father,

Scoop me up, Lord, and keep me safe in the hollow of your hand.
Give me the courage to step out on a limb for you.
I trust that you will not let me fall. I trust that you will take care of me and love me for obeying you. Amen.

october 27

GODLY THOUGHTS

Finally, brothers, whatever is true, whatever is honorable, whatever is just, whatever is pure, whatever is lovely, whatever is gracious, if there is any excellence and if there is anything worthy of praise, think about these things. Keep on doing what you have learned and received and heard and seen in me. Then the God of peace will be with you (Philippians 4:8–9).

When I was a teenager, I needed surgery. Knowing that hospitals terrified me, my mother encouraged me to fill my mind with thoughts of all things lovely and pleasant, particularly Jesus. She reminded me that God was always with me and all I had to do was call out and he'd be there. Now, whenever I find myself in a precarious situation, I remember my mother's sage advice and take comfort in her words. God is always with me. What circumstances have been occupying your thoughts? Are you thinking about your kids struggling with school, wondering what kind of experiences they're having?

The Bible teaches us to have good, moral minds centered on God. That enables us to act the way we think, with our actions always revolving around God. Consider what you fill your mind with: mindless TV shows about killing, infidelity, or violence? What websites do you visit? What type of books do you read? What thoughts occupy your mind?

REFLECT

When bad thoughts enter your mind, say to Jesus, "If the thoughts are not from you, take them away!" Then replace them with lovely thoughts of God: how he changed water into wine when Mary asked him to do something for the bride and groom at Cana. Think about how he multiplied the loaves and fish and fed so many. You have the power to change your thoughts. Let God do the rest.

✠ PRAY ✠

Dear Heavenly Father,

Fill my head with wondrous thoughts of you.
Chase evil thoughts away before they take root in my mind.
Let me dwell on your loveliness, Lord. I love you. Amen.

october 28

DO GOD'S WORK

So they said to him, "What can we do to accomplish the works of God?" Jesus answered and said to them, "This is the work of God, that you believe in the one he sent" (John 6:28–29).

On occasion I have asked God, "Is this really what you want me to be doing with my life?" Maybe I was surrounded by toys, folding mountains of laundry, or selling school stuff with my daughters. It didn't feel fulfilling at the time.

Jesus answers our question of, "What shall we do to accomplish God's works?" with the answer: "Believe in the one he sent." It sounds simple and easy. All we have to do is believe in Jesus and imitate him. It's not easy to emulate God, but that's exactly what we all have to do. Maybe it's helping our kids sell candy bars happily when we would rather be doing something else. It could be complimenting a stranger, praying for the persecuted or for peace within our hearts, our nation, and the world. Whatever job you are doing, remember that your primary goal is to believe in Jesus Christ. It is through Jesus Christ that we find true fulfillment.

REFLECT

What have you been doing lately that might make you question the value of your time or the way you are living your life? Are you devoting too much time to your day job and not enough time to your family? Or are you doing too much for your teenagers and not giving enough time to developing your spirituality? Perhaps you feel like you're being stretched too thin with too many tasks and not enough time to complete everything. How can you refocus your tasks on Jesus?

✠ PRAY ✠

Dear Heavenly Father,

I believe in Jesus and want to imitate him in all I think, say, and do. I ask this in Jesus' name. Amen.

october 29

GOD IS THE WAY

Jesus said to him, "I am the way and the truth and the life. No one comes to the Father except through me (John 14:6).

When my daughter was in her third year of college, we gave her a GPS to help her get from point A to point B. Her sense of direction and map-reading skills were mediocre. A GPS would help her navigate to her job, internships, and volunteer work in the community. What the GPS couldn't do was help her stay on the straight path of righteousness or direct her to heaven. She can only do that by living the word written in the Bible. Jesus clearly states that he is the way. If we want to go to heaven, we get there through Jesus.

We tend to believe that life is long and we have forever to get to heaven, when, in fact, we don't know when our last day will actually be. Is it tomorrow? Would you be ready? If you were going on a trip to France you would make preparations like packing a suitcase, having an up-to-date passport, and an airline ticket. Living each day in Christ is preparing you to get to heaven. Jesus tells us there are many roads we can take, but he is the only true way to go to the Father in heaven.

REFLECT

We get caught up in the busyness of our lives by making lists of things to do, prioritizing our goals, and planning how to accomplish them. That's great until something goes awry. When you find yourself going the wrong way, remember to trust in Jesus. Focus on his divinity and your crooked paths will be made straight.

✠ PRAY ✠

Dear Heavenly Father,

I trust in you, Lord and will follow you all the days of my life,
even the stormy ones when my path becomes muddled.
You are my beacon of hope and I won't take my eyes off you.
You are all I need. I love you, sweet Jesus. Amen.

october 30

ANGEL'S DAY

The person who acts in righteousness is righteous, just as he is righteous. Whoever sins belongs to the devil, because the devil has sinned from the beginning. Indeed, the Son of God was revealed to destroy the works of the devil (1 John 3:7–8).

The night before Halloween is known as "Devil's Night," where mischievous youths engage in acts of vandalism such as egging homes, soaping windows, or toilet-papering trees. While these acts are a far cry from works of the devil, this date can remind us to focus on extending kindnesses to people instead of mischievous deeds.

Call it "Angel's Day" where you go out of your way to spread joy, peace, and love to those around you. Maybe your coworkers will benefit from your kindheartedness, or perhaps you could reach out with compassion to total strangers. You don't have to be Mother Teresa, but you could invoke St. Thérèse of Lisieux to foster your own "little way" to Christ's heart by doing small gestures of love. Consider starting a yearly tradition with your teen where you do little acts of kindness with great love. Sometimes the smallest gesture means the most.

REFLECT

What small gestures could you include in your daily activities today? What small gesture could you do for your teen today?

✠ PRAY ✠

Dear Heavenly Father,

Expand my heart to contain the abundance of love that you pour into it each day. Let me use that love to make others happy. Teach me how to enjoy being small and do little acts of goodness to those around me. I ask this in Jesus' name. Amen.

october 31

HALLOWEEN TRICKS

Then Moses and Aaron went to Pharaoh and did just as the Lord *had commanded. Aaron threw his staff down before Pharaoh and his servants, and it turned into a serpent. Pharaoh, in turn, summoned the wise men and the sorcerers, and they also, the magicians of Egypt, did the same thing by their magic arts. Each one threw down his staff, and they turned into serpents. But Aaron's staff swallowed their staffs* (Exodus 7:10–12).

You might not expect to find magic in the Bible, but the Pharaoh used it to one-up Moses. Tricks have been popular since the beginning of time. In the Garden of Eden, the serpent tricked Eve to eat the forbidden fruit. Tricks are a big part of Halloween. Do you or your kids enjoy dressing up in costumes, carving pumpkins into jack-o'-lanterns, visiting haunted houses, or watching horror films? This fun time of year allows families an opportunity to step "outside the box" and create characters with gourds and crafts or simply celebrate the harvesting of autumn fruits and vegetables.

Instead of focusing on ghosts, scary creatures, and sorcerers remember that Halloween is a time of the liturgical year reserved to remember all the faithful departed believers, including saints and martyrs. Consider how you can integrate the liturgical celebration into your family's Halloween plans.

REFLECT

Perhaps your teens would like to throw a party with a small cluster of friends at your home. Consider encouraging them to wear costumes of their favorite saints, like Joan of Arc or Francis of Assisi. Inspire them to study the saint they select to promote a lively discussion.

✠ PRAY ✠

Dear Heavenly Father,

Help me to weave religion into Halloween for (name) and his friends.
Let me make my home welcoming to foster love and growth.
I love you, Lord. Amen.

november 1

ALL SAINTS' DAY

Call now! Will anyone respond to you?
To which of the holy ones will you turn? (Job 5:1).

Many people believe that if you have misplaced something, St. Anthony is the saint to pray to; he will help you find it. When you are traveling, pray to St. Christopher; he will keep you safe. If you have vision problems, pray to St. Lucy; she will enable you to see clearer. Isn't it marvelous that there is a saint for every need? Who is your special saint, the one you pray to when you are in need? When I hit rough patches raising two teenagers, I prayed to St. Jude, the patron saint of desperate situations.

On the feast of All Saints' Day we set aside this day to honor Church members believed to be in heaven. This feast is a joyful day to remember the saints who are watching over us from heaven. As Catholics, we believe that death doesn't end our life but changes it. The Bible states that people who lived virtuous lives and died with faith in Jesus will partake in his resurrection.

On earth we share in unity with other Christians. Even when one of us dies, we continue to share that communion. Therefore, saints can remain close with many of us on earth. Going to a saint with our prayer requests is the same as asking a friend, relative, or church congregation to pray for you. The difference is, these friends are already in heaven with God.

REFLECT

When you attend Mass on this holy day of obligation, remember to invoke the saints to watch over you while you parent your daughter. Saints have a direct line to the Lord.

✠ PRAY ✠

Dear Heavenly Father,

Soothe my trembling heart, Lord, and fill me with the peace I need to be a better parent. Carry me close to you, through the whirl of din and disastrous difficulties that are derailing me. Don't let me suffocate. Hold me up high, sweet Jesus, to see above it and get through it. I ask this in your holy name. Amen.

november 2

ALL SOULS' DAY

For we know that if our earthly dwelling, a tent, should be destroyed, we have a building from God, a dwelling not made with hands, eternal in heaven. For in this tent we groan, longing to be further clothed with our heavenly habitation if indeed, when we have taken it off, we shall not be found naked (2 Corinthians 5:1–3).

My college roommate persuaded me to camp in the woods in a tiny tent. A torrential rain fell that night. Two days later we were, thankfully, back at the dorm—a safe building I came to appreciate. In today's Bible passage, our earthly body is referred to as a "tent," while the future body is called a "building." After spending a weekend in a tent, I can attest to its temporariness. A building is made for the permanent habitation of a resident.

Saint Paul uses the tent as a symbol of the body we currently occupy, while the building is the glorious body we hope to occupy in heaven some day. Today, we are living in transitory tents. After my camping experience, I understand how temporary my body is, that it is aging, weakening, and deteriorating from the many storms of life. The good news is that God has a sturdy body, better suited for life in heaven. When we become cognizant of our failing earthly tent, transitioning toward death, we groan to be clothed in our heavenly dwelling. The groaning is of elation for wanting to occupy that other body, the eternal building from God.

REFLECT

On the feast of All Souls' Day, let us observe those who died and might exist in purgatory. Catholic doctrines say that our prayers can help cleanse these departed souls and prepare them for heaven. Who will you pray for today?

✠ PRAY ✠

Dear Heavenly Father,

Hear my prayers, merciful Lord, for (name), who has passed on before me. Lift up (name), drawing him near your compassionate heart, washing your child in the source of life that surged out for souls. Fount of Life, I cry out with a voice of agony, please don't reject my earthly prayer. Empty yourself upon (name). I ask this in your name, Lord. Amen.

november 3

DRINK FROM THE WELL

Jacob's well was there. Jesus, tired from his journey, sat down there at the well. It was about noon. A woman of Samaria came to draw water. Jesus said to her, "Give me a drink." His disciples had gone into the town to buy food. The Samaritan woman said to him, "How can you, a Jew, ask me, a Samaritan woman, for a drink?" For Jews use nothing in common with Samaritans (John 4:6–9).

Soon after the fall of Communism in Romania, my husband and I walked through state-run orphanages attempting to adopt. Pat and I interacted with gypsies and black-marketers; people we normally wouldn't speak to. It was a surreal experience.

John paints a similar scene where Jesus does something odd: he interacts with a Samaritan woman at the well at noon when only outcasts are there. Jews scorned Samaritans because they were a mixed race. Jews refused to worship with them, speak to them, or touch them. Yet, Jesus deliberately met this Samaritan woman.

This passage teaches us to reach out to those living on the edge of society. In order to follow Jesus, we will have to cross racial, cultural, and social barriers. Jesus models for us a way to connect with the unfortunate, desperate, and needy individuals who might have been pushed to the fringe of our communities. It's not an easy thing to do. However, to help those pitiful souls means you are imitating Christ—which is exactly what he wants of us.

REFLECT

What are you doing to get your teenager to reach across those racial, cultural, and social barriers Jesus calls us to cross? Could you and your daughter make sandwiches together to distribute to the homeless population in your community? Where is God leading you?

✠ PRAY ✠

Dear Heavenly Father,

Take me to the well, Lord, and teach me how to drink from it when I am afraid and alone. I want to do your work as tenderly as you. I trust in you, Jesus. Amen.

november 4

ELECTION DAY

Before me no god was formed, and after me there shall be none. I, I am the Lord*; there is no savior but me* (Isaiah 43:10–11).

I always brought my daughters into the voting booth with me each Election Day to instill the importance of voting. Each Election Day we went through this ritual so they could see the significance of voting. As some get voted out, others move in with great hope for a brighter future. But these legislators are not saviors. While it's good to teach teenagers about government and politics, it needs to be done with an understanding that God's laws come first.

The Bible says there is only one true Savior: Jesus. God is the only one who gives us genuine hope for the future. God can meet all of our needs. He forgives sins, nourishes our soul, and guides our path. He walks with us on our long and cumbersome journey, bringing us to an eternal kingdom that never ends and will never disappoint. God is our only rescuer, saving us for all time, not just the short term.

REFLECT

The laws God gives us to obey are the Ten Commandments (Exodus 20). Make sure your teens understand the importance of these laws in their lives and how God's laws and humanity's laws work together.

✠ PRAY ✠

Dear Heavenly Father,

Savior of the world, I adore you! I only want to honor you, follow you, and live by your rules. You are such a kind and merciful God, always willing to forgive my sins and embrace me in your love. I am here, Lord. Call on me. Amen.

november 5

REMOVE YOURSELF

Do not be friendly with hotheads, nor associate with the wrathful, lest you learn their ways, and become ensnared (Proverbs 22:24–25).

I know a man who needs an ongoing anger-management program. When approached by him, my heart races as my body gets tense. I pray for strength to stay positive, loving, kind, and encouraging. However, after he leaves I always feel drained, as if his negativity and rage rubbed off on me! Even though I work mightily not to be like this hothead, his language and tone inevitably follow me. There is truth in the phrase "we become like those we surround ourselves with."

Perhaps you give in to anger when your teenager's annoyances pile on top of each other, making a mountain of gloom. Do escalating problems at work make you feel like a volcano ready to explode once you get home? Maybe you have misdirected anger toward your family. Take a long look at yourself in the mirror and decide who you want to be.

Consider the type of kids your daughter befriends. Do they use foul language or have a bad attitude? Do they have good morals and values? Your teenager's friends do much more than influence her. Their anger and annoyances can rub off on your kid.

REFLECT

Ponder healthy ways you can incorporate positive influences in your teen's world. Can you get her involved in a community soup kitchen or food pantry? Perhaps she could volunteer a few hours each week at a nearby nursing home. Not only will she expand her horizons, adding richness to her college applications, but she will also be doing God's work.

✠ PRAY ✠

Dear Heavenly Father,

Cool my temper, Lord, and ease my pain. I'm balancing too many things and making a mess of it all on my own. I need your help, Lord. Teach me to be more like you: loving, kind, and merciful. I truly love you. Amen.

november 6

PITCH IN

Then he said to his disciples, "The harvest is plentiful, but the laborers are few" (Matthew 9:37).

I chaperoned a school event that was clearly understaffed. There were too many kids and not enough adults for the experience to be a success. I completely understand the message Jesus was trying to convey: There's a lot of work but not enough workers.

There is a profound reason for our existence on this earth, but we may not realize what that reason is. We have to trust in God's plan for us. Eventually, if we're lucky, we will come to know and appreciate it. While we put the puzzle pieces of our life together, God wants us to be good, kind, and merciful to everyone.

God calls us to enhance the lives of strangers and those around us, too. There is no end of people who need some of the joy of God in their lives, but some days it seems as if too few of us are answering that call to work. God wants us to reach out to everyone regardless of whether or not we know them. We have to trust that God brought these people into our lives for a reason; maybe to offer comforting words or steer them in the right direction. Do any of your kid's friends fit this profile? Maybe one of your child's friends is depressed or wants to lash out at authority figures. Maybe he just needs to know there is an adult who cares about him and shows an interest in his life. Step up, even if you're unsure how to act or feel busy enough with your own life. It's the right thing to do.

REFLECT

Listen carefully to hear God's messages for you by reflecting on the image of Jesus. Ask our Lord to enlighten you. Roll up your sleeves and pitch in to do God's work. With God, you can do anything. There's a lot to do, but not many are willing to do it. Are you?

✠ PRAY ✠

Dear Heavenly Father,

Work through me, Lord. I am yours. I am here to do your will, whatever it is. Use me, Lord! With you I can do anything and am not afraid. Amen.

november 7

ASK IN JESUS' NAME

Amen, amen, I say to you, whoever believes in me will do the works that I do, and will do greater ones than these, because I am going to the Father. And whatever you ask in my name, I will do, so that the Father may be glorified in the Son. If you ask anything of me in my name, I will do it (John 14:12–14).

It took forever to fill a moving van with all of my daughter's belongings as she left for her first apartment. Thankfully, we hired a few professional movers to unload the truck at her new place on the outskirts of New York City. One mover said to me, "Pile on the boxes; I can carry several at a time." I was amazed that he could do that because I knew just how heavy those boxes were. I think of this scenario whenever I feel God asking me to do something.

Jesus says, "Whoever believes in me will do the works I do." In the Bible, Jesus did a lot of astonishing things: the sick were cured, the lame walked, the dead came back to life. If we truly believe, we can tell Jesus to pile it on. We can handle any weight with the Lord because he says whatever we ask in his name, he will do. Wow! What a magnificent gift.

REFLECT

The road of life is full of twists and turns and is sometimes difficult to navigate when we are parenting teenagers with all of their drama, worries, and woes. Remember to call out to Jesus in your hour of need. He will help you by giving you the strength to carry more than you think you can. All you have to do is believe, trust, and ask in Jesus' name.

✠ PRAY ✠

Dear Heavenly Father,

Thank you for filling me with your indelible love today. Thank you for fortifying my bones to carry the weight of the world that (name) brought home for me to deal with. Thank you for safeguarding my heart in the hollow of your hand so I can do your work here on earth. I ask this in your name, Lord. Amen.

november 8

LOVE ONE ANOTHER

I give you a new commandment: love one another. As I have loved you, so you also should love one another. This is how all will know that you are my disciples, if you have love for one another" (John 13:34–35).

A mother bear will go to great lengths to safeguard her cubs. The news media reported recently about a cub who wandered onto a busy freeway; the mother bear reached over the embankment and pulled it to safety. The furry family moseyed away unscathed.

Have you acted like a mother bear protecting your children? When you rescue your teen from a precarious situation, do you read your son the riot act, instill a punishment, and fester over it? Or do you let it go as if it were another day? It isn't easy to forgive and forget when our kids act imprudently, because we want them to learn and don't want them to repeat the mistake.

Jesus says we are to love one another the way he loved us. He doesn't say "after they have learned a lesson about their transgression." Jesus' love is unconditional, steadfast, and everlasting. Regardless of the indiscretion, Jesus' love for us will never die. Therefore, we must love others the same way, even if it's our teenager who just wrecked the car, flunked out of school, got a tattoo or piercing, or lied for the umpteenth time. God gave us a new commandment. And it's not a proposition—it's a requirement.

REFLECT

How can you be more like the mother bear who felt that "close call" and then kept loving the way God intended? It isn't easy to have unwavering love for our kids when they mess up. However, God instructs us to love one another just as he loves us with all of our faults and failures.

✠ PRAY ✠

Dear Heavenly Father,

Help me to move past (name)'s mistakes and continue to love just as you love me. Please, Lord, pour out your love over my pain. Let your love heal every affliction and fortify me to continue on, doing the work you intended for me. Amen.

november 9

GIVE THANKS TO GOD

I give thanks to my God always on your account for the grace of God bestowed on you in Christ Jesus, that in him you were enriched in every way, with all discourse and all knowledge, as the testimony to Christ was confirmed among you, so that you are not lacking in any spiritual gift as you wait for the revelation of our Lord Jesus Christ (1 Corinthians 1:4–7).

Upon requesting services for Andrea when we first brought her home from Romania, I had to present a list of her limitations to social workers who had to evaluate our daughter's needs. At the top of the list I included Andrea's talents: she had a killer smile and giggled frequently with a twinkle in her sparkling brown eyes. I wanted the professionals to remember that she had attributes, too. We often tend to focus on our kids' problems and overlook the positive. Do you do that with your daughter? What glaring issue has been overshadowing the good?

In this passage, St. Paul was thankful for a church that had numerous problems because he identified with God's benevolence. He could have easily focused on their shortcomings, but instead he focused on thanksgiving. Paul found a way to spin the situation in a positive light.

Living with teenagers requires much patience, diligence, and enduring love. Sometimes their faults are evident and we have to decide whether to overlook them or discuss them. This balancing act consumes so much energy, but recognizing their talents can be effortless. Therefore, strive to identify God's grace in their life instead of their mistakes.

REFLECT

We all make mistakes because we are human. Our kids will make more mistakes because they are young, they're still learning, and their brains are not fully developed. Dwell on their smile and gregarious laughter. Thank God for it because it's a gift.

✠ PRAY ✠

Dear Heavenly Father,

Thank you for making (name) especially for me.
You created this wondrous person with much tenderness and love.
Thank you, Lord for this very special child. Amen.

november 10

SEEK AND YOU SHALL FIND

A time to seek, and a time to lose; a time to keep, and a time to cast away (Ecclesiastes 3:6).

When my daughter was very young, she was hospitalized at the National Institute of Health (NIH). While she had x-rays taken, the housekeeping staff cleaned her room, including changing the bed sheets. To her despair, when she got back her dearly loved blankie was missing; presumed lost in the gigantic industrial washers. Finding that blankie would be like searching for a needle in a haystack. Thankfully, with many prayers and divine intervention, I found the blankie.

There are times in our life that God can be like my daughter's blankie – presumed lost. Maybe you feel like you've been praying in vain for a situation to change, and when there's no progress you feel like quitting. Perhaps you have been praying earnestly and wonder if God is listening. Maybe something has you questioning your faith altogether. God said, "When you look for me, you will find me. Yes, when you seek me with all your heart, I will let you find me" (Jeremiah 29:13–14). He is there. He is listening.

REFLECT

Sometimes we feel like the needle in the haystack: lost. But just as I took the time and diligence to look for and retrieve my daughter's blankie, God will be diligent in his search for us. Therefore, be persistent in your prayer. Be patient and remember that God knows exactly where you are and what you want. God will provide on his terms, on his timetable, according to his will. He knows what is best for you. Trust in his ways. God is the light and the way.

✠ PRAY ✠

Dear Heavenly Father,

Help me through this difficulty. You know what's in my heart. Take the pain from me, Lord, and give me rest in your loving embrace. Breathe life into me and invigorate my soul to forge onward. This road is hard and long and I need to feel you near me. Please, Lord, don't give up on me! Amen.

november 11

VETERANS DAY

There was heavy fighting with the Philistines during Saul's lifetime. Whenever Saul saw any strong or brave man, he took him into his service (1 Samuel 14:52).

My mother's advice to parenting teenagers is to pick your battles. While she feels not everything needs to be about a lesson, I look for those teaching moments and seize them the way Saul took any strong brave man into his service. The teaching-moment method of faith-building informs teenagers about God by capturing their attention with a topic they can relate to that occurs on the spot.

First, seek a catalyst or an event that exemplifies a spiritual point. A conversation starter could be that today is Veterans Day, where we pause to reflect on the service that our military forces have provided to ensure our freedom. As U.S. citizens, we have the freedom of speech and are not persecuted for voicing our opinions. We also have the freedom of religion to worship God. This conversation could go in many different directions depending on the message you want to deliver to your teenager.

If you want to keep the focus on honoring the servicemen and women of the armed forces, encourage your teenager to write thank-you letters to be sent to a veterans hospital. Maybe you know someone who served, and you could honor that individual today. A word of thanks goes a long way to someone who made great sacrifices for your freedom. One of the best things you can do for members of the armed services is pray for them.

REFLECT

Use today as a teaching moment, spinning it however is necessary to instill in your daughter a lesson that she can think about for years.

✠ PRAY ✠

Dear Heavenly Father,

Form the words in my heart to relay a message to (name). Bless my intentions, Lord. I want to instruct (name) to grow into a person of good moral character. Help me to guide her to walk the path you have laid out before us. I trust in you and your infinite wisdom. I love you, Lord. Amen.

november 12

JESUS SAVES

Because I came down from heaven not to do my own will but the will of the one who sent me. And this is the will of the one who sent me that I should not lose anything of what he gave me, but that I should raise it [on] the last day. For this is the will of my Father, that everyone who sees the Son and believes in him may have eternal life, and I shall raise him [on] the last day" (John 6:38–40).

If you could relive your life, would you do it? Was your childhood so wonderful and harmonious that you would go back to infancy to do it all over again? Were your teenage years so magnificent that you'd jump at the chance to go back? Most people would decline this opportunity. They don't want to relive the heartaches, the disappointments, the fights, and the many pains that come with growing up.

As the Son of God looked on the human race observing and discerning, what ran through his mind? He came off his heavenly throne to be created in flesh and dwell among us. He could already see from heaven the pitfalls, disenchantments, and wretchedness that ensnared earthly creatures. I wonder if he thought, "You people make something that's supposed to be easy into something so difficult and discombobulated. I'll show you how it's done."

Jesus' Incarnation had to be difficult. Can you imagine agreeing to live someplace other than your comfortable home for the next thirty-three years, knowing that your friends and neighbors will slaughter you in the most excruciating manner? Jesus did this to wash away our sins so we could spend eternity with him in heaven. Jesus suffered to save us.

REFLECT

The next time your teen makes a choice you just can't comprehend, keep in mind that you've done it all before. Try to lead by example.

✠ PRAY ✠

Dear Heavenly Father,

I'm sorry I complain about (name) and the suffering I endure by parenting him. It isn't easy being a teen today. Bless me with understanding and love to wash away the irritations that annoy me. With you, I can do anything, Lord. I trust you and love you. Amen.

november 13

STAY WELL

He restores my soul. He guides me along right paths for the sake of his name (Psalm 23:3).

This is the time of year when everyone seems to catch a cold easily and the flu season is about to begin. Indoor pathogen exposure rises with cold weather. Cooler temperatures stress the immune system, and attempts to stay warm sap our energy. Decreasing sunlight reduces vitamin D, leaving many people vulnerable in flu season. Fresh fruits and vegetables are less prevalent in grocery stores, leaving many people with fewer nutrients going into the winter months.

Parents dislike their child missing school or having to miss work themselves and stay home with a sick kid. Sometimes kids are too sick to even do homework. It's a delicate balancing act between not allowing your daughter to fall behind academically while giving your child enough time to recover from an illness. To keep this from happening we often spend time trying to prevent our kids from getting sick in the first place. Whether it's getting a flu shot, stocking up on fruit high in vitamin C, or prompting them to wash their hands more frequently, we spend a lot of time trying to keep our kids healthy.

It's essential for your teenagers to be well physically in order for them to do well academically, but how often do you think about the health of your teen's spirituality? What do you do to promote prayer, quiet time for reflection, or time for reading the Bible?

REFLECT

Invite your kids to participate in your own personal prayer time so they can understand the importance of it and how it can be done. When families pray together, it strengthens the ties that bind you together.

✠ PRAY ✠

Dear Heavenly Father,

Enable me to welcome (name) into my prayer rituals.
Empower me with the capability to teach and encourage my kids to reach out to you every day for strength and encouragement.
Help me to lead and guide them down the right path so they are well physically and spiritually. I love you, Lord. Amen.

november 14

SECOND CHANCES

I will sprinkle clean water over you to make you clean; from all your impurities and from all your idols I will cleanse you. I will give you a new heart, and a new spirit I will put within you. I will remove the heart of stone from your flesh and give you a heart of flesh. I will put my spirit within you so that you walk in my statutes, observe my ordinances, and keep them (Ezekiel 36:25–27).

We bought a hodgepodge of old furniture with nicks and dents from a rummage sale for my daughter. She spent months scrubbing away filth, sanding scratches out of table tops, refinishing old dressers, polishing grime off brass fixtures and lamps, and bringing new life to the old pieces. As my daughter worked through this process, she realized she was also fixing herself up, cleaning up her act, attending Mass regularly, praying daily, and discovering what she's made of.

Transformations don't happen easily or quickly. It's a slow process that comes with determination and grit. Do you have a teenager who is taking a second chance at something? Maybe your son is taking another road test or trying out for a sport that he didn't qualify for last year. Was your teen accused of shoplifting and you are rebuilding trust between you?

God is patient and forgiving; he therefore wants us to be patient with and forgiving of our kids when they mess up. God gives us second chances, so we should give them to our kids when they need it. Giving them a second chance means we allow them another chance to earn our trust. Trust must be earned over time. We need to have a loving and forgiving heart to help us through these difficulties.

REFLECT

Call out to the Lord to keep you strong during trying times.

✠ PRAY ✠

Dear Heavenly Father,

Fill me with your love while I try to imitate your ways. Let your Spirit guide each step I take while (name) rebuilds trust with our family and me. I trust in your ways, Lord. Amen.

november 15

CELEBRATE ACCOLADES

We ought to thank God always for you, brothers, as is fitting, because your faith flourishes ever more, and the love of every one of you for one another grows ever greater. Accordingly, we ourselves boast of you in the churches of God regarding your endurance and faith in all your persecutions and the afflictions you endure
(2 Thessalonians 1:3–4).

The path of the just is one of loveliness, beaming with truth, light, and grace, making each day splendid in God's perfect love. The righteous don't get the glory, God does. He makes all things right. Love arises from faith, which is useful when trials come because it enables us to endure all tribulations. Ponder if the path you are walking is one of righteousness. Do you get sidetracked with dishonesty or immorality?

If your kids hear you lie, dishonesty is what they'll learn. If your kids witness your tolerance of corruption, that is what they'll learn. Your teenagers will mimic what you say and do. You are their best teacher, so strive to be honorable. Each time you do the right thing, celebrate it! Use it as a teaching moment to convey to your kids how they should act when something similar happens to them.

REFLECT

Shower your teen with accolades when she acts fairly or decently, especially if took great effort to achieve. Maybe your youngster stood up to bullies on the school bus or shared lunch with an ostracized student because it was the right thing to do. Recognize all successes of your child and all the steps she takes in the right direction, no matter how big or small.

✠ PRAY ✠

Dear Heavenly Father,

Thank you for granting me the ability to know right from wrong and walking the path of righteousness. Thank you for illuminating my trail so I don't stumble and fall. There are so many deviations that could lead me astray; thank you, Lord, for safeguarding my heart. I love you, Lord. Amen.

november 16

CONTROL YOUR THOUGHTS

Jesus rebuked him and said, "Be quiet! Come out of him!" Then the demon threw the man down in front of them and came out of him without doing him any harm. They were all amazed and said to one another, "What is there about his word? For with authority and power he commands the unclean spirits, and they come out" (Luke 4:35–36).

Sometimes the devil creeps into our lives without us realizing it. Maybe an upbeat thought turns sour or an optimistic afternoon turns horrific and we can't figure out why. The devil camouflages what he does so we don't know it's him. His works are disguised by deceit. Have you ever had a thought, idea, or suspicion that didn't seem quite right but you thought was your own? Under this ruse you accept it, believing it's yours, while it's really his. Perhaps you began wondering if your son and friends are really where they said they would be. You jump to conclusions and become upset over these thoughts. Maybe you begin to worry frantically that your teenager is unsafe: a siren signals a car accident, lateness indicates trouble, your teen doesn't respond to your texts so he must be lying.

Our imaginations run wild, and these thoughts can even make us physically ill. Worry does no good whatsoever. But prayer can do much good. The next time Satan places a worm of worry in your thoughts, say, "Get away from me!" Call out to God to chase the devil away and keep you strong. Being a parent is tough enough; you don't need the devil making the job more difficult.

REFLECT

Rely on the Lord's strength to carry you through stressful moments, temptations, and unfounded fears.

✠ PRAY ✠

Dear Heavenly Father,

If the thoughts in my head are not from you, Lord, take them away from me; I do not want them. Bless my thoughts with holiness as they are formed in my mind. Grant me the intelligence to distinguish what is from you and enable me to act on them in a loving and compassionate manner. All I do, I do for you.
You are my Savior. I love you, Lord. Amen.

november 17

MOTHERS

The man gave his wife the name "Eve," because she was the mother of all the living (Genesis 3:20).

An Army chaplain told stories about his wartime experience in German-occupied France. He observed gravely injured soldiers lying on the battlefield calling out to their mothers. In their last moments of life, the person they wanted most was Mom. For some, in our time of need, we turn to our mothers for consolation, encouragement, and love. During moments of discord, it can be challenging to reach your teenager. Maybe you could make a special meal or bake his favorite dessert with an accompanying note saying how much you love him. Maybe you could pray with him in addition to praying for him. Positive words of affirmation also increase his security with you.

When kids handle their life's challenges poorly, it can be draining on mothers and fathers. Both parents need to remember not to shift all of the focus on the teen with troubles. The parents also need to take care of themselves and each other. One of the best ways they can do this is to pray as a family. You have the power to strengthen the ties that bind you together. If there has been a misfortune in your home, choose to be the one your child clings to, to weather it. If your teenager feels safe with you, he will be less likely to turn to unhealthy measures for comfort, like drugs and alcohol.

REFLECT

Consider if you offered sufficient support to your teenager recently. What new event brought you and your youngster closer together?

✠ PRAY ✠

Dear Heavenly Father,

Strengthen me while (name) struggles through his difficulties. Allow me to be extra tender and caring during this time. Empower me with the right words to be inspirational to him and keep you in our daily conversations. Thank you, Lord, for giving me the right tools at the perfect time. Amen.

november 18

REFLECTIONS

Reflect on what I am saying, for the Lord will give you understanding in everything (2 Timothy 2:7).

These days I won't make any major decision until after I have had ample time to mull it over and pray on it. When I was younger, I made quick decisions hoping for the best outcome. I sometimes paid dearly for bad choices. Today, kids have tools to make speedy decisions since they seem to be constantly wired to the internet. Any question they have can be instantly resolved with a swipe of a finger or click of a button.

When you were a teenager, how long did it take you to do research for a school paper? Did you have to use encyclopedias and typewriters? Did you have a cell phone when you were a teenager? Laptops and smartphones make life easier and learning faster for kids today, which can be both good and bad.

In this passage, Paul tries to convince Timothy to spend ample time reflecting on his words by allowing the Holy Spirit to provide understanding. Paul wanted Timothy to turn to God and not him for enlightenment. It might have been faster for Timothy to ask Paul, "What do you mean?" but Paul wanted Timothy to have a more profound explanation from God.

We also need to ask God to give us understanding. The rewards will be greater when we spend time reflecting on passages and questions.

REFLECT

In today's world where we don't have enough time in the day to do everything that we need to do, make the time to reflect on God's words. His words are more important than anyone else's.

✠ PRAY ✠

Dear Heavenly Father,

Thank you for shedding light into my world, for granting me understanding and wisdom to recognize the messages you intend for me. You are perfectly sublime, and I am profoundly satiated in your grace and endless love. Amen.

november 19

NOT BREAD ALONE

He therefore let you be afflicted with hunger, and then fed you with manna, a food unknown to you and your ancestors, so you might know that it is not by bread alone that people live, but by all that comes forth from the mouth of the LORD (Deuteronomy 8:3).

We do not live by bread alone but also on the word of God. What's interesting about today's passage is that God allows the travelers to be afflicted with hunger before he provides nourishment. Have you ever noticed how good food tastes when you're really hungry? Likewise, when I'm feeling despondent, it's then that I see God's hand the clearest, guiding me up and out of the darkness I'm in. It's then that I am truly appreciative of being rescued and all that God does for me and gives to me.

Everything that God engages in leads to our nourishment; God's blessing makes it ample to support life. Sometimes we forget that we depend on the Lord for life and all things. God's words, the bread of life, are nourishment for our spiritual life. The next time you feel down or that you are lacking what it takes to be a good parent and role model, look to heaven. God is waiting for you to reach out to him.

REFLECT

Have you taken God's gifts for granted? Whatever affliction you are struggling with, remember that your sustenance will come. The path to a greater union with God goes through the cross. Suffering cleanses the soul.

✠ PRAY ✠

Dear Heaven Father,

Help me through this disparity. I feel so tired and weak, I need your nurturing and love. Wrap your merciful arms around me and safeguard my heart for the torment of our cruel world. All good things come from you, Lord Jesus. Shine your grace, your power, and your light around me so I can lead (name) into the way of salvation. I ask this in Jesus' name. Amen.

november 20

SET GOOD EXAMPLES

Like obedient children, do not act in compliance with the desires of your former ignorance but, as he who called you is holy, be holy yourselves in every aspect of your conduct, for it is written, "Be holy because I [am] holy" (1 Peter 1:14–16).

We tell our kids to eat well-balanced meals, get plenty of rest, and exercise to maintain a strong body. How good is this advice if they see their parents skip meals or eat junk food, get insufficient shuteye, and become couch potatoes every night? If we talk the talk, we also need to walk the walk. Parents need to practice what they preach.

Think about how you can start setting good examples for your kids beginning today. Kids learn by watching their parents. They will pick up your good habits as well as your bad ones. Maybe you could set the cruise control on your car to ensure you only drive the speed limit. Never drink and drive. Don't talk on the phone or text behind the wheel. Always buckle up. As soon as you get in the car, say a prayer asking God to protect you on your journey regardless of the distance you are going. Keeping God in your thoughts will help you avoid road rage.

Stop telling little white lies. A lie is a falsehood no matter how you look at it. Your teenager will respect you for being truthful, and she will grow into an adult of good moral character if she sees you as an example of one.

Be forgiving. Not only does Christ want us to, but it will strengthen your family unit and teach your child to be merciful, too. Don't use foul language. If Jesus was standing beside you, would you swear? Promote healthy dialog by using open and honest communication skills and compassionate language.

REFLECT

Pray often, and give credit when credit is due, especially if it's directed to the Lord.

✠ PRAY ✠

Dear Heavenly Father,

Help me to be the best possible version of myself.
Thank you for keeping me healthy throughout my child's teen years.
Amen.

november 21

GIVE THANKS TO THE LORD

Give thanks to the LORD on the harp; on the ten-stringed lyre offer praise. Sing to him a new song; skillfully play with joyful chant. For the LORD's word is upright; all his works are trustworthy. He loves justice and right. The earth is full of the mercy of the LORD (Psalm 33:2–5).

I tried to instill thankfulness in my daughters. While they were young, it was easy to emulate gratitude at home. However, once they became teenagers mingling with friends, I could only hope that they extended appreciation appropriately when they were away from home. Some teens express their gratitude better to friends, classmates, and even strangers than to their parents. I have been known to do too much for my kids and then feel resentful when my acts of kindness go unnoticed or unappreciated. I want to hear my kids say, "Thanks, Mom! You're the best!"

I imagine God feels similarly when we don't notice or acknowledge each and every little thing he does for us. God allows us to open our eyes each morning to enjoy another new day. He provides clean air and unpolluted water. We have food to eat and a roof over our heads. How often do we thank God for those little things that are often taken for granted? God wants us to have a thankful heart and sing praises to him.

REFLECT

The next time you feel the resentment building because of someone in your circle of friends or your family, stop to consider if you have forgotten to thank God for all he has given to you.

✠ PRAY ✠

Dear Heavenly Father,

Thank you for all you give to me each day: the ability to function and think clearly as I parent (name). Thank you for providing the blessings that carry me through the difficult moments and the stamina to forge on to do it all over again tomorrow. You are my loving Lord, full of kindness and mercy. Amen.

november 22

SEEK WITH PATIENCE

*The two disciples heard what he said and followed Jesus. Jesus turned and saw them following him and said to them, "What are you looking for?" They said to him, "Rabbi" (which translated means Teacher), "where are you staying?" He said to them, "Come, and you will see." So they went and saw where he was staying, and they stayed with him that day (*John 1:37–39).

Many times throughout my life I have asked God, "Is what I'm doing what you want me to be doing?" I ask because I want reassurance. Parenthood is a seemingly endless and thankless job with a lot of heartache, and while there are many rewards and benefits in the thick of it, my mind focuses on the difficulties at hand.

Sometimes I want something more from my life; fulfillment in another form. When I get restless, I think about President John F. Kennedy's words reminding us not to ask what our country can do for us, but what we can do for our country. Say that phrase to yourself, but this time insert "God" in place of "our country." Ask not what God can do for you, but what you can do for God. Maybe what we can do is be satisfied with being a good parent.

In today's Bible passage, Jesus asks the disciples, "What are you looking for?" If you met Jesus on the roadside and he asked you that question, how would you reply? Consider including in your response the reasons why you are seeking meaning in your life through Jesus. The disciples probably just wanted to stay where Jesus was in order to learn from him. What is your purpose in seeking to follow Jesus?

REFLECT

What can you learn from the disciples' passion to seek Jesus, and how can you change the way you seek Christ in your life? Maybe it's being content with the role you play in your teenager's life while inviting Christ to be a bigger part of your journey.

✠ PRAY ✠

Dear Heavenly Father,

Help me to be satisfied with my role as parent because I can include you in everything I do. Tell me, Lord, what can I do for you? Amen.

november 23

A NOURISHED SOUL

One who is full, tramples on virgin honey; but to the man who is hungry, any bitter thing is sweet (Proverbs 27:7).

When I was in Romania in 1991 adopting our daughter, I witnessed people starving for the basics: food, clothing, and shelter. I saw mile-long breadlines and empty shelves in grocery stores. It wasn't long before my own stomach growled. I missed the comforts of home: cupboards stocked with food, stores overstocked with merchandise, and banks with plenty of money. In America, I took those things for granted. My security was dependent upon things. At home, while my physical needs were fulfilled, my spiritual needs were unsatisfied with stuff. Here my soul was nourished with something totally different: God's word.

In times of trouble, I often seek comfort through food and shopping online. Sometimes I forget to open the Bible and let God's words, sweeter than honey, satisfy me. Are you like one who is full and dislikes honey? Those individuals have enough. Allow your soul to be hungry because you can satisfy your cravings with the Lord's sweet words.

Dwell on God's words, allow the sweetness to wash over you and settle into your bones. His message will coat the bitterness of your tribulations and allow you to move past them. Walk hand in hand with Jesus. He knows true suffering because he endured a dreadful crucifixion. Regardless of what your burdens are, God will help you carry them. Don't waste your time and energy trying to find satisfaction yourself with worldly possessions. Instead, gobble up God's word; only then will you be truly satisfied.

REFLECT

Do you try to achieve satisfaction by surrounding yourself with things: a new car, a nicely decorated home, frequent trips to the shopping mall for stuff you don't need? How can you refocus so you turn to God for fulfillment?

✠ PRAY ✠

Dear Heavenly Father,

Nourish my soul, dear Lord, with the sweet words my heart longs to hear. I want to devour your message and be content only with you. I can live without things. I cannot live without you in my life. I love you! Amen.

november 24

THANKSGIVING

So, as you received Christ Jesus the Lord, walk in him, rooted in him and built upon him and established in the faith as you were taught, abounding in thanksgiving (Colossians 2:6–7).

Thanksgiving is one time of the year when we gather together with family and friends to ponder all that we are truly thankful for: family, friends, our jobs, and our health. In my home, our tradition is to take turns sharing our feelings of thankfulness with each other as we feast on a smorgasbord of food. But we don't do this only one day of the year; we do it every day. We feast on a banquet of each other's kind words. Why should we only voice our thanks one day out of the year?

It's easy to become entangled in other people's lack of thankfulness, their insincerity, or their lack of appreciation. Some people are chronic complainers. Don't get ensnared in that negativity because it will inevitably drag you down, too. Is your appreciation more abundant than your complaints? If you are unhappy with your job, can you at least be thankful that you *have* a job when so many are unemployed? If you are unhappy about how poorly your stocks are doing, can you at least be happy that you have money? If you are unhappy with your kid, can you at least be content that he is with you today?

REFLECT

When you have a teenager with issues, it's hard to be thankful when there are so many problems surfacing; you get through one and something else pops up. Ask yourself if your teen is better today than yesterday and if so, be thankful for that. Look for one aspect of your kid to rejoice over, even if it is simply a warm smile. Be grateful for it.

✠ PRAY ✠

Dear Heavenly Father,

Through you, I have all that I need. I appreciate what you have done for me, sending your son to be crucified for my sins so that I might spend eternity with you. I truly love you, Lord. Amen.

november 25

BLACK FRIDAY

Nothing that my eyes desired did I deny them, nor did I deprive myself of any joy; rather, my heart rejoiced in the fruit of all my toil. This was my share for all my toil (Ecclesiastes 2:10).

Black Friday, the day after Thanksgiving, marks the beginning of the Christmas shopping season. Stores open earlier than usual offer deals too good to pass up. In 2011, some stores opened at midnight; in 2012, stores began opening on Thanksgiving Day; and in 2013, some families abandoned their traditional Thanksgiving feast for shopping. They encountered aggressive crowds with throngs of people trampling each other to grab certain items before supplies ran out.

What happened to the day reserved for giving thanks? Has our nation become so materialistic that we cannot bother with Thanksgiving because we are in a hurry to scoop up retail discounts? What would Jesus think of this?

Has the devil riled merchandisers to offer phenomenal deals to lure families away from the dinner table and into their stores? Use this time to reflect on the essence of the holiday season. We are called to give thanks, show appreciation, offer gifts of service to others, show tolerance, offer peace, and be patient, loving, and kind. The Christmas season is not about the best deals or the most presents. It's about celebrating the gift God gave to us by sending his Son to walk among us.

REFLECT

During this holiday season, boycott the crowded malls. Give from the heart. Only display religious trinkets and ornaments. Make your Nativity set a showcase in your home. Christmastime is about preparing for the birth of Christ, not the coming of Santa Claus.

✠ PRAY ✠

Dear Heavenly Father,

Let me be more loving to my family. Help me to say "yes" to them when they need my help. Don't let me become materialistic and focus on stuff. Enable my heart to expand this Christmas, to feel more love and compassion. I ask this in Jesus' name. Amen.

november 26

WONDERFUL LIFE

God in the beginning created human beings and made them subject to their own free choice. If you choose, you can keep the commandments; loyalty is doing the will of God (Sirach 15:14–15).

At this time of year, my daughters begin watching Christmas movies. We each have our personal favorites; one we all enjoy is *It's a Wonderful Life*. It reminds us how important it is that our life has meaning. God gave each of us a wonderful life. It's our responsibility to use it to the best of our ability and lift up those around us who have fallen, or perhaps point out our neighbors' gifts and talents if they can't see them.

Oftentimes, my daughters need to be reminded that their young lives have value and purpose. They might fail to see their talents or perhaps don't know how to use them to serve others. That's where parents need to be supportive and creative, helping their kids search for avenues to make wise choices with their lives.

Each person's life touches numerous other lives, and when he isn't around a void is felt. An obvious point of *It's a Wonderful Life* is that without George, many things would have been different. Consider how different your life would be without your kids. Would it be better or would your life lack meaning? Oftentimes we have no idea how significantly our lives affect others or vice versa. However, we can thank God that he brought such amazing people into our lives to be our family. We can choose to embrace them. God gave each of us the ability to make our own decisions. It's up to us whether or not we will make wise decisions and keep the commandments.

REFLECT

What are your kid's gifts and how can he use them to become lifelong productive citizens?

✠ PRAY ✠

Thank you for giving me a wonderful life and family.
Thank you for the difficulties because they make me wiser and stronger.
Thank you for the blessings because they make my heart light.
I truly love you. Amen.

november 27

HOPES AND DREAMS

His sons did not follow his example, but looked to their own gain, accepting bribes and perverting justice (1 Samuel 8:3).

Imagine having a youngster who won't follow your example. Imagine that youngster becomes corrupt, accepting bribes and misrepresenting honesty and integrity. That's not what parents dream for their kids. Parents have high hopes that their children's futures will be promising and bright.

Some parents hope their children will fulfill their own unrealized ambitions. Is this the case in your situation? If you feel your children are an extension of you, then you might be more likely to expect your teenager to fulfill your failed dreams. Are you pushing your teenager to study law or medicine because you always wanted to be a lawyer or doctor? Have a heart-to-heart conversation with your teen to hear what her hopes and dreams are, irrespective of what you want for her. As long as your daughter feels and can count on your continual love, guidance, and support, she will do well.

Many parents enjoy basking in the glory of the accomplishments of their children. There are parents who live vicariously through their kids. Our job as a parent is to steer our kids in the right direction, nurturing them as individuals, and helping them to realize their passions. Once you start believing in your child's hopes and dreams, she will believe in them, too.

REFLECT

Contemplate your desires for your teenager's future.

✠ PRAY ✠

Dear Heavenly Father,

Help me to let go of unrealistic expectations I have for (name). Enable me to work through her issues so that together we can learn her strengths and build on them. Thank you for giving me this beautiful child to raise into the person you created her to be. Amen.

november 28

ALWAYS LOVE GOD

Therefore, you shall love the LORD, your God, with your whole heart, and with your whole being, and with your whole strength. Take to heart these words which I command you today. Keep repeating them to your children. Recite them when you are at home and when you are away, when you lie down and when you get up. Bind them on your arm as a sign and let them be as a pendant on your forehead (Deuteronomy 6:5–8).

This passage reminds us to always love God in everything we think, say, and do. It sounds impossible when your teenager is rolling his eyes at something you've just said. Put your hands together, look to heaven, and pray out loud, "Dear Lord, Thank you for my brilliant teenager, whom I adore! Bless him with kindness, insight, and purpose today. I ask this in your name, Jesus. Amen."

Take a look around your house and notice the religious articles you have displayed. If you don't have crucifixes on your walls or statues on your shelves, it's time to get some. Your children need to know that God is more important than paintings of landscapes or vacation souvenirs. If Jesus knocked on your door, would he feel important in your home if his picture was nowhere to be found? If your teenager is embarrassed by such things, now is the perfect opportunity to discuss how important God is in your life. Wear holy medals and encourage your teenager to wear them, too. Explain the significance behind them and everything else you do.

REFLECT

Oftentimes when you don't know what to do, the best thing to do is pray. God will hear your words and answer you. Go for a walk and let God fill your heart with his infinite wisdom.

✠ PRAY ✠

Dear Heavenly Father,

Compassionate Lord, you are the light of my world and the reason for everything I do. Cast a merciful gaze onto me and onto (name) so he can come to know you as I do. Draw him into your light and grant him joy. I truly love you, Lord. Amen.

november 29

DISCIPLINE

Folly is bound to the heart of a youth,
but the rod of discipline will drive it out (Proverbs 22:15).

Discipline is tough for any parent. Rules and consequences are critical when negotiating your way through the teenage years. Using rewards can encourage your teen to follow rules and behave appropriately. When my daughter followed our family rules, she could drive the family car. The consequence of misbehaving meant the keys were taken away. Punishments need to match the misconduct. Screaming and hitting are ineffective forms of discipline that will teach your teenager violence and yelling are acceptable.

Have you considered having your teen pay restitution for a penalty? That's an opportunity to correct her mistake. If your teenager breaks something, allowing her to pay for its replacement gives her a chance to redeem herself by seeing how the consequence fits the action.

Inevitably while parents dole out punishments, they are bound to get a degree of "talking back" challenging the rules. There's a slippery slope between developing autonomy and being rude. Maintain your composure while you address it with, "Please be respectful. It's OK to disagree, but you have to be polite about it." This lets your teenager know her opinion matters, but she must be respectful, which will improve future debates.

REFLECT

How well are your current discipline techniques working? Do you use the loss of privileges as a punishment for your teenager? Every kid is different, so what works with one teenager might not work for another. For example, changing a curfew for my daughter wouldn't be a big deal because she didn't stay out late. However, grounding her by keeping her away from friends would be a sentence with meaning.

✠ PRAY ✠

Dear Heavenly Father,

Empower me while I discipline (name). Help me say the
right words so I build her up while making a point.
Help (name) to feel my love knowing I forgive transgressions.
I ask this in your name, Jesus. Amen.

november 30

CHILDREN ARE GIFTS

Certainly sons are a gift from the Lord,
the fruit of the womb, a reward (Psalm 127:3).

God rewards us with children. They are gifts. We must treat these gifts with love and respect—even if at times their actions make it seem impossible to do. Teenagers know how to push your buttons and say the worst things at the poorest of times. Does your teenager get embarrassed by the way you dress or style your hair? Maybe your teen thinks he is smarter than you because he appears to know everything.

If you are being tormented by the metamorphosis of your kid, think back to the day you first held him. Remember how blissful those first moments were. Remember the awe you felt wondering who that tiny creature would be some day. Today you have a glimpse of that individual blossoming before your eyes. Our best possessions are our own dear offspring, with whom God blessed us.

In 1956, Hungarians tried to escape Communism by sneaking across the border into Austria late at night. Many people carried valuables, dropping cumbersome objects along the way. My neighbors left their belongings behind and carried only their most priceless possessions: their two children. Having their priorities straight laid the foundation for a happier life for them in America.

REFLECT

It's impossible to know why we have different circumstances from our friends and neighbors, but we have to trust in God's plan. Imagine if God said, "Oops! You weren't supposed to have your teenager this long. He must come back with me now." You would do anything to keep your child a little while longer, bad attitude and all. Remember that you were once a teenager, too. God has a reason for everything that happens. Trust God.

✠ PRAY ✠

Dear Heavenly Father,

Even though I'm at the end of my rope, I trust your plan, Lord. I don't see the things you see; I don't know what you know, but I do trust in your ways. Bolster my endurance so that I don't falter on my journey. My path is long and the journey is arduous. Rejuvenate me with your love. I ask this in Jesus' name. Amen.

december 1

PRAISE IS NOTEWORTHY

Worry weighs down the heart,
but a kind word gives it joy (Proverbs 12:25).

There is much to be anxious about as we begin a new month: Advent, Christmas, end-of-the-year activities, and winter weather. Just one of those things is enough to deal with, but altogether it's quite a lot—especially with your kid's events piled on. Don't allow the frenzy to morph into a gigantic problem. Try to enjoy the upcoming holiday with your family by untangling your obligations and prioritizing them. Delegate some responsibilities to your teenagers; don't try to do everything yourself. If something isn't done perfectly, let it slide. If something doesn't get done, let it go. Focus on the big picture: the coming of the Lord.

In everything that you do to prepare for Christmas, do it with love. If it's done with anger or anxiety, how good is that? Start your day with prayer and positive actions. Speak lovingly to your family. Give your spouse and teenagers a smile and kind word. Hug them and thank God for them. They are gifts from God. Your positivity can build up your kids to do wondrous deeds. Praise doesn't cost anything, it doesn't require much effort, you can do it as often as you like, wherever or whenever you want, and no one will ever get tired of it.

REFLECT

Consider which family member needs to hear the most praise. Recognize her beautiful smile and twinkling eyes. Acknowledge the slightest optimistic behavior and compliment it frequently. Do this every day, not just today. You can make every day special with praise, love, and cheerfulness.

✠ PRAY ✠

Dear Heavenly Father,
Fill my heart with abundant love; let it overflow onto everyone I meet.
Let my kids and spouse feel my love and respond accordingly.
With authentic praise filling our home, anything can happen.
Thank you for allowing me to choose all that is good, hopeful,
and bright. I love you, Lord. Amen.

december 2

BELIEVE THE UNBELIEVABLE

Then the angel said to her, "Do not be afraid, Mary, for you have found favor with God. Behold, you will conceive in your womb and bear a son, and you shall name him Jesus. He will be great and will be called Son of the Most High, and the Lord God will give him the throne of David his father, and he will rule over the house of Jacob forever, and of his kingdom there will be no end." But Mary said to the angel, "How can this be, since I have no relations with a man?" And the angel said to her in reply, "The holy Spirit will come upon you, and the power of the Most High will overshadow you. Therefore the child to be born will be called holy, the Son of God" (Luke 1:30–35).

Imagine your daughter telling you that she is pregnant, and insisting that she is still a virgin! Then, you are informed that an angel appeared and informed her that this child will be the Savior of the world. You might be disgusted with her, call her a liar, or have her committed to a psych ward. The story sounds unbelievable, yet it happened. And Mary accepted the impossible situation, embracing the ramifications of it; what would she say to her parents, what would Joseph think, how would she raise the Messiah? I pictured an unplanned pregnancy as a mistake until I read today's passage. Mary's pregnancy wasn't planned, but it was perfectly orchestrated in God's colossal plan. Has an untimely pregnancy disrupted your life? Think of Mary as you work through it, trusting in God as she did. There is a reason for everything that happens, even if you do not like it or understand it. In time you might appreciate it.

REFLECT

Thinks about how great Mary's faith was to trust in such an undertaking. Whatever circumstance you are dealing with, accept the unbelievable, just as Mary did. God has control over the situation. When it comes to your faith, believe what seems humanly unbelievable.

✠ PRAY ✠

Dear Heavenly Father,

Teach me to be flexible and accept the unexpected.
Open my heart and my mind to you, Lord. Amen.

december 3

A CHRISTMAS RELEGATION

Have among yourselves the same attitude that is also yours in Christ Jesus, who, though he was in the form of God, did not regard equality with God something to be grasped. Rather, he emptied himself, taking the form of a slave, coming in human likeness; and found human in appearance, he humbled himself, becoming obedient to death, even death on a cross (Philippians 2:6–8).

Each year my family decorates our Christmas tree with a theme. One year it might be silver ornaments, the next year, gold. Some years it's an old-fashioned theme, other years the ornaments are homemade. We follow that theme throughout Advent, basing our gifts around it. This joyful practice allows us to reflect on past Christmases with great fondness as we recall the silliness of stringing popcorn garlands or the somberness over difficulties.

One Christmas was minimalist because my daughter needed surgery. I wasn't able to do much decorating, baking, or shopping. As we struggled through it in a hospital, with tests and long periods of waiting and uncertainty, somehow our Christmas was perfect. We didn't focus on what we lacked. Instead, we spent hours making a gingerbread house, decorating it with leftover Halloween candy. The powerful emotions of Christmas make the memories linger—some are bittersweet.

God the Father must have bittersweet memories, too. I cannot imagine God sending his Son knowing that he would be tortured and crucified. Today's Bible verses are especially poignant. Jesus relinquished his divine place with God in heaven. Imagine leaving paradise with all of the angels and saints to become human. I never could have done that. Jesus did. He became fully human to experience the same emotions we feel and to appreciate and understand them. He became like us to be a closely personal God and to die for each of us.

REFLECT

If your Christmas is not the way you hoped it would be, shift the focus away from yourself and onto those who might need your help, your smile, or loving embrace. Dwell on God's love as he gave his only Son this Christmas.

✠ PRAY ✠

Dear Heavenly Father,

You have given so divinely to us. I truly thank you for it all. Amen.

december 4

CHRISTMAS GIVING

Whoever cares for the poor lends to the Lord, who will pay back the sum in full (Proverbs 19:17).

When my daughters were little, I taught them the importance of giving anonymously. In early December we shopped for something extra to include in the food baskets that were distributed to underprivileged families in our community. One year we bought candle centerpieces, another year we bought cloth napkins and place mats. My daughters delighted in this special practice as our ideas would change and develop year after year. When I had the talk about Santa Claus' identity, they understood because they had been playing the role of a "special helper" themselves.

It isn't easy to raise a responsible child, willing and able to help others in a "me" society. You can start by setting a good example by taking your son with you when you volunteer at a church or a community event. Include him in aspects that he will be successful with. Perhaps your teenager could help assemble bags of food at the local food pantry or visit residents at a nursing home.

Volunteering provides teenagers an opportunity to gain important life skills while learning to put others' needs first. It allows them the opportunity to discover the world beyond their back yard. It teaches them to give unselfishly with no expectation of return or reward. These invaluable lessons are gifts that will serve them well throughout their entire lives. They will become good models for their friends as they live Christ-centered lives.

REFLECT

What charitable acts will you involve your kids in during the Christmas season?

✠ PRAY ✠

Dear Heavenly Father,

Show me ways to be more charitable. I'm afraid to work outside of my comfort zone. Take my hand and lead me to where you need me most. With you, I can do anything. Amen.

december 5

ADVENT WREATH

"Lord, God of heaven, great and awesome God, you preserve your covenant of mercy with those who love you and keep your commandments. May your ears be attentive...to hear the prayer that I, your servant, now offer in your presence day and night for your servants the Israelites, confessing the sins we have committed against you, I and my ancestral house included (Nehemiah 1:5–6).

The beginning of Advent is the best time to pray together as a family. One way to do this is through an Advent wreath on your kitchen table. Take turns lighting it and holding prayerful discussions around it. You could make one from a circular garland of evergreen branches signifying eternity. There are three purple candles, one pink, and occasionally one white in the center, each representing facets of the spiritual preparation for Jesus' birth.

Begin by lighting the first purple candle, called the "prophet's candle," which symbolizes the hopefulness of Isaiah, who predicted the messiah's arrival. Discuss as a family your own hopes and how you can try to fulfill others hopes during Advent.

The next week's candle is called the "Bethlehem candle," which represents love as people prepare for Jesus' birth. Look for opportunities in your neighborhood when you can shower elderly neighbors with love.

The third purple candle is called the "shepherd's candle," which represents the angel's joy proclaiming Christ's birth.

The fourth (pink) candle is referred to as the "angel's candle" embodying peace. Consider ways that your family can be more peaceful both within your home and in the community.

The white candle in the center, known as "Christ's candle," is lit on Christmas Eve, signifying that Christ has come into the world.

REFLECT

Use this time to reconnect with the people who mean the most to you.

✠ PRAY ✠

Dear Heavenly Father,

Help me to establish new Advent traditions within our family to help serve others who need our prayers and loving touch. Amen.

december 6

PRECIOUS WORDS

The Lord God has given me a well-trained tongue, that I might know how to speak to the weary a word that will waken them (Isaiah 50:4).

At my daughters' doctor's appointment, the physician asked if the girls were "real sisters." Juliana laughed and said, "Have you ever seen a 'fake' sister?" If the doctor used positive adoption language, referring to the girls as "biological siblings," he wouldn't have needed correcting.

There are sensitive topics that require using correct language to avoid hurt feelings. Because you might not know when you're approaching a delicate matter, always think before speaking. God has given us the ability to speak; therefore, rely on the Holy Spirit to direct the meanings of the messages you want to convey. Ask God to help you form the words in your heart and mind.

Maybe your teen needs to hear more positive reinforcement from you. Consider how you can transform your ordinary language into something more supportive. Maybe your child requires more coaching or encouragement. What would it hurt to provide more praise to each family member throughout Advent? Your precious words could make a world of difference in how your family views the world and measures success.

REFLECT

During Advent, in the spirit of giving, try to give someone a compliment each day. Kind words are gifts. They are free, and you can give as much as you want to build up those around you. You never know what kind of impact your thoughtful words can have on someone. Allow God to speak through your voice. Who will you bless with compassionate words today?

✠ PRAY ✠

Dear Heavenly Father,

Speak through me to uplift and encourage everyone I meet today, regardless of who it is. Enable me to put smiles on faces and warm people's hearts through sublime words that roll off my tongue. Let my words be your words, Lord. Amen.

december 7

LOVE AND PEACE

Therefore the Lord will give them up, until the time when she who is to give birth has borne, and the rest of his brethren shall return to the children of Israel (Micah 5:2).

The second week's candle on the Advent wreath, the Bethlehem candle, represents love and peace as we prepare for Jesus' birth. It reminds us that Jesus, a king, was born in a manger in Bethlehem. It's a story so ingrained in us that we don't need to be reminded of it. However, we do need to be prompted to offer peace and love to those we are not fond of. They could even live in the same house with us!

Consider who you are struggling with: a spouse, your teenagers, a neighbor, a coworker, a sibling. Think of ways you can offer an olive branch. Perhaps you could write heartfelt messages on Christmas cards, telling them what a difference they have made in your life. You could remember these people in your daily prayers and let them know you are praying for them. Prayers are the best gifts you can offer anyone, and they could help rebuild peaceful relationships.

REFLECT

Ask God to fill you with the love you need to carry out an intended kind behavior for people you have been struggling with. Maybe you could buy presents for them. If you don't know what to buy, shop online for religious books, movies, or CDs. Have gifts shipped to their homes as a surprise! You might decide to bake Christmas cookies. It takes great effort to do kind deeds for folks who have rubbed you the wrong way, but God will bless you for them. You will be teaching your kids how to be Christlike during Advent.

✠ PRAY ✠

Dear Heavenly Father,

Fill me with your endless stream of love as I try to lay a path of peacefulness with (names). Show me how to love unconditionally, as you do. I ask this in your sweet name Lord, Jesus. Amen.

december 8

THE IMMACULATE CONCEPTION

And coming to her, he said, "Hail, favored one! The Lord is with you" (Luke 1:28).

The Solemnity of the Immaculate Conception celebrates preserving the Blessed Virgin Mary from original sin. Because of God's foresight that Mary would bear Jesus, God kept Mary free from original sin at the time of her conception in St. Anne's womb. On this special feast day we revel in the belief that Mary lacked having a sinful nature; other than Jesus, she was the only person to walk the earth who was sinless.

For today, set a picture of Mary on the kitchen table or a place of prominence in your home where you will see it throughout the day. Pray a rosary, as it's a powerful prayer to God. Praying the rosary gives glory to Jesus and Mary and is more praiseworthy than any other prayer. In various apparitions throughout the world, Mary has appeared holding a rosary and has asked that we continue to say the rosary. Mary leads us to Jesus and presents our needs before him. This prayer cultivates our relationship with God by loving him more.

Consider giving rosary beads as gifts to your family for Christmas. Maybe you could start a new family tradition by praying the rosary altogether on Mary's special feast day. The old adage is true: families who pray together stay together. Conflicts have been resolved because people prayed the rosary; hearts have been converted and implausible intentions answered also. Your life can be blessed by praying the rosary today.

REFLECT

We begin the rosary by praying the Apostles' Creed, one Our Father, three Hail Marys (for an increase in faith, hope, and charity), and one Glory Be. Then there are five decades, each allowing you to meditate on a set of mysteries from Jesus' life: joyful, luminous, sorrowful, and glorious. Each decade begins with an Our Father, followed by ten Hail Marys, and ending with a Glory Be and, if you chose, the Fatima Prayer. After five decades you conclude with the Hail Holy Queen.

✠ PRAY ✠

Dear Heavenly Father,

Thank you for the reminder to pray the rosary today.
I love you. Amen.

december 9

NOTHING IS IMPOSSIBLE FOR GOD

Nothing will be impossible for God (Luke 1:37).

In 1991 I didn't have a clue how to complete an international adoption, but my husband and I were convinced that God was leading us to Romania. We put all of our trust and faith in him and believed that he would help us through it. And he did. Even though we didn't know anyone there, we couldn't speak a word of Romanian, had limited funds and knowledge of the paperwork, we still were successful with our adoption. When you turn over your life to God, allowing him to steer your life's journey, you will be amazed at what can happen.

Reflect over times when you wanted to trust in God. Were you able to put your complete faith in him? Remember that there is a purpose for everything that happens. Don't be afraid to ask for a miracle. If it is God's will, he will grant it, according to his time line for you. Mary conceived a child through the Holy Spirit, which sounds impossible, but with God it was possible. Jesus rose from the dead. That sounds impossible, except it happened. The Bible is filled with miraculous stories, emphasizing that nothing is impossible for God.

How will you remember to call out to God today to ask for help with difficult, circumstances? In your humanity you cannot do everything yourself. Turn your difficulties over to the Lord and allow him to work miracles in your life.

REFLECT

During this hectic time of shopping, baking, volunteering, and kid activities, spend alone time with Jesus, your Lord and Savior. Be still with him. In the silence of your heart, listen for his message for you. He wants the best for you, just as you want the best for your kids. Take time for God. He makes all things possible.

✠ PRAY ✠

Dear Heavenly Father,

Surround me with your love. Scoop up the brokenness of my heart and put it back together. Fill my heart with the love that once was there. I have been feeling so empty, so cold, and isolated. Warm my soul and bring me near, for nothing is impossible in you.

I ask this in your sweet name, Jesus. Amen.

december 10

ASK FOR A SIGN

And behold, the star that they had seen at its rising preceded them, until it came and stopped over the place where the child was. They were overjoyed at seeing the star (Matthew 2:9–10).

Have you looked up at an evening sky and wondered what it was like for the Magi to follow a star? It must have taken strong faith for them to do such a thing. It was an arduous journey, an enormous undertaking. The Wise Men had hope, faith, and—once they saw the Christ Child—love. All because God sent them a star to follow.

Consider an undertaking you have been contemplating but want a sign to know if you are doing the right thing or making the right choice. Ask God for a sign. Perhaps God will send you a subtle indicator or a certain "feeling" that will confirm you are on the right path. Pray for guidance and understanding.

Sometimes the divine realm is beyond human comprehension and steadfast faith is necessary to move you forward. Trust that God will stop you if you are on the wrong path. Trust that God has a magnificent plan, even if you do not know it or feel it yet.

REFLECT

What activity have you been consumed with lately? Maybe you are too close to a certain problem and need to step back from it in order to see the bigger picture. Give that issue to God. He knows how to handle such things and will lead you to the right solution. Remember that with God, you can do anything.

✣ PRAY ✣

Dear Heavenly Father,

Show me the way, Lord, or give me a sign to enlighten me.
I trust in your plan for my life, even when it feels hectic and I can't seem to make any sense of it. I know that you know. I'll be patient, Lord, while I wait for you. Wrap your loving arms around me.
I need you, sweet and merciful Lord. Amen.

december 11

DECIPHERING SIGNS

Ask for a sign from the LORD, your God; let it be deep as the nether world, or high as the sky! But Ahaz answered, "I will not ask! I will not tempt the LORD!" Therefore the Lord himself will give you a sign; the young woman, pregnant and about to bear a son, shall name him Emmanuel (Isaiah 7:11–12,14).

Have you ever traveled to a foreign country and saw a road sign you didn't understand? There are plenty strange road signs in America that are difficult to interpret, too. Often, a tourist must think about his surroundings in order to figure out the meaning of a certain sign.

When doctors prescribe new medications to patients, they warn patients of possible side effects and encourage them to look for signs of adverse reactions.

God gives signs. The problem is that we might not feel worthy to ask, or we might not want to bother God, similar to Ahaz's reply that he didn't want to tempt God. The Lord grants a sign anyway: a virgin shall bear a son. Ahaz might as well have heard that somewhere on earth a pomegranate will be full of priceless diamonds. Where would this woman be? What was her name? How would she conceive? When would this happen? How would he know? There were many unanswered questions. Yet, the sign was from God.

REFLECT

Often we may see something and not recognize it as a miraculous sign because we don't know the entire story. Therefore, it is essential to pray on every little thing. Eventually, when the time is right, God will make it known. Trust in God that he will enable you to decipher the signs he gives.

✠ PRAY ✠

Dear Heavenly Father,

Help me to see the signs you have given. Enable me to act on them and praise you for blessing my life in such a marvelous way. I adore you! Amen.

december 12

SAVING YOUR LIFE

He summoned the crowd with his disciples and said to them, "Whoever wishes to come after me must deny himself, take up his cross, and follow me. For whoever wishes to save his life will lose it, but whoever loses his life for my sake and that of the gospel will save it" (Mark 8:34–35).

Jesus puts in this passage the way to save your life. You must deny yourself being the center of the universe; only God is. Taking up your cross means taking up the consequences of following Christ. Following Jesus also means that for the sake of God's love through Jesus Christ you're willing to die. Therefore, if you live only to please yourself, you will lose your life eternally. But those who lose their life for Jesus' sake by giving it in service or sacrifice to God will save their life by gaining eternal life.

In December, when the nights are long and the air is cold, remember that winter is a period of restfulness necessary for flowers to blossom in the spring. In order for apples trees to bear fruit, they need this break. In order for maple trees' sap to flow, they must rest. The winter is a splendid opportunity to rest as it allows us a time of reflection on the many gifts that God provides, not just in the springtime, but all the time. What gifts are you most thankful for?

My father-in-law loved to make meatballs in the winter because it warmed up the house and his heart while he worked. His recipe made 100 meatballs; he never mixed small batches. He believed meatballs were best when shared. His ability to give left people feeling full and loved.

REFLECT

During the winter months, contemplate what you can do to be more giving. It is in giving that we receive.

✠ PRAY ✠

Dear Heavenly Father,

Keep me strong as I live for you. Bless every act of kindness and charity that I do in your sweet name. Amen.

december 13

SEEK THE LORD

Glory in his holy name; let hearts that seek the Lord *rejoice! Seek out the* Lord *and his might....Recall the wondrous deeds he has done, his wonders and words of judgment* (Psalm 105:3–5).

To end a beautiful day, God gives us spectacular sunsets. When the sunsets are complete, God provides billions of twinkling stars to fill the evening sky. And when daybreak arrives, God gives us another incredible day to live as we see fit. It's all how we look at it. If you can't see the beauty in something, wait a few moments and keep searching, because eventually you will find it. Everything has its beauty, but not everyone sees it, experiences it, or appreciates it.

Perhaps you are not feeling your best because of a growing pile of concerns surrounding the growth and development of your daughter. Maybe she needs an attitude adjustment or maybe you need to change your perspective. If you are unable to see the beauty in your situation or your child, simply wait and ask God to point it out to you. Search for it like a hidden treasure.

If you are feeling exceptionally blue and nothing seems right in your world, focus on how much the Lord loves you. Dwell on Jesus' face smiling down on you, warming you to the bone. Give thanks for the Holy Spirit within you and ask him to lift you from your funk so you can reside in God's loving mercy.

REFLECT

Seek the Lord in all things. If you struggle to find him, look at the sunset, marvel over the twinkling stars that dot the night sky. God is there in it all.

✠ PRAY ✠

Dear Heavenly Father,

Help me to find you when I feel burdened by life's troubles.
Help me to climb out of my misery and focus on your goodness.
Help me to open my eyes to see it. Help me reach out to feel it.
Help me, Lord. I know you are there. I know that you care.
I ask this in Jesus' name. Amen.

december 14

REJOICE: THE LORD IS NEAR

She will bear a son and you are to name him Jesus, because he will save his people from their sins (Matthew 1:21).

As the third week of Advent approaches, allow joy to fill your heart because the Lord is near. The jubilant spirit is marked by the rose-colored candle of the Advent wreath. On Gaudete Sunday (*Gaudete* means "rejoice" in Latin), prepare your heart by removing any sadness and ask for grace to fully experience the joy that God wants you to feel. Your longing has prepared you for the belief that the reign of God is near. Rejoice in the hopefulness that God's presence will grant.

It sounds wonderful to be constantly cheerful, but what if you are overwhelmed by work, obligations, and your teen's activities? How can you let God's shining light into the dark places of your life? How can you avoid patterns of sinfulness?

Don't get caught up in believing that Christmas is all about buying and wrapping gifts, baking and preparing foods, housecleaning, and decorating. Throughout the third week of Advent, celebrate the gifts God has given to you; pause in gratitude for them. Whatever each day brings, be thankful for it all—good and bad—because there is a reason for it all. Regardless of how busy you are, take a few moments to talk to the Lord and give thanks.

REFLECT

Try to experience God's mercy and healing through the sacrament of reconciliation. Offer a gesture of kindness to someone who least expects it: a forgotten friend, a lonely neighbor, a critical relative, your cranky teenager, or an unfriendly coworker. You could apologize for a mishap, overlook an annoyance, or patch up a broken relationship.

✠ PRAY ✠

Dear Heavenly Father,

I lift up my heart to you, thanking you for continual blessings. I rejoice as I prepare my heart to receive your immense, unending love. Bring my family and me into everlasting life. I love you. Amen.

december 15

SIGNS OF HOPE

The needy will never be forgotten, nor will the hope of the afflicted ever fade (Psalm 9:19).

Signs of hope can be found all around this time of year. Witnessing them warms the heart and lifts the soul. Last Christmas I was responsible for providing seventy gifts to indigent families; however, I was only able to offer ten. I was apprehensive that people might not receive a present, so I prayed. At the end of my prayers I remembered the parable about Jesus feeding a gargantuan crowd with just a few fish and loaves of bread. Somehow I knew God would provide. As I began the distribution, unexpected visitors dropped off gift cards and extra presents. By the time we completed the holiday delivery, we had presents left over!

God really does work in miraculous ways. You can experience these miracles by reaching out into your own community. If you want to see the face of God, look into the eyes of a homeless man. Give him a warm pair of socks and gloves; it will comforting him as well as Jesus. When you feed the hungry, you satisfy them as well as the Lord. Consider what acts of service you could do with your daughter. Strive to be a sign of hope for those around you.

REFLECT

Is there a soup kitchen in your community? Does your parish volunteer to hand out presents and necessities to impoverished neighborhoods? Bring your kids to these places so they can see and experience Jesus.

✠ PRAY ✠

Dear Heavenly Father,

I humbly request that you guide me to those who need me most during this season. Give me the tools that I need to do your work, whatever that may be. Let me find you in the sick, the lonely, the hungry, the poor. Let me put my arms around you, let me smile and make you feel welcome. Let me build a fire in the hearts of those whose hearts have grown cold. Amen.

december 16

UNPLANNED PREGNANCY

Joseph her husband, since he was a righteous man, yet unwilling to expose her to shame, decided to divorce her quietly (Matthew 1:19).

I always imagined if my daughter experienced an unplanned pregnancy I would be so angry that I might stop loving her. I thought about the shame, the disappointment, and fear of the unknown that it would bring into my life. Then I thought about how St. Anne must have felt when Mary told her she was pregnant. If my teenage daughter told me she became pregnant by the Holy Spirit, I wouldn't believe it. How did Anne have the grace to embrace her daughter? To love and support her as she departed with Joseph to Bethlehem?

If you are experiencing an unplanned pregnancy, think of St. Anne and ask God to bless you with tolerance, wisdom, and understanding to get you through the ordeal. Initially, you may not understand it, the way Anne couldn't fathom how Mary could get pregnant. Yet Mary was carrying the Savior of the world. You may not feel it now, but later you might know the true blessing of the child.

REFLECT

If you are struggling to accept an unplanned pregnancy or any other unplanned change of plans in your teen's life, take comfort in knowing that you are not alone. Mary experienced it, too, and the Holy Spirit dwells within you. Whatever you do, know that God is always with you. He will never leave you, especially in your time of need. Pray whenever you feel alone, sad, or scared.

✠ PRAY ✠

Dear Heavenly Father,

Thank you for taking me on an incredible new journey. Ease my fears and trepidations and replace them with excitement and love. Guide each step I take, Lord, walk this path with me. I ask this in your sweet and holy name. Amen.

december 17

PUT GOD FIRST

You expected much, but it came to little; and what you brought home, I blew away. Why is this?—oracle of the LORD of hosts— Because my house is the one which lies in ruins, while each of you runs to your own house (Haggai 1:9).

When the people of Judah returned from captivity, they tried to rebuild God's Temple. They stopped during construction because they wanted their homes built before God's. Their excuse (dwindling materials) was for naught because there were plenty of building supplies to construct fancy houses for themselves. This passage reminds me to put God first in all aspects of life.

In the early years we set high goals for our children, planning ways to achieve them and mark our success. Often God isn't included in those plans. You might look back on your plans and identify missteps. What could you have done better? It's especially poignant during the holidays when shopping malls are bustling with shoppers devoted to buying the perfect gifts for their loved ones. While it's nice to give thoughtful gifts, it's even better to spend quality time away from packed shopping centers, away from online shopping sites, and in soup kitchens and food pantries, or even just quality time in your own kitchen.

REFLECT

Throughout the holidays, let the Holy Spirit swell your heart with love for others. Think about them before you think of yourself. Then you will truly make God happy.

✠ PRAY ✠

Dear Heavenly Father,

Move me with your divine Spirit so I follow your lead to do the work you have designed for me even though I don't know what it is. Whisper it in my ears, murmur it in my heart, and envision it in my mind so that I do your will here on earth. All I want is to live in heaven with you for eternity.

Amen.

december 18

LEAN ON THE LORD

Surely then you may lift up your face in innocence; you may stand firm and unafraid. For then you shall forget your misery, or recall it like waters that have ebbed away. Then your life shall be brighter than the noonday; its gloom shall become as the morning, and you shall be secure, because there is hope; you shall look round you and lie down in safety (Job 11:15–18).

Just because the Christmas season has arrived doesn't mean that all of your troubles will disappear. Sometimes pains, disappointments, and sorrows dampen the holiday season. Maybe there was a depressing diagnosis that has left you feeling empty, or the death of a loved one has left your heart feeling especially heavy. What is causing your sadness right now and what can you do to change your attitude about it? If you cannot change the situation, consider changing your approach to it.

Throughout the Christmas season, try to find Jesus in the faces of others who might have bigger troubles than you and then pray for those people. Make a list of everything you might enjoy doing with your teenagers and do the top three things on it. Perhaps you could build a snowman or spend an afternoon sledding with your kids. Warm up with hot cocoa afterward while discussing how you could make someone's Christmas extra special. Consider singing Christmas carols at a nursing home with your teens and some of their friends.

Lean on the Lord to guide you through the holidays. Trust in his ways. Your kids are a gift from God. Enjoy the Christmas spirit that emanates from them.

REFLECT

Gather your teens in the kitchen and bake Christmas cookies with them. Decide together who you should give some of the cookies to. Include your family in the entire process. You'll be making wonderful memories for the future.

✠ PRAY ✠

Dear Heavenly Father,

Thank you for supporting me through my difficulties and diverting my energies into positive happenings with (name). Thank you for giving me my splendid family. They make my life complete. Amen.

december 19

A NECESSARY RESPITE

And the angel said to her in reply, "The holy Spirit will come upon you, and the power of the Most High will overshadow you. Therefore the child to be born will be called holy, the Son of God. And behold, Elizabeth, your relative, has also conceived a son in her old age, and this is the sixth month for her who was called barren; for nothing will be impossible for God" (Luke 1:35–37).

This passage reminds me that when you say "yes" to God, he will help you complete his work. God informed Mary about Elizabeth's condition; therefore, she would be safe to stay with her relative during her pregnancy. When Elizabeth heard Mary's greeting, the infant leaped in her womb, and Elizabeth—filled with the Holy Spirit—cried out in a loud voice and said, "Most blessed are you among women, and blessed is the fruit of your womb. And how does this happen to me that the mother of my Lord should come to me?" (Luke 1:41–43). God paved the way for Mary to stay with Elizabeth to mull over her feelings in her heart before returning to Joseph and her family. Take advantage of every opportunity God sets in your path, for you don't know where those trails will take you. God knows, so trust in his ways, as Mary did.

REFLECT

Perhaps Mary needed some time away from her family to pray over her future without stress or pressure from her parents or Joseph. Contemplate if you might need a brief respite away from your family. Maybe you and your spouse need to step away for a minivacation or a get-away weekend to revive your parenting skills, to pray, or simply to rest. Is God calling you to rest to mull over those feelings in your heart?

✠ PRAY ✠

Dear Heavenly Father,

Sometimes I grind away at problems, making them bigger than they really are. Help me to step back and breathe in your divine grace. Bolster my spirits. Help me finish the task you have set before me. Show me the way and I will follow. Amen.

december 20

WHAT IS YOUR PURPOSE?

Mary said, "Behold, I am the handmaid of the Lord. May it be done to me according to your word." Then the angel departed from her (Luke 1:38).

Each time I gaze at my Nativity set, I reflect on Mary's response to the angel who had such a momentous message: a request from God. It would be hard to say "no" to God, but what he asked was not to be taken lightly. It was an enormous petition. Mary must have realized that Joseph would divorce her or, worse, have her stoned to death. What would her parents think, and how would they believe her? The neighbors would ridicule her and speak poorly about her and her family. No one would believe that Mary conceived miraculously from the Holy Spirit. Instead of getting to know her new husband, Mary had to go away and have a baby without family to support her.

Mary is someone we can admire and respect for her bravery and tenacity. God chose her: a simple and plain girl, a hard-working manual laborer. He didn't want a wealthy princess to be the Mother of God. He picked a humble girl with steadfast faith who lived only to serve him. Mary is a shining example of the mother we can aspire to be. Live to satisfy God's desires of you.

There have been many moments where I have said, "I'm just a mom." Mary was "just a mom," too, and what a marvelous role model she became by being meek, humble, and ordinary. Mary didn't brag to other women at the well that her Son was the Messiah. She simply kept him on the path to do God's work on earth.

REFLECT

Reflect on times when you have boasted about your kid's accomplishments. Could you have handled them differently? Consider times when you felt you didn't measure up because you are just a parent. How are you doing God's work in that role?

✠ PRAY ✠

Dear Heavenly Father,

Thank you for blessing me with the role of parenthood. You must believe I am capable. Help me to raise (name) the way you chose. Guide me down the right path. I trust in you, Jesus. Amen.

december 21

WHERE IS GOD DRAWING YOU?

But when the fullness of time had come, God sent his Son, born of a woman, born under the law, to ransom those under the law, so that we might receive adoption (Galatians 4:4–5).

Two thousand years ago, you might expect the Savior of the world to be born to a royal family; not born of a simple carpenter and his teen bride. You could presume that Jesus would enter the world in a cushy Roman palace, not a measly stable in Bethlehem surrounded by foul-smelling animals. Shepherds and outcasts were the first to be invited to see the newborn king. God planned for Jesus' arrival into the world differently than we imagined.

What is something you imagined but discovered God had planned differently? Maybe you expected your child to be a prodigy but instead she must cope with a learning disorder. Whatever the difference between reality and expectations, remember that God has a reason. As the shepherds did with the babe in the manger, it is good if you search for the goodness in situations. Keep searching until you find it.

REFLECT

Consider other areas of your life, opportunities, or happenings that you could have missed out on because your way of thinking was different from God's. Try to be open-minded to embracing things that you otherwise might not do. Maybe it's inviting a lonely neighbor to Christmas dinner or buying a gift for someone you might not normally give a present to. Step outside your comfort zone and offer a gesture of kindness because God might be drawing you there.

✠ PRAY ✠

Dear Heavenly Father,

Open my eyes to those who need my smile during the Christmas season. Point me in their direction, Lord, so that I can offer a loving embrace or a shoulder to cry on. Let me be the stone they step on. Let me be the brace they use to stand up. Let my arms carry them, warm them, and love them, the way you do for me each day. Amen.

december 22

GOD LOVES THE LOWLY

Now there were shepherds in that region living in the fields and keeping the night watch over their flock. The angel of the Lord appeared to them and the glory of the Lord shone around them, and they were struck with great fear. The angel said to them, "Do not be afraid; for behold, I proclaim to you good news of great joy that will be for all the people. For today in the city of David a savior has been born for you who is Messiah and Lord. And this will be a sign for you: you will find an infant wrapped in swaddling clothes and lying in a manger" (Luke 2:8–12).

While adopting my daughter, we toured the Romanian countryside hoping to have a picnic with the family we were staying with. They parked the car at the side of the road and we walked through a field of sheep to speak with a shepherd. He reeked and was filthy, wearing ragged clothes and mud-encrusted boots. After realizing we were about to have a lamb picnic roast, I persuaded everyone to give the gentle man the granola bars I brought from home. The image of the raggedy shepherd stayed with me.

In every Christmas story I've read, angels announce to the shepherds that the Messiah has been born and they will find him in a manger. My Nativity set's manger is surrounded by several shepherds. Each year I arrange the figurines differently: close to the infant Jesus, behind the Wise Men, or scattered randomly about. Each time I display the set, I recall the shepherd I met in Romania. That is the type of person God invited first to the *crèche*. Imagine how startled they must have been to have an angel appear to them and then invite *them* to see the Messiah! They must have thought they were dreaming as God reached out to the meek of the earth.

REFLECT

Consider reaching out to the "shepherds" in your own community during Advent. Offer them a smile, a prayer, a granola bar. Or all three.

✠ PRAY ✠

Dear Heavenly Father,

Thank you for embracing the lowly people; for I am one! Thank you for reminding me how important they are to you; for I will make them important to me, too! I love you, sweet Lord. Amen.

december 23

ARE YOU PREOCCUPIED?

She wrapped him in swaddling clothes and laid him in a manger, because there was no room for them in the inn (Luke 2:7).

On our last family vacation, we were driving home from Florida and figured we would find a hotel when we got tired and needed a rest. We were surprised to discover no vacancy in one hotel after another. We were exhausted and craved a clean room with crisp white linens to cradle our tired bodies.

I wasn't like Mary: urgent to find a place to give birth to the Savior of the world. The innkeeper was probably like the ones we encountered at the hotel chains along I-91; with his rooms filled, his hands were tied. It was unfortunate being turned away, but what else could he do? The innkeeper in Bethlehem was preoccupied with his own guests, making them a priority. But he wasn't cold-hearted because he offered Joseph and Mary a stable.

Consider the preoccupation of that innkeeper. What a gift he turned away. If he had known the significance of Jesus, he probably would have vacated his other guests or given his own room to Jesus. But he was preoccupied and turned the Holy Family away. Don't become so involved with other things that you fail to welcome Christ into your life.

REFLECT

Are you so preoccupied that you turned away something profoundly special? Are you too busy baking Christmas cookies to notice improvements in your kid's behavior? Are you too busy shopping for the perfect presents that you overlooked her accomplishments in school this week?

✠ PRAY ✠

Dear Heavenly Father,

Remove the blinders that have prevented me from seeing you.
Allow me to feel you, Lord, in everyday happenings.
I don't want to be distant from you. Draw me near and keep me close to your heart. That is where I want to spend every day of my life, starting today. Amen.

december 24

THE PERFECT GIFT

For God so loved the world that he gave his only Son,
so that everyone who believes in him might not perish
but might have eternal life (John 3:16).

Christmas is a glorious season where we celebrate the birth of the Christ Child. He came to the world in an insignificant manner in an out-of-the-way place. Even so, God sent his Son to us as an incredible gift wrapped in flesh.

As we buy and wrap gifts, we put so much pressure on ourselves to buy the perfect presents for those we love. When my two-year-old daughter Andrea asked for Aladdin's magic lamp one Christmas, I was determined to find it for her. I had everyone in New York State on the hunt for it. I was elated when a businessman called to say he found one. Christmas has become synonymous with helping others in the spirit of goodwill. A stranger went out of his way to ensure my daughter's delight. I couldn't have been happier knowing the magic lamp was wrapped under our tree. I wanted Christmas to be special for my daughters. Who doesn't?

We put such an emphasis on having the perfect gift because that is exactly what God gave us in his Son. At Christmas we are reminded to celebrate Jesus' Incarnation with generosity and goodness to others. Not only as the businessman did for me, but to dig deeper and give unselfishly to those who need it most: the homeless, the destitute, those forgotten in nursing homes. This Christmas, teach your teen to give abundantly to others.

REFLECT

What is your perfect gift?

✠ PRAY ✠

Dear Heavenly Father,

Teach me how to be a conduit of your love this Christmas.
I pray for chances to emulate your generosity.
Let me be moved by the Holy Spirit in all I think, say, and do. Amen.

december 25

MAKE ROOM

While they were there, the time came for her
to have her child, and she gave birth to her firstborn son.
She wrapped him in swaddling clothes and laid him in a manger,
because there was no room for them in the inn (Luke 2:6–7).

My daughters always enjoyed sleepovers with friends. Sometimes they invited so many kids to our house I didn't think they would all fit. No one was left out; we could always squeeze in one more friend, or two, or three. Somehow we could always make room. If Jesus, Mary, and Joseph knocked on our door, we could find a place for them. But, I realize sadly, in today's world not everyone is willing to make room.

God is still on the fringes of so many lives. He is worked in only when it is convenient or popular to do so. One popular time is Christmas. For some families, Christmas is the only time during the year they come together to attend church services. While that is good, it would be so much better to go to Mass every Sunday. Some people say they are too busy to go to Mass each week. Their lives are filled with obligations and activities. Kids are involved in sports, musical events, and social experiences. All of this is great, but there still has to be a place for God.

Give your teenagers the gift of attending Mass each week as a family. Teach them about the Lord. Expose them to the Gospels. Let them lift their songs of praises to the Lord and you will be blessed for it.

REFLECT

God needs to be the most important presence in your life. How will you make room for God in your life today?

✠ PRAY ✠

Dear Heavenly Father,

Teach me how to invite you into my life and family.
Teach me how to be a better parent and a better Catholic.
Let me sing your praises every day of my life. I adore you, Lord.
Amen.

december 26

ALL ARE WELCOME

And Mary kept all these things, reflecting on them in her heart
(Luke 2:19).

After her long and exhaustive journey, Mary gave birth in the lowest of places. Shortly afterward, she had unexpected company drop in: young and old shepherds and wise men—all were in awe of what they saw. Mary shared the Christ Child while quietly reflecting on all of it, safeguarding her thoughts in the silence of her heart.

After Christmas, many people drop by my home, some young, others old. Everyone is welcome, but there are occasional visitors who rile me: the relatives with rude comments, the loud neighbor, or the know-it-all kids. I especially dislike the annoying guest who criticizes my parenting skills or boasts about her accomplishments and her children's endeavors. Sometimes I want to control these visits, limiting each stay or turning them away.

Then I think about Mary, how unselfishly she welcomed guests to see her newborn son. She didn't set boundaries for the shepherds, nor did she turn anyone away. She probably invited everyone to see the Savior of the world. Mary had to be worn out but never complained. Instead, she probably smiled lovingly while welcoming each visit patiently.

Today, if an unexpected visitor drops by, think of Mary and how kind she was after giving birth. Recall her fortitude as she carried out God's wishes. Maybe God wants you to strengthen your tolerance or share your abundance with the next person who rings your doorbell. Perhaps God wants you to be welcoming to all of your guests, not just a special few.

REFLECT

How will you treat the next person who shows up on your doorstep unannounced?

✠ PRAY ✠

Dear Heavenly Father,

Teach me patience and kindness as I endure unpleasant guests. Let me be a good role model for my children by welcoming cold visitors into my home. Let me warm them and be more tolerant of their differences. Teach me to love all people. Amen.

december 27

GIVE OF YOURSELF

And suddenly there was a multitude of the heavenly host with the angel, praising God and saying: "Glory to God in the highest and on earth peace to those on whom his favor rests." When the angels went away from them to heaven, the shepherds said to one another, "Let us go, then, to Bethlehem to see this thing that has taken place, which the Lord has made known to us" (Luke 2:13–15).

During our first year of marriage, my husband and I attended his company picnic. I was unprepared: I wore the wrong clothes and forgot to bring a dish. Unbeknownst to me, there were subtle unwritten rules. If an angel invited me to the *crèche,* would I spiff up and bring a gift?

Now imagine what went through the shepherds' minds as they witnessed "a multitude of heavenly the host." Their evening must have been unassuming and boring until celestial praises filled the sky. What did they think approaching the manger beside lavishly dressed learned men with camels draped in silks, presenting elaborate gifts of gold, frankincense, and myrrh? The shepherds stood in awe of the Christ Child, empty-handed and poorly dressed. Undoubtedly, God was pleased.

In reflecting over the best presents I have received, all were gifts of the heart: a sincere smile, a warm embrace, a genuine compliment, or a gift of time. When a doctor delivered bad news, a friend let me cry on her shoulder. When I doubted the world, my daughter wrote a note, saying, "I love you."

REFLECT

Maybe God summoned the shepherds to remind us to give of ourselves from our heart and not to worry about our outer appearances. Use this time to reflect on the ultimate source of your joy.

✠ PRAY ✠

Dear Heavenly Father,

Thank you for enabling me to stand before you empty-handed. Thank you for overlooking my weaknesses and finding my talents and rejoicing in them. I will sing your praises every day of my life.

Amen.

december 28

COME AS YOU ARE

Then the shepherds returned, glorifying and praising God for all they had heard and seen, just as it had been told to them (Luke 2:20).

When my daughters were young and I retold the Nativity story each Christmas, I glossed over the shepherds. Instead, I focused on the three kings and their gifts, both costly and symbolic. They traveled from afar. There were songs about them. They were revered. They had massive camels.

But my girls never played with the Nativity set's camels or wise men, though. They adored playing with the shepherds and sheep. They rearranged them several times a day and spoke about how Jesus loved the sheep near him.

As teenagers, my daughters barely glanced at the Nativity, and I fought a useless battle trying to encourage them to dress respectfully to attend Mass. They wanted to wear jeans and T-shirts, while I had something different in mind. Then, one Christmas I noticed the garb of the shepherds in my Nativity set. They were the motley crew God invited to the manger first. Does God care what my kids wear to church as long as they're there, listening to the word, participating in the service, bringing home and living the message? I don't think God cares about my daughters' disheveled appearance.

The shepherds reminded me that when the angels announced Jesus' birth, they went. They didn't change their clothes or spruce up. They just went. That's what Jesus wants, too. He doesn't care what we look like or how we dress for Mass. I don't have to wear anything special to honor God. I just have to hear his call and answer it. God doesn't judge, so why should we?

REFLECT

Is there something about your teen's faith life that you wish you could change? Is it truly important or could you overlook it and just be grateful he's showing up for church?

✠ PRAY ✠

Dear Heavenly Father,

Sometimes I get hung up on all of the wrong things, like how we dress and how we look. Remind me what is really important. I love you, Lord. Amen.

december 29

KEEP GOING

The angel of the Lord appeared to Joseph in a dream and said, "Rise, take the child and his mother, flee to Egypt, and stay there until I tell you. Herod is going to search for the child to destroy him." Joseph rose and took the child and his mother by night and departed for Egypt (Matthew 2:13–14).

Imagine walking eighty miles from Nazareth to Bethlehem wearing flimsy sandals, Mary heavily pregnant, dusty hot trails in daytime and chilly evenings for camping with few blankets. It sounds like a brutal journey, but they completed it in time for Mary to give birth to Jesus. Just when they thought they could rest, an angel tells them to flee to Egypt, about 100 miles away.

I have spent many mornings snuggled under warm bed covers unwilling to start my day because I felt too tired from holiday celebrations. I have hit the snooze button on the alarm clock so many times that I expect it to yell, "Enough, Lazy Bones! Get out of bed!" Yet Joseph awakes from a dream, gathers up their stuff, and the family makes another long and arduous journey. Joseph's faith was simple yet unwavering to the point that he could act on a dream. How many strange dreams have you had? And which ones have you acted on? Consider asking God to reveal himself to you in a dream; maybe then you could start acting on them the way Joseph did.

REFLECT

The flight to Egypt reminds me that God lets us rest every now and then, but he gently nudges us to keep going. We might think our work is done, but in reality, God wants us to continue on. Mary and Joseph probably dreaded another trip with a newborn infant, but they did what they were told and, because of it, their lives were spared. When God asks you to keep going, what will you say?

✠ PRAY ✠

Dear Heavenly Father,

Give me the strength to keep going, if that is your will.
I trust in your ways. Amen.

december 30

GIFTS

They were overjoyed at seeing the star, and on entering the house they saw the child with Mary his mother. They prostrated themselves and did him homage. Then they opened their treasures and offered him gifts of gold, frankincense, and myrrh (Matthew 2:10–11).

Consider if your kids have grumbled after Christmas that they didn't get the present they most wanted, or perhaps they got bored with their gifts or experienced a letdown after they were opened and put away. Remember that God gave us the ultimate gift: his Son. And the Holy Spirit fills us with many other gifts, too: joy, love, the ability to lift up each other as we do God's work. Think on the spiritual gifts you were given and how you will use them in the upcoming year. Gifts are marvelous things that hold us near to those who give them.

At some point after Jesus' birth, the three Magi—Caspar, Melchior, and Balthasar—arrived to set before the Christ Child three symbolic gifts: gold, fit for a king; frankincense, perfect for a priest, and myrrh, a burial ointment for one who would die. The gifts were for *the* king, God, and for a suffering redeemer. After the gifts have been opened under your Christmas tree, do you feel satisfied with the preparations you made, the presents you selected, and the good deeds you did for others? It's important to identify gifts of virtue, prayer, and suffering, too.

REFLECT

As we prepare to celebrate the feast of the Epiphany, we must be mindful of our duty to adore our Lord through prayer, worship, and self-sacrificing good works. Contemplate ways you might be able to do this with the help of your teenagers.

✠ PRAY ✠

Dear Heavenly Father,

You have showered me with countless gifts over the years. Now it is my turn to offer myself to you. Let me use my hands to serve others and you. Let me use my words of kindness to transform a cold stone heart into one with rich, abundant love and warmth. Use me, Lord, to do your work. It is my gift to you. Amen.

december 31

GOD'S PERFECT LOVE

Beloved, let us love one another, because love is of God; everyone who loves is begotten by God and knows God. Whoever is without love does not know God, for God is love. In this way the love of God was revealed to us: God sent his only Son into the world so that we might have life through him. In this is love: not that we have loved God, but that he loved us and sent his Son as expiation for our sins. Beloved, if God so loved us, we also must love one another (1 John 4:7–11).

Jesus commands us to love each other. We might get tired of hearing the same thing repeatedly, but it's what God wants. If you can only do one thing, make sure it is what God wants: to love each other. God doesn't say to pick the people to love; he wants us to love everyone. Everyone means every person. It's not an option, it's mandatory. And this love is not a fleeting, sentimental type of love, but more of a selfless, compassionate promise that is revered in seeking the very best of the loved one. It isn't our duty, it's our pleasure.

It is extremely difficult to love your teenager after she has just yelled, "I hate you." It's challenging to love your teen when she looks you in the eye and lies to you. It is tough to love your child when she does the complete opposite of what you asked. How can you love someone who is constantly pushing your buttons? Jesus wants us to do it prayerfully, peacefully, and kindheartedly.

Immerse yourself in God's merciful and limitless love. Soak it up and bask in it; God's might can strengthen and empower you to do incredible things, including loving the unlovable. Begin by filling your head with positive thoughts of God's compassionate heart. Dwell on the gifts he has given to you in the past, and be thankful for them.

REFLECT

Invoke the Holy Spirit to help you to be kind to your teen. This obligation requires self-sacrifice. Remember that while you are not perfect, God's love is.

✠ PRAY ✠

Dear Heavenly Father,

I'll try harder to be better at loving everyone, especially (name). You gave this child to me for a reason, and I trust in your remarkable ways. Amen.

january 1

FEAR NOT

It is the LORD *who marches before you; he will be with you and will never fail you or forsake you. So do not fear or be dismayed* (Deuteronomy 31:8).

There will be many places you will have to go; not because you want to, but because you have to. Maybe you have to accompany your kid to an x-ray department to have a procedure that you are uncertain of. Or you might have to approach a boardroom full of people to ask for something you doubt they will grant. What monumental place will you have to go as a result of your child, and how will you find the courage and strength to face your fears to carry it through?

The Lord your God will walk with you wherever you go, no matter how far or how intimidating the journey seems. When you are frightened, remember that God stands beside you always; he will never leave you. If you become alarmed, call out to God for strength. Ask him to sift through your discombobulated thoughts and make sense of them. No matter what you are asked to do, have faith that you will not have to go through it alone.

REFLECT

Go outside in the crisp air and take a few long, deep breaths to allow the oxygen to clear your thoughts, remembering that the Holy Spirit is within you. Hold your head up high and take a step forward, regardless of how big or small, with the Lord.

✠ PRAY ✠

Dear Heavenly Father,

Energize me with the fire of your indelible love that I long to feel burn within me. I desire your warmth as I conjure the courage to do what needs to be done. I am the perfect one for this job. I am capable and qualified because you are with me. You will empower me with the abilities I need to be successful. Thank you for being there and believing in me. I love you, Lord. Amen.

january 2

SEEKING CLARITY

Trust in the L*ORD* *with all your heart,*
on your own intelligence do not rely; In all your ways be mindful of him, and he will make straight your paths (Proverbs 3:5–6).

Have you had bad news delivered from a doctor, therapist, teacher, or school principal? Perhaps it was a diagnosis you didn't want to hear. Or maybe it was learning that your teen did something that you struggle to make sense of. Whatever it is, don't worry about trying to fathom it because God doesn't expect you to understand everything. Some things are not meant for you to comprehend.

Instead, give it to God. He wants you to trust in him with your heart, your mind, and every ounce of your being because he knows what he is doing. There is a reason for everything, even if you do not understand it now; you may later. Or, you may never understand it completely. But for now, for this particular instance, don't waste time trying to grasp it. God wants you to simply acknowledge him, and he will allow your direction to unfold exactly the way he planned it. Trust in God.

REFLECT

Consider what emotions are weighing you down with this news and how you can free yourself from it. Contemplate your preferred method of self-soothing. Do you like to take a long hot shower, crank up the music and dance crazily, or run on the treadmill? Whatever you enjoy, do that today while remembering how good God has been to you in the past.

✠ PRAY ✠

Dear Heavenly Father,

Watch over me as I struggle to comprehend the senselessness of the news I received. Teach me how to absorb it and trust in your ways. If it is your will, allow me to understand and cope with clarity. I trust in you and your ways. Where you lead, I will follow. Thy will be done, Lord. Thy will be done. Amen.

january 3

BE UPLIFTING

Therefore, encourage one another and build one another up, as indeed you do. We urge you, brothers, admonish the idle, cheer the fainthearted, support the weak, be patient with all. See that no one returns evil for evil; rather, always seek what is good (both) for each other and for all (1 Thessalonians 5:11, 14–15).

Have you ever felt like not getting up in the morning because you just didn't feel like facing the day? Maybe you went to bed upset or perhaps you had a rough night. Sometimes when you're feeling down from the difficulties of parenting, it's understandable why you might bring everyone else around you down, too. Instead of wallowing in self-pity, take comfort in the knowledge that you will live in the Lord.

Try to build others up. Perhaps you need to help your spouse. Allow them to lean into your love so that you strengthen each other as you journey through life's challenges together. If your partner stumbles, give a hand to bolster him along.

It's difficult to wait and have patience, to offer repeated forgiveness, and perform acts of goodness. But that's exactly what God wants. He says to help those who are mentally challenged, weak, and cowardly. If someone upset you with harsh words or actions, let it go. Christians are to turn the other cheek and not return evil for evil. Avoid trying to get even for a wrong that has been done. Be kind to those you consider an enemy.

REFLECT

Maybe right now you are feeling weak or depressed. Perhaps you need to focus on self care. Take extra time for yourself to build your strength back up so you are refreshed to tackle the issues at hand.

✠ PRAY ✠

Dear Heavenly Father,

When I open my eyes each morning, let me thank you for another day, another chance to make the world right. Don't let me pull the covers over my head and attempt to sleep the day away. Fill me with energy and stamina to withstand all that I must face. Remind me to smile and be kind to everyone, especially those who give me grief. I ask this in Jesus' name. Amen.

january 4

ASK WITH CONVICTION

But if any of you lacks wisdom, he should ask God who gives to all generously and ungrudgingly, and he will be given it. But he should ask in faith, not doubting, for the one who doubts is like a wave of the sea that is driven and tossed about by the wind. For that person must not suppose that he will receive anything from the Lord, since he is a man of two minds, unstable in all his ways (James 1:5–8).

Have you stood over the bed of your sleeping child and wished she could stay that angelic and peaceful? Maybe nightmares or fever woke her in a fitful rage. Walking the floors in the middle of the night with an unsettled teenager can be unnerving while you wonder what is causing the uneasiness. Instead of doing the typical things you did in the past, do what works: steadfast prayer.

Whatever is weighing heavy on your heart, give it to God, for he knows how to handle such complicated things. If your daughter needs a miracle, ask for it without reproach, and it will be given to you if it is God's will. Don't ask for something halfheartedly. Ask with unwavering faith that you deserve what you are seeking. Trust implicitly in the Lord. His way is the only way.

REFLECT

What special intention do you need to pray to the Lord for today?

✠ PRAY ✠

Dear Heavenly Father,

I beseech you, Lord, to fill me with the knowledge to overcome the obstacles that are cluttering the path I am trying to maneuver. Please, Lord, fill me with your wisdom and guidance. Reveal your will and guide me in the right direction. Thank you for always directing my footsteps and sheltering me from harm. I love you, Lord, and trust in your ways. Amen.

january 5

REASONS FOR EVERYTHING

We know that all things work for good for those who love God, who are called according to his purpose (Romans 8:28).

Often, when stuck in the middle of a dilemma, it's extremely difficult to see the good in it. For instance: a flat tire. Have you ever wondered why you get a flat tire at the worst possible time? It rarely happens in your driveway when you have plenty of time to fix it. It usually happens when you're running late for an important meeting, in the pouring rain, when you're wearing a suit. Maybe what you didn't know is that if God didn't slow you down with a flat tire, you could have been in a serious car accident. There is a purpose for every little thing. Even though God doesn't reveal the motive to you right away—or ever—trust in his ways because they are divinely purposeful.

There is a reason for everything God does. It's important to thank God for everything he does: good and bad. It's not easy to be thankful for something you think is bad, like a root canal. However, each life event is meaningful.

REFLECT

When you make a cake, each ingredient in itself tastes bad. But when all of the ingredients are blended together, they make something magnificent. While it isn't easy to thank God for a root canal, maybe you could appreciate that you had a good dentist to care for you. Give thanks that you could afford it and after the procedure, you were fine.

✠ PRAY ✠

Dear Heavenly Father,

Thank you for all of the happenings of this day: good and bad. Thank you for bringing the right person into my life to help me through my difficulties. Thank you for safeguarding me when I was frightened. I truly love you, Lord. Amen.

january 6

CRY OUT TO GOD

Hear my cry, O God, listen to my prayer! From the ends of the earth I call; my heart grows faint. Raise me up, set me on a rock, for you are my refuge, a tower of strength against the foe. Let me dwell in your tent forever, take refuge in the shelter of your wings (Psalm 61:2–5).

As I was barreling down a highway, my car died in the middle of heavy traffic. My mind raced with ideas of things I could do. Then I remembered to quiet myself and pray. In that instant, I felt calm and knew exactly what to do. If you find yourself in a precarious position, call out to God for help before you call anyone else. When your heart is overwhelmed, remember that Jesus is the rock of your salvation; he can help you through anything, no matter how outrageous it is. Trust in God's protection.

Are you facing a seemingly impossible situation in your family life? Maybe your son is being bullied at school, or his academic problem is giving you grief? Give the problem to God because even though your heart is troubled and the situation feels like more than you can take, it's not more than God can handle. When there is nothing else you can do or think of to solve a problem, all you need to do is pray.

Prayer is the answer to everything. The problem will resolve on God's terms and God will tell you what to do. When you get discouraged and you don't know what to do, give it all to Jesus because he is watching over you.

REFLECT

Sit in the quiet of your home and dwell on Jesus' face. If your mind wanders to the problem, simply say, "Jesus."

✠ PRAY ✠

Dear Heavenly Father,

Bless my mess. I don't know how to get out of this situation, Lord.
I need you to rescue me. Let me find comfort in your loving embrace.
Amen.

january 7

SERVE WITH LOVE

For you were called for freedom, brothers.
But do not use this freedom as an opportunity for the flesh;
rather, serve one another through love (Galatians 5:13).

Driving on ice in a Northeast winter can be unnerving. When the car skids, I steer into it even though it seems unnatural. It works every time. In life it can feel peculiar to steer into problems, especially when you want to avoid them. Try tackling your next problem head on.

My church needed a ninth-grade religion teacher. Even though I lacked teaching experience, I volunteered. I worried that I didn't know enough or couldn't keep the students' attention. But God made sure that each lesson was insightful and meaningful. The freedom I had to devise the lesson plans was amazing, the kids were wonderful, and overall the experience turned out to be a spiritual awakening for me, too. Sometimes you just have to face your fears, walk headfirst into the wind, and trust that God will work through you for the greater good.

Initially, steering into life's problems might feel unnatural; however, decide if what you are doing is good, honest, and just. The freedom God provides must be used responsibly, not for your own personal gratification or as a personal reward. Love God with all your heart, and love others as you would yourself.

REFLECT

Consider an issue you have been grappling with and question what you can do about it. Is your teenager being deceitful or irresponsible? Can you face it head on knowing God is with you?

✠ PRAY ✠

Dear Heavenly Father,

Fill me with your unwavering love. Use me as your earthen vessel to inspire, educate, heal, and embrace those who need it the most. Let them be drawn to me like an intense magnetic force and I will serve them as you desire. I am but a handmaiden waiting to do your work, whatever it is. I trust you. Amen.

january 8

CHOOSE WISELY

Indeed, the word of God is living and effective, sharper than any two-edged sword, penetrating even between soul and spirit, joints and marrow, and able to discern reflections and thoughts of the heart (Hebrews 4:12).

There is only one letter difference in the words "champ" and "chump." If you call your teenager a champ, she will act like a winner. If you call your daughter a chump, she will be gullible or an easy target for ridicule. Why treat your daughter pathetically when you have it within your means to be respectful and build her up?

It's easy to fall into the parental role of guiding, controlling, and ruling your youngster's life because it's your job to help your daughter be her very best. But sometimes parents can become narrow-minded and end up steering their teens the way they want things to turn out, disregarding the feelings, desires, hopes, and dreams of the teens.

It's important to hear them and not steamroll over them because you (as a parent) know what's best. Maybe you act the way you do because you learned that technique from your parents, but that doesn't mean you have to raise your kids the same way. God gave you the freedom to decide what's best for each circumstance, so invoke his will each time.

REFLECT

When you gaze at your teen, remember that God created her in his image. The Holy Spirit dwells within her, so speak to your daughter with the same respect and love that you want to show to the Lord.

✠ PRAY ✠

Dear Heavenly Father,

Filter my words so that each one is sanctioned and blessed by you. Enable me to guide (name) lovingly under your care and watchful eyes. Give me the tools to be the very best parent I can be. Amen.

january 9

GIVE THANKS

And one of them, realizing he had been healed, returned, glorifying God in a loud voice; and he fell at the feet of Jesus and thanked him. He was a Samaritan. Jesus said in reply, "Ten were cleansed, were they not? Where are the other nine? Has none but this foreigner returned to give thanks to God?" (Luke 17:15–18).

Have you ever received a gift you didn't like? How did you respond? You probably acted politely, showing thanks for the present and vowing to have several uses for it. And then you never touched it again. Gifts are wonderful. They should be appreciated regardless of what they are. Sometimes we don't appreciate a gift until we really need it.

What if Jesus gave you a gift? What if it was something ordinary like a bright sunny day? How would you react to that gift? Many people wake up each day and never thank him for it. When was the last time you woke up and said, "Thank you, Lord, for this beautiful day?" Even if it's a dark, dreary, rainy day, be thankful for it. It's not too late to express your thankfulness for all God has given you.

What if God gave you an extraordinary gift, something magnificent that was full of potential, love, and glory? What if that gift was your teenager? Maybe you don't consider your offspring a gift right now, but some day you will. You have no idea who he will grow up to be. Take comfort in knowing that the story of your child's life is still being written. Don't worry about being appreciated or thanked for all you do for your teen. Instead, focus on your job, and praise God for all he continues to give you each day.

REFLECT

Give praise to God for the gift of your teenager today. Do not be like the ungrateful nine who were healed but did not return to thank God.

✠ PRAY ✠

Dear Heavenly Father,

Thank you for the many gifts that you give to me each day.
I want to spend the rest of my life adoring you,
thanking you, worshiping you. I truly love you. Amen.

january 10

PRAY CONTINUOUSLY

Pray without ceasing. In all circumstances give thanks, for this is the will of God for you in Christ Jesus. Do not quench the Spirit (1 Thessalonians 5:17–19).

What are you worrying about? Perhaps you think something is wrong with your teenager, like a mysterious illness or a learning disorder. Maybe your doctor thinks she is fine, but you disagree with the assessment. Worrying does no good, like pacing the floors. Instead, pray unceasingly. All things are possible with God, but nothing good comes from worry. Ask God to enlighten you and point you in the direction of the cause for the symptoms that are troublesome to you. Ask God to bring the right person into your life to help you with this dilemma. God will not let you down.

If you think you don't have time to pray, then vow to say one prayer each time you find yourself waiting for something: a red light, in line to buy something, for a web page to load....You waste so much time waiting for things. Make that time productive by reaching out to God in your time of need. Even if you only have a minute to dwell on his image in your mind, that will satisfy the Lord.

REFLECT

Put a holy card in your wallet so that each time you pay for something you will be reminded to talk to God. Put a holy medal in your car or on your key ring to prompt you to pray while you drive. Carry rosary beads in your pocket to remind you to seek Mary's comfort during difficult times. Mary knows firsthand how painful it is to watch a child suffer.

✠ PRAY ✠

Dear Heavenly Father,

Remove the qualms that cause my stomach to churn in anguish. Release the troubles that weigh me down and the worries I carry on my shoulders. Remind me to give these problems to you; for you know what to do with them. Thank you for your love, wisdom, and generosity. I trust in you. Amen.

january 11

CELEBRATE LIFE WHILE YOU WAIT!

But they who wait for the Lord shall renew their strength; they shall mount up with wings like eagles; they shall run and not be weary; they shall walk and not faint (Isaiah 40:29–31).

When your child first learned to walk, you didn't assume that some day his legs would carry him across the Boston Marathon finish line. All you knew was that your child was at the beginning of something great: a full and meaningful life. Celebrate it; rejoice over the places you child might go. You might have dreams of those legs carrying him through college graduation with marvelous employment opportunities. But what if your kid's dreams are different than yours? What if an accident or illness confines him to a wheelchair? What if your son takes a wrong turn? Will you be there to pick him up and offer help the way Jesus would?

Recognize the small events in life; rejoice over them, for even though they might seem insignificant, they are all gifts from God. While you wait for your teenager to fully develop and strengthen, find God's gifts, peace, love, and joy each day. It can be excruciating waiting for your child to heal and grow; however, while you wait, God is refueling you for something magnificent. From God's perspective, what may feel like idleness is resolute preparation. When you wait patiently, you emerge resilient after God renews and refreshes you.

REFLECT

If God is rejuvenating you, imagine how robust you will become. How might this "waiting period" for your child be preparing you both for something greater?

✠ PRAY ✠

Dear Heavenly Father,

Bless the time I spend waiting for a change in (name)'s life. Enable me to be patient, kind, loving, and supportive of (name). Teach me how to be grateful for all you give to me each day, especially if I struggle to identify it. Open my eyes and instill in me the grace to do the job you set before me, no matter how difficult it is. I trust in you, Jesus. Amen.

january 12

ENDURANCE IS POSSIBLE WITH GOD

No trial has come to you but what is human. God is faithful and will not let you be tried beyond your strength; but with the trial he will also provide a way out, so that you may be able to bear it (1 Corinthians 10:13).

One of the worst things that can happen to any parent is having a sick kid. It's gut-wrenching to watch her suffer, regardless of how old she is. While you're going through it, remember you are not alone. God is with you. Lean into his love for strength. If something awful happens like blindness, the loss of a limb, or a cancer diagnosis, don't stay angry at God. While anger is a natural human emotion, ask God to help you work through it.

Ask God to transform any negative feelings you might be experiencing into something positive. Maybe you've developed a closer relationship with your spouse or teenager as a result of the difficulty. Maybe a friend or neighbor has been particularly supportive of you throughout this situation. Has your spirituality strengthened as a result of your hardship? If you are unable to find anything positive in your situation, ask God to point it out to you.

REFLECT

If you are stuck, trust that God has a plan for you, your teen, and your family. Your suffering won't last forever. If it feels too overwhelming, remember that God won't allow you to be tested beyond what you can tolerate, and he always provides a way out of your misery. Trust in God.

✠ PRAY ✠

Dear Heavenly Father,

I am hurting so badly that I can barely focus on prayer.
Take my pain and enable me to see the good in it.
Teach me how to carry my burden with grace by remembering that you are with me, and you will never give me more than I can bear.
I'm at that point, Lord. Carry me through this in your indelible love.
I ask this in Jesus' name. Amen.

january 13

YOUR CRITICAL JOB

For to me life is Christ, and death is gain. If I go on living in the flesh, that means fruitful labor for me. And I do not know which I shall choose. I am caught between the two. I long to depart this life and be with Christ, (for) that is far better. Yet that I remain (in) the flesh is more necessary for your benefit. And this I know with confidence, that I shall remain and continue in the service of all of you for your progress and joy in the faith, so that your boasting in Christ Jesus may abound on account of me when I come to you again (Philippians 1:21–26).

Paul thought his death would be a gain; he dearly wanted to depart his life on earth and live in heaven with Christ. Yet he realized God had a purpose for him on earth and he needed to stay and complete it. Whatever task you are doing, know that it's God's purpose for you. He has chosen you as his special servant because he knew you were capable and you would be successful. Even if you feel like you are not doing much, know that to God you are productive in his love. If you feel what you are doing isn't important, remember that you're doing the critical assignment God selected you to do.

It's not easy to untangle a web of problems spun around you by the difficulties you have encountered with your son. Maybe he has a bad attitude. Could God want you to demonstrate a healthier way around the brashness? Perhaps your adolescent's outlook needs an adjustment. God feels you are qualified to help your son through this difficulty. All you have to do is call out to our Lord. He longs to hear your voice.

REFLECT

If you feel inadequate for the job of parent, remember that you never act alone. God will never abandon you, especially in your time of need.

✠ PRAY ✠

Dear Heavenly Father,

Empower me to do the work you chose for me. Whatever it is, I will do it because of my great love for you. Please, help me to succeed in all I think, say, and do. I ask this in Jesus' name. Amen.

january 14

GOD'S TESTS

Remember how for forty years now the Lord, your God, has directed all your journeying in the desert, so as to test you by affliction, to know what was in your heart: to keep his commandments, or not (Deuteronomy 8:2).

What do you remember from your tests in high school or college? Were they easy or pleasant? Where you a nervous wreck taking your road test? Tests are not supposed to be enjoyable. God tested his people in order to know what was in their hearts; whether they would keep his commandments or not. Consider that you might be tested now so God can determine your reactions and the genuineness of your heart.

In today's passage, God humbled Israel by bringing them to the desert where they had to depend on him because they had nothing else. Has God humbled you recently? While you are in a humbling place, consider if your heart is being transformed. God is concerned about the metamorphosis of your heart, especially if you long for something different. God wants us to be content in our humble place because that is where our education begins. If you are not humble and not teachable, the rest of God's education is pointless. God requires total dependence on him.

REFLECT

Give your troubles to God and trust in his ways. Accept your humility gracefully and open your heart, body, and mind to absorbing God's loving teachings. Ask for the courage to see it through to fruition on his terms, not yours.

✠ PRAY ✠

Dear Heavenly Father,

Take my hand and guide me down the path you have chosen for me. Give me the courage to endure, especially now when I feel pathetic and powerless. I surrender unto your divine mercy, today, tomorrow, and always. I adore you, sweet and loving Lord. Amen.

january 15

DEPEND ON GOD

For to this you have been called, because Christ also suffered for you, leaving you an example that you should follow in his footsteps (1 Peter 2:21).

At the beginning of Christmas break, I was driving my daughter home from college when I encountered a freak snowstorm. There was zero visibility on a long stretch of highway with no place to stop. My car slowly crept behind the one in front as I focused on his flashing hazard lights.

When an unpredictable storm blows into your life and you can't see a way out, remember that you don't have to see the road in front of you. Simply look straight ahead and fix your sights on God. Allow the Lord to steer you through each storm you encounter. God knows the right way out; depend on him.

What kind of storm is creating havoc in your life right now? Is your teenager out of control? When this happens, it's hard to know what to do. How do you decide between what's best for your kid and what's best for you and your family? Prayer will help; it's like turning on your hazard lights. It signals to God that you are in trouble and seek his divine intervention.

REFLECT

Don't allow this rift between you and your teenager to undermine your parenting. Think about times in the past where you have met rough weather without warning. You might have tightened your seatbelt, turned off the radio, and concentrated on driving techniques. Do the same with God. Pick up your rosary beads, open the Bible, and call out God's name.

✠ PRAY ✠

Dear Heavenly Father,

Illuminate my path to enable me to travel down the road that leads to you. Keep me focused on your ways, Lord; don't let me go astray. Point me in the right direction and walk with me. I feel so alone and afraid. Please help me through this disparity. I need your loving embrace. I ask this in Jesus' name. Amen.

january 16

FERVENT PRAYER

He was in such agony and he prayed so fervently that his sweat became like drops of blood falling on the ground (Luke 22:44).

My parents taught me to pray when I was in trouble, for thanksgiving, and most importantly to talk to God every day as my friend. I designated a recliner as my prayer chair where I sat whenever I chatted with God, my friend. If I felt distressed, I bypassed the chair and got down on my knees. I closed my eyes and envisioned Jesus kneeling against a rock at the Mount of Olives before he was put to death. I imagined the fervent prayers he spoke to God the Father as his sweat became like drops of blood. If Jesus prayed that frantically that night, you can send desperate prayers to heaven when you are in crises, too.

Whatever predicament you are in, pray fervently to the Lord. Jesus understands your humanness. He knows your fear, your sadness, and your disparity. Perhaps your teenager is being ostracized at school or there is a medical illness that separates her from her classmates. It's difficult to watch your child suffer. In your desperation, give the problems to God and trust in his ways. He has a reason for what is happening. Maybe it's teaching your daughter empathy, leading to a career as a school psychologist, social worker, or doctor. Maybe it will inspire your child to become a sister. Remind your daughter that the Holy Spirit dwells within and can be called upon at any moment of need. Remind your teen that a host of heavenly angels encircle and protect her.

REFLECT

Teach your adolescent to pray earnestly. Give her the coping skills and tools that will be needed to encounter problems in the future. Teach her how to look for the good that is woven into the suffering caused from any crisis.

✠ PRAY ✠

Dear Heavenly Father,

I call out to you in my time of need. Please save my family and me. I ask this in Jesus' name. Amen.

january 17

HOPE IN GOD

In you, LORD, I take refuge; let me never be put to shame. In your justice rescue and deliver me; listen to me and save me! Be my rock and refuge, my secure stronghold; for you are my rock and fortress. My God, rescue me from the power of the wicked, from the clutches of the violent. You are my hope, Lord; my trust, GOD, from my youth (Psalm 71:1–5).

When your faith is tested through trials and tribulations, maintain hope that you will not be shaken. What has gone wrong? Did your teenager get a poor test score and you worry that some underlying problem caused it? Perhaps he failed a class and you worry about social or emotional issues. Does your child need to repeat the entire year?

Maintain hope in God that he will give you the wisdom to know how to handle the situation you and your teen are in. If your mind is racing, try to quiet it by focusing only on Jesus' face. In the stillness, listen for his message. He will tell you what to do. In your patience, God will speak to you. Trust that he knows what is best.

REFLECT

Sometimes, God doesn't want you to do anything except be nice. Go for a long walk and marvel at the beauty in the trees, the gentle breeze that rustles the leaves, the chirping birds, the brilliant sunshine, the billowy clouds. God made them for you to enjoy. Take this time to thank God for all he has given you.

✠ PRAY ✠

Dear Heavenly Father,

I struggle to maintain hope when I am wallowing in sorrow, suffering from the consequences caused by (name). Let me rest in your warm embrace while I wait for you to point me in the right direction. You entrusted me to parent (name). Tell me how to do it in your love. I trust in you, Lord. Amen.

january 18

EXERCISE FOR JESUS

Your curving thighs [are] like jewels,the product of skilled hands.
How beautiful you are, how fair, my love, daughter of delights!
Your very form resembles a date-palm, and your breasts, clusters
(Song of Songs 7:2, 7–8).

Are you the very best version of yourself, or could you be a little bit better? What could you do to improve yourself? Could you drop a few pounds? Whenever I get stressed out, I reach for a bag of M & M's. Maybe my daughters said something annoying or hurtful and I replay the events of the day in my mind. Sometimes I will justify the candy by saying I had a rough day, I deserve a treat, and chocolate is good for me. Eating a bag of candy is not good for my waistline or my heart.

I hate to exercise! I hung up a sign over my treadmill that reads: "Trust in God—exercise for Jesus." A crucifix hangs beside the sign. It reminds me that Jesus suffered greatly in his lifetime. He didn't want to be tortured and nailed to a cross, but he endured that brutality for my sins. I think of that whenever I get on the treadmill. I vow to walk for thirty minutes every day whether I want to or not. I do it for Jesus.

REFLECT

God created our bodies in such a beautiful way that after exercise, endorphins flow through our system, giving us a lift. Regardless of the type of day you had, can you exercise for Jesus?

✠ PRAY ✠

Dear Heavenly Father,

Fill me with the energy I need. Give me the strength to carry out the tasks that I must do. I love you, Lord. I want to do your will. Amen.

january 19

BLESS MY THOUGHTS

Lord, you have probed me, you know me: you know when I sit and stand; you understand my thoughts from afar. Even before a word is on my tongue, Lord, you know it all (Psalm 139:1–2, 4).

Do you ever have irrational and foolish thoughts about your teenager being in danger when he was probably safe at a friend's house? Or have you thought your child's sore throat was really the bubonic plague? Sometimes, when so many things go wrong at once, it's easy to allow your imagination to run wild and think the worst. But don't allow your thoughts to spiral out of control, taking you on crazy journeys. Maybe they come in a fleeting moment and then take off like a jackrabbit, bouncing here, there, and everywhere. How do you stop feeding negative thoughts?

The best thing you can do when this happens is to invoke the Holy Spirit who dwells within you, asking to quell your apprehensions and fears and send guardian angels to watch over your son, to safeguard him in your absence. Try to fill your head with loving thoughts, both positive and productive.

REFLECT

Light a holy candle in your kitchen and say a prayer for your teen each time you see it. Use the candle as a symbolic means of carrying your prayers to heaven, blessing your good intentions.

✠ PRAY ✠

Dear Heavenly Father,

If the thoughts in my mind are not from you, take them away. If my thoughts need shaping and realigning, please do it quickly so I can make sense of it and act appropriately. If these thoughts are from you, build them into something I recognize.

I trust and love you implicitly. Amen.

january 20

GOD LISTENS

Say to the fearful of heart: Be strong, do not fear! Here is your God, he comes with vindication; With divine recompense he comes to save you. Then the eyes of the blind shall see, and the ears of the deaf be opened; Then the lame shall leap like a stag, and the mute tongue sing for joy.... Waters will burst forth in the wilderness (Isaiah 35:4–6).

If Jesus still walked the earth, would you petition him for a miraculous cure for your child? Just because you don't see God doesn't mean you shouldn't ask. He can hear you no matter where you are, no matter what you are doing. God listens.

When my daughter was little, she was diagnosed with a rare and incurable disease. The National Institute of Health (NIH) in Bethesda, MD, managed her medical care. They warned me that no child with this condition ever went into remission, so I shouldn't hope for that. All I could hope for was to slow down the progression of the disease. My mother disagreed. "There is hope!" she said. "Ask for a miracle." My parents and I prayed fervently for a miracle. After two weeks the doctors called me to say my daughter went into remission. And she has been perfectly fine ever since. That was nearly twenty years ago.

God hears your prayers. He knows what's in your heart. He walks with you always, wherever you go, whatever you do; he is beside you. No trouble is too big or small for him. God longs to hear from you.

REFLECT

With God, all things are possible. Whatever is troubling you, whether it is an illness or behavioral issues, ask God for a miracle.

✠ PRAY ✠

Dear Heavenly Father,

I am burdened, distressed, and suffering in excruciating pain.
I cry out to you today in my anxiousness to take this problem away.
Please, Lord, if it is your will, grant a miracle for (name).
I ask this in your sweet and merciful name, Lord Jesus, creator of heaven and earth, to bless me with a miracle. Amen.

january 21

LET PEACE RULE

May the Lord of peace himself give you peace at all times and in every way. The Lord be with all of you (2 Thessalonians 3:16).

I get upset when my kid is sick. I feel defensive and willing to go to war with anyone who crosses my path, whether they are doctors, therapists, or lab technicians. I don't need a medical degree to know when something is wrong with my kid. It's challenging to hear a doctor say, "There's nothing wrong," when I know he's mistaken. One of my daughters was misdiagnosed for eighteen years! When I finally discovered I was right, I wanted to tell all the professionals of their errors because they made my daughter suffer needlessly.

Instead, I let God's love and peace flow over me and through me, like a cleansing rainfall on a sultry summer evening. Releasing that pent-up pain was liberating. It allowed me to be peaceful, light, and jubilant. I replaced my vengeance with serenity over the bliss of seeing my daughter get well. I rejoiced and celebrated in God for bringing the perfect doctor into our lives to obtain the correct diagnosis and treatment. I could be more thankful than angry. Peace ruled.

REFLECT

If you find yourself in the midst of a rage, remember that the Lord is with you always, filling you with peace. You can choose to let his graces go and hold on to your anger or you can keep them as the gift he intended.

✠ PRAY ✠

Dear Heavenly Father,

Thank you for filling me with your unconditional love, your infinite stream of grace and abundance of peace. Thank you for sending your only Son and allowing him to take my sins on the cross with him. I truly love you, Lord. Amen.

january 22

GOD'S MASTERFUL WORK

For I know well the plans I have in mind for you—
oracle of the L*ORD—plans for your welfare and not for woe,*
so as to give you a future of hope (Jeremiah 29:11).

God has a mysterious plan for your life. Right now it may not seem wonderful, but you might be focusing on one small piece of the puzzle. If you stand back, away from it, you might be able to see the bigger picture and how remarkable it really is. It's reminiscent of viewing Claude Monet's paintings: from a distance they are priceless masterpieces; but up close, it's hard to tell what you are looking at. Don't focus on the brush strokes or blobs of paint. Search for the bigger picture because then you will see God's masterful work.

Sometimes it's critical to step away from your adolescent's problems to see life from a different perspective, perhaps to focus on your other youngsters for a while. Perhaps they have been feeling neglected. Stepping away doesn't mean you don't care; it means you need to reenergize and prevent burnout. Maybe you and your spouse could take a walk to get fresh air or go on a date.

I spent a week beside my daughter after surgery to remove a bone tumor. I refused to leave her side until one nurse insisted I take a shower and go to the cafeteria to eat a complete meal instead of picking from my daughter's meal tray. Stepping away that brief time rejuvenated me, and I was a much better mother as a result.

REFLECT

Allow friends and family members to pull you away from time to time. God works through people; you never know who.

✠ PRAY ✠

Dear Heavenly Father,

I trust in your glorious plan for me, even though I can't see it. Pull me back so that I can see the whole picture and understand what it is you want of me. Thank you for giving me a future full of hope!
Amen.

january 23

LISTEN FOR HIS VOICE

When you call me, when you go to pray to me, I will listen to you.
When you look for me, you will find me.
Yes, when you seek me with all your heart,I will let you find me—
oracle of the Lord—and I will change your lot (Jeremiah 29:12–14).

Do you ever feel like you are praying to God, but he is not there? Do you ever feel like he doesn't hear your prayers? He is like oxygen; there to keep you alive, but you can't see him or feel him. But he is there and he hears your prayers. He may not answer your prayers the way you want. He will either give you what you asked for or he may not. He may say, "This isn't the right time," and make you wait longer. Or, he may say, "No, that is not what I want for you at this time." You have to be receptive to the Lord's responses. He has a reason for everything he does and every answer he gives.

Maybe you cannot hear his voice. If that is the case, quiet yourself. Be still. In the silence of your contemplative heart, you will hear his reassuring voice.

REFLECT

Go outside and gaze upon the clouds that float across the sky and ask God the Father, the Holy Spirit, and the Son of God to come to your aid. He will not abandon you in your time of need.

✠ PRAY ✠

Dear Heavenly Father,

I have been crying out to you, sweet Jesus, and I hear not your reply.
Hear me, Lord, and take pity on me! I am suffering and need your
healing touch. Please, come near me now, when I need you
the most, and whisper in my ear the words I long to hear.
I ask this in your name. Amen.

january 24

TRANSFORM YOUR WAITING

And so, after patient waiting, he obtained the promise (Hebrews 6:15).

Even on the best day, it's difficult to be patient. Have you ever had to wait for a bus that was running late while it was raining outside? Waiting for a doctor to return your call can be unbearable, especially when your kid is sick. It can be agonizing waiting for test results to come back, or waiting a few months for a medication to work. Waiting for your child to come out of surgery can be excruciatingly difficult. It's also awful to wait for your teenager to change a negative behavior. Waiting is never easy.

Ask God to bless your waiting period. Ask God to transform the negative energy surrounding your waiting into something positive, productive, maybe even a little exciting. For instance, instead of being miserable while waiting for a bus, find the humor in it. One time my mom and I looked like drenched rats while we waited for a bus in the pouring rain; we laughed ourselves silly over how dreadful we looked. We still recount that day with much fondness. While waiting for your doctor, pray that God grants him the ability to treat your teen, or yourself, quickly and accurately. If you are waiting for test results, pray that there's not a problem. Joy comes in the hope that you are on the verge of the ending of your trials.

REFLECT

Trust that God has an amazing plan for you and waiting for it to unfold can be as exciting as waiting to unwrap the gifts nestled beneath your tree on Christmas morning. How you want to approach the wait is entirely up to you.

✠ PRAY ✠

Dear Heavenly Father,

Lift the dark cloud that has loomed overhead for so long.
Enable me to see the silver lining in it and to be grateful for it.
Reveal the messages you want me to know. I want to live in your love.
Amen.

january 25

EVERYTHING COMES FROM GOD

Do you not know? Have you not heard? The LORD is God from of old, creator of the ends of the earth. He does not faint or grow weary, and his knowledge is beyond scrutiny. He gives power to the faint, abundant strength to the weak (Isaiah 40:28–29).

God reveals through Scripture that he is everlasting, he has always been and will always be, and he is constant and never changes. You can rest assured that no matter how problematic your teenager's issues are, you can always count on God to do what he promised. God will provide everything you need because he knows and understands everything. Maybe God will send the right person to help you through your crises at the perfect moment. That could be in the form of a social worker, a therapist, or a counselor. It's never coincidental when you find the right person; God intended that individual to help you.

Furthermore, you never have to worry about overtaxing God because he does not grow weary. Even if you feel as if you are bringing him too many problems, nothing is too much for the Lord. Don't worry that your troubles are too convoluted because God's knowledge is beyond scrutiny; he can untangle any mess. No mountain is too big for him to move.

REFLECT

Consider what wonderful idea came to you out of the blue or what information God blessed you with to solve a problem. Remember: Everything comes from God.

✠ PRAY ✠

Dear Heavenly Father,

Thank you for the air I breathe, the food I eat, the love you put in my heart, and the knowledge you fill my head with. You are truly an amazing God. I love you, Lord. Amen.

january 26

ALLOW GOD IN

Now, when Pharaoh let the people go, God did not lead them by way of the Philistines' land, though this was the nearest; for God said: If the people see that they have to fight, they might change their minds and return to Egypt. Instead, God rerouted them toward the Red Sea by way of the wilderness road, and the Israelites went up out of the land of Egypt arrayed for battle (Exodus 13:17–18).

In this passage, God opted against the shortest route. Sometimes God wants to take you on a longer trail instead of the shortcut. Trust that he has a good reason for it. Consider if God is using a delay or a longer journey to prepare you for something important in your life. In today's Scripture the Israelites were slaves, totally unprepared for war. God knew if they went to battle they would be slaughtered. God might use a delay in your situation to prepare you to overcome the difficulty you are currently experiencing with your teenager. This delay will strengthen your faith and increase your stamina.

Sometimes God uses delays to examine your response under pressure and to test your obedience to him. God also uses delays to retrain your bad habits or negative thought processes and transform them into God's way of doing things. Your routines and behaviors might be ingrained in your heart and mind; it might take a long time to overcome them. Try to be patient when things don't happen on your terms.

REFLECT

What journey is God taking you on right now? Allow God to work in your life, and let him lead the way. In the end, you will be glad you did.

✠ PRAY ✠

Dear Heavenly Father,

Thank you for nourishing my heart, body, and soul.
With you I can do anything. If it's on your terms and not mine,
I understand. I trust your method, for you know more than I. Amen.

january 27

RESTING FAITH

Consider it all joy, my brothers, when you encounter various trials, for you know that the testing of your faith produces perseverance (James 1:2–3).

When I was accepted into x-ray school, I first had to pass a general physics exam. When I looked at the test I panicked because I was unprepared, lacked the understanding, and was unsure of myself. After I spent two years learning the concepts, I was elated when I knew the answers to the questions on the physics final exam. Today's Bible passage reminds me of those physics tests. I learned when you have the knowledge and confidence in God, life's tests can be joyful.

Ponder if your faith is currently being tested. If so, how strong is your conviction? There are three kinds of faith: *struggling faith*, like the unsure student; *clinging faith*, like the student who desperately clings to the teacher, books, and notes; and *resting faith*, like the student who knows the material and aces the exam. Having faith is essential to get through life. However, having a resting faith in God means you can trust implicitly in him and his mighty ways, even if you do not understand them completely. This is what God wants from all of us.

REFLECT

If your faith is being tried because of a difficulty you are experiencing with your teenager, surround yourself with religious pictures to remind you to stay focused. Make signs that read: Trust in God; hang them around you house. Display your rosary beads to remind you to pray. Remember that tests don't last forever; you just have to see it through and God will be there.

✠ PRAY ✠

Dear Heavenly Father,

Help me to stay strong and true to you during my hardships.
I want to cry out but I'm afraid you won't hear me in my despair.
Catch me when I fall and buoy my faith during this storm. I want my faith to rest in your love. I ask this in your holy name, Lord Jesus.
Amen.

january 28

JESUS ALWAYS REMEMBERS

Can a mother forget her infant,be without tenderness for the child of her womb? Even should she forget, I will never forget you. See, upon the palms of my hands I have engraved you; your walls are ever before me (Isaiah 49:15–16).

It's easy to understand a comparison between a mother's love and God's love. Just imagine the anguish Mary endured while she watched Jesus be persecuted, tormented, and put to death in such a gruesome way. Who would have that kind of strength? Stories have surfaced about mothers who lifted cars that trapped their child. When it comes to the depth of a mother's love, it can't be accurately measured because it is so vast, so strong, so determined. The same is true with God's love for us, his children. God says he will never forget you.

When you hear discouraging news about your daughter, God has his arms wrapped around you. When you cry because your heart aches from unfavorable reports, God is there to catch your tears and wipe them away. How do I know? When you look into the palm of Jesus' hands, you will see your name etched in the nail marks that caused him to die to save you.

REFLECT

In the misery you are currently experiencing with your teenager's issues, know that you are not suffering alone; God is right beside you, holding you up and embracing you when you stumble or fall.

✠ PRAY ✠

Dear Heavenly Father,

Thank you for always sticking with me during good times and bad.
I feel as if I am drowning in misery, but each time I go under,
you pull me back up and breathe life into me again.
Thank you for your unwavering love and steadfast dedication. Amen.

january 29

CHANGE WITH GOD'S GRACE

Yet even now—oracle of the LORD—return to me with your whole heart, with fasting, weeping, and mourning.
Rend your hearts, not your garments,and return to the LORD, your God, for he is gracious and merciful, slow to anger, abounding in steadfast love, and relenting in punishment (Joel 2:12–13).

God says to bring all of your brokenheartedness to him with fasting, weeping, and mourning. Open your heart to God and allow him to fill it with his merciful love. Show humility while serving God with a pureness of heart, not with rote ceremonies. Consider what outward expression of sorrow and shame you can show, knowing that if you repent of your sins, God will forgive them. Remember that your salvation is worth more to God than all material things because those will eventually fall by the wayside.

In order to achieve this, you might need to change. Most people don't like change because they are comfortable with their routines and habits. Some people accept their sins, shortcomings, or weaknesses by calling it their "humanness." Maybe you have tried to change, but it was so hard that you stopped trying and settled into your old rut.

Have you ever tried to convince yourself that you are as good as you can be? There is always room for improvement. Open your heart to the Lord and ask him to help it be transformed by his merciful love.

REFLECT

Do you need to be more accepting of an unruly teenager? Or more forgiving? Perhaps you handled a situation with your son poorly and now have regrets. Take one small step closer to change and try to fix it with God's grace.

✠ PRAY ✠

Dear Heavenly Father,

Help me to become the very best version of myself.
I want to improve for you and my family.
You are my saving grace, sweet and loving Lord.
I ask this in Jesus' name. Amen.

january 30

ASK, BELIEVING YOU WILL RECEIVE

Amen, I say to you, whoever says to this mountain, "Be lifted up and thrown into the sea," and does not doubt in his heart but believes that what he says will happen, it shall be done for him. Therefore I tell you, all that you ask for in prayer, believe that you will receive it and it shall be yours (Mark 11:23–24).

Have you ever asked a store for a discount thinking you won't get it, but you ask anyway? When it comes to asking God for something in prayer, ask believing that he will give it to you. What you ask of God must have just motives (meaning you can't ask for the right numbers to win the lottery). Instead, ask God if what you desire is in accordance with his plan. God hears your prayers when you ask him for the things that please him.

Consider what you could ask of God today that would be in accordance with his plan. Maybe your teenager was given a diagnosis that you wish would be less intrusive. Could you ask God to help you overcome it? Maybe your daughter needs special services to enable her to do well in school. Consider asking God to bring the perfect person into your life to help you.

REFLECT

Sometimes when you are struggling with a difficulty surrounding your child, it is hard to see past it. Trust in God that he can see you through any problem.

✠ PRAY ✠

Dear Heavenly Father,

I am drowning in a sea of misery. Pluck me from the sorrows that keep pulling me under and save me, Lord God almighty. Lift me up in your glory if it is your will. Spare (name) from the disparities that consume our family. Shine your healing love on us, Lord and let us sing your praises as long as we shall live. Amen.

january 31

GOD FORGIVES

Jesus said to them in reply, "Those who are healthy do not need a physician, but the sick do. I have not come to call the righteous to repentance but sinners" (Luke 5:31–32).

This passage reminds us that when we are sick, we go to the doctor. And when we have sinned, we seek forgiveness from the Lord. Give your contrite heart to God and he will forgive you because he is kind and merciful. The Church makes the process easy and painless through the sacrament of reconciliation. Not only do you receive special graces, but you welcome God's cleansing and purification of your conscience and soul.

Would you take a spotlessly clean car to the car wash? No, but you would feel good if you drove a filthy car through a car wash. Your vehicle emerges sparkling clean, which pleases you, and it's only a car! Imagine how good you will feel when your integrity, heart, and soul get a thorough cleaning.

Sometimes when you become overloaded with obligations, you fail to see the buildup of grime that accumulates on your moral compass. Therefore, it's good to set aside time to reflect each day on the good and bad. If you hear yourself say, "I could have handled that situation better," maybe you need to get to confession. Try to examine your conscience each day.

REFLECT

Take some time, even if you can only spare five minutes, to meditate with God today. Sit in silence and concentrate on Jesus' face.

✠ PRAY ✠

Dear Heavenly Father,

Thank you for reminding me to seek you throughout each day. I give you my jumbled-up heart and ask that you wash it with your tender mercy and your loving touch. Let me shine with your love the way you intended. I love you, sweet Lord. Amen.

february 1

LAY THE GROUNDWORK

For here the saying is verified that "One sows and another reaps." I sent you to reap what you have not worked for; others have done the work, and you are sharing the fruits of their work (John 4:37–38).

This passage reveals that after Jesus talked to a Samaritan woman at the well, a gathering of people clustered around him. Jesus told the disciples that the spiritual harvest they were witnessing resulted from the work of others who tilled the ground, planted, and watered the seeds. The disciples were experiencing the fruits of their work.

If you have grown frustrated raising your teen because of various difficulties, consider the others who have helped you in tilling the soil, planting, and watering the seeds. Maybe they were counselors, doctors, therapists, or teachers. Many people influence the way your kid is being raised and nurtured. It's understandable to become consumed in reaping the fruits of your work, but it's also wise to acknowledge the others who have helped in the process.

After I privately adopted our children, I told prospective couples seeking to adopt that my husband and I did it on our own. They didn't see the social workers who performed home studies; the agencies who cleared us legally, medically, and financially; the lawyers who went to court; the judges who reviewed the case; the consulate staff who appraised our case and issued visas; the passport officials and airlines. We didn't do our adoption "alone." We did it with the help of many people. I was caught up in the reaping like the disciples in today's Bible verses.

REFLECT

When it comes to your kids, it's easy to focus on the reaping and ignore the tilling, planting, watering, and cultivating that made it happen. Who do you need to thank for the positive things that happen in your kid's life? Remember to make sure God makes the list.

✠ PRAY ✠

Dear Heavenly Father,

Teach me to be patient with laying the groundwork.
While this task seems insignificant now, remind
me that later the investment will be worth it.
Thank you for the people you have brought into my life to help me.
Amen.

february 2

GOD IS GREAT

Bless the L*ORD*, *my soul; and do not forget all [God's] gifts, who pardons all your sins, and heals all your ills, who redeems your life from the pit, and crowns you with mercy and compassion, who fills your days with good things, so your youth is renewed like the eagle's* (Psalm 103:2–5).

When I would come home from school, my mother greeted me with the typical question: How was your day? After rough classes filled with tests and homework assignments piled on, I would tell her my day was the pits. She would put her warm arms around me, remind me that she loved me, and pour me a tall glass of milk with a scooter pie, which I loved. Mom knew exactly what to do to breathe new life into me.

Today's Bible passage reminds me of my mother's love when I was feeling low. God's love is given in many forms. One is the endless gifts he provides. God grants so many favors and showers us with so many generosities that if you stop to think about all of them, you would spend the entire day thanking him. God's love is also kind and merciful. His infinite stream of forgiveness is so vast that it's incomprehensible for the human brain to fathom.

REFLECT

It is within God's power to heal your ills. Whatever is keeping you down, give it to God and ask him to restore you. Has your life been the pits lately? Maybe school functions have you feeling despondent or an evaluation turned out poorly. Give it to God.

✠ PRAY ✠

Dear Heavenly Father,

Thank you for your unwavering love and commitment to me.
You are always there for me when I cry out to you.
You hold me safely in the hollow of your hand.
There is no greater place to be. Amen.

february 3

GOD ANSWERS

Blessed be the LORD, who has heard the sound of my pleading.
The LORD is my strength and my shield, in whom my heart trusts.
I am helped, so my heart rejoices; with my song I praise him
(Psalm 28:6–7).

Have you ever called a friend when you were upset only to get voice mail? It's frustrating when you need a friend to talk to and no one is around to listen. In times of trouble, remember that God is always with you, he will listen at all times, and he can help you through any difficulty. All you need to do is call out to him. Close your eyes and envision his face gazing upon you with love-filled eyes. He will protect you and keep you strong despite your problems. Let God shield you from your foes, whatever they might be. Whatever test you and your teenager must endure, know that it will not last forever.

Even if God does not give you everything you asked for, thank him anyway. He gave you what you were meant to have. Don't question his motives. Instead, sing his praises. God answers by giving you what you asked for, by making you wait, or by saying no. While you may not understand, he has a reason for his response, so thank him loud and long. I remember as a child when my father said "no" I would be angry, not understanding his reasoning behind it. But he knew what was best for me, just as God knows now.

REFLECT

How does your teen respond when you tell her "no" even if you're doing it for her benefit? How do you respond when God says "no" to you? What are some ways you can teach your teen to handle a response of "no" better whether it's coming from you, God, or anyone else?

✠ PRAY ✠

Dear Heavenly Father,

Mend my brokenness, Lord. Teach me how to go on despite my hardships. I need you in my life more now than ever before. I ask this in Jesus' name. Amen.

february 4

HAVE FAITH

He said, "Come." Peter got out of the boat and began to walk on the water toward Jesus. But when he saw how [strong] the wind was he became frightened; and, beginning to sink, he cried out, "Lord, save me!" Immediately Jesus stretched out his hand and caught him, and said to him, "O you of little faith, why did you doubt?"
(Matthew 14:29–31).

Sailing in a storm, the apostles became frightened when they saw Jesus walking on water. Peter tried to walk toward Jesus, but when he took his eyes off the Lord and focused on the storm he began to sink. Peter cried out to Jesus, who reached out and saved him. Have you recognized the Lord approaching you in the middle of one of your storms? Peter didn't sink until he noticed the intensity of the storm. Learn from that—don't take your eyes off Jesus. Focusing on your problems makes them seem worse and bigger than they are. Instead, call out to the Lord. When Jesus extends his hand, take it.

If your faith falters like Peter's did, all is not lost. Cry out to God in your desperation. Peter could have yelled to his buddies in the boat to help him, but he chose Jesus. As soon as Jesus got in the boat, the storm stopped. If you invite Jesus into your boat, the storms in your life will be calmed, too.

REFLECT

How strong is your faith when the storms roll in? Consider the storm that's brewing in your life with your teenager. How will you keep your faithfulness to God?

✠ PRAY ✠

Dear Heavenly Father,

Help me to keep my eyes on you and not get derailed by distractions. Calm the rough waters that crash around me and climb into my boat and rescue me. I need you, Lord. Amen.

february 5

EMBRACE POSITIVITY

I too will speak my part; I also will declare my knowledge!
For I am full of words; the spirit within me compels me.
My belly is like unopened wine, like wineskins ready to burst.
Let me speak and obtain relief; let me open my lips, and reply
(Job 32:17–20).

Jackie Robinson broke baseball's color barrier in 1947 when he played for the Brooklyn Dodgers. Segregation made life challenging. Hotels and restaurants refused him. Teammates and fans rebuked him. He endured cruel injustices because he loved to play baseball. Despite the negativity and racism that surrounded him, his game was unaffected. He played like the champion he was.

Life is full of negativity, but it is also bursting with optimism. Dwell on all that is hopeful and good. Seek it in all things, embrace it, and build on it.

Reflect on the negativity that has been growing in or around your life. Maybe your teenager is struggling with establishing or maintaining friendships. Treat the negativity like weeds in a garden. Pull them out so the real harvest can flourish. Tell your teen to avoid negative influences even if that means turning off her phones, blocking former friends, or staying off of social media. Teach your teen that when you align yourself with people who build you up, you become the best version of yourself.

REFLECT

Who in your life has been more of a hindrance than a help? If you can, try to distance yourself from that person's influence.

✠ PRAY ✠

Dear Heavenly Father,

Replace all of my evil thoughts with loving thoughts of you. Fill my head and heart with your loveliness. Teach me how to find and embrace constructive actions so that everything I think, say, and do all revolve around you. Enable me to cultivate loving relationships with (name) and everyone who interacts with her. Amen.

february 6

INVOKE THE HOLY SPIRIT

In the same way, the Spirit too comes to the aid of our weakness; for we do not know how to pray as we ought, but the Spirit itself intercedes with inexpressible groanings. And the one who searches hearts knows what is the intention of the Spirit, because it intercedes for the holy ones according to God's will (Romans 8:26–27).

Have you ever been in such a deplorable situation that you didn't know how to pray? Perhaps you didn't know what to say or maybe you were too upset to pray. Maybe stress inhibited your prayerfulness or your heartache was so tremendous you were simply unable to focus spiritually. This happened to me when a suspicious finding was noticed on my mammogram. While I waited for the technologist to confer with the doctor, I wanted to pray but I was bereft of words. I simply said, "Lord, help me." And that was enough.

The Holy Spirit helps you in times of desperation. The Holy Spirit knows your heart, your intentions, and your needs. Even if you can only say, "God," that is enough. Your Spirit will carry that word and set it before God the Father.

REFLECT

Did you receive a troubling phone call about your son's behavior or a medical diagnosis that you didn't comprehend? Whatever the misery, give it to God for his keeping.

✠ PRAY ✠

Dear Heavenly Father,

Lift me out from the disparity that I am wallowing in.
Fill me with your divine grace to enable me to carry on. Amen.

february 7

DON'T LOOK BACK

"Are you not satisfied with having led us here away from a land flowing with milk and honey, to make us perish in the desert, that you must now lord it over us? Far from bringing us to a land flowing with milk and honey, or giving us fields and vineyards for our inheritance, will you also gouge out our eyes? No, we will not go" (Numbers 16:13–14).

God freed the Israelites from slavery in Egypt. They cried out to God and he rescued them, but he never said their journey to the Promised Land would be easy. God provided for them, but some of the people were disgruntled and reflected on their Egyptian slavery, viewing it as a place of milk and honey, which was what the Promised Land was supposed to be. The Israelites considered their freedom inconsequential because they feared perishing in the desert.

The changes God has called you to might not be easy to make. You might be commuting longer and need to juggle carpooling with complicated work schedules. Your journey could seem bewildering. Often your experience getting through the wilderness is the hardest. Like the Israelites, you could reflect on the past with bittersweet admiration, seeing it through rose-colored glasses, or you can look toward the land flowing with milk and honey that God has planned for you. As you come to that crossroad you have a choice to make: You can look back or keep moving forward with confidence.

REFLECT

Is God bringing you or your teen to a life change like the Israelites? Once you make the decision to move on, you need to stop looking back.

✠ PRAY ✠

Dear Heavenly Father,

Don't let me dwell in the past. Remind me about the green pastures that await me. Hold my hand, Lord, and walk with me. I trust in you, Lord. Amen.

february 8

SHARE YOUR SUFFERING

It was good for me to be afflicted, in order to learn your statutes. The law of your mouth is more precious to me than heaps of silver and gold. God, your hands made me and fashioned me; give me understanding to learn your commandments (Psalm 119:71–73).

I was a "difficult" child to raise. I was the one always getting into trouble. My siblings were angels. I was always getting sick. My siblings were healthy. I was the clumsy kid who always fell or broke something. My siblings were careful. I gave my parents every gray hair on their heads. But I doubt they would have traded me in if they were given the chance.

I never understood why I was the only one in my family to get tumors, ulcers, and cancer. I didn't know back then that God was preparing me to raise children with medical issues. The skills I acquired as a child enhanced my tolerance, increased my awareness, soothed irritations, and taught me patience. We might not understand why we suffer when we do, but God has a reason for it and we will be better people in the end for having lived through it.

REFLECT

Are you in the midst of suffering, perhaps as a result from your son's illnesses or misfortunes? It isn't easy to sit on the sidelines while your offspring agonizes over something you cannot fix. If your heart is aching, ask God to mend it. God is pained over watching you suffer the same way you hate to see your teen suffer. Try to find something positive in the suffering. Ask God for enlightenment.

✠ PRAY ✠

Dear Heavenly Father,

Take my broken heart and make it whole again.
Hold onto it with the love and fortitude that only
a father can have for his child.
I love you, Lord, and trust in your ways. Amen.

february 9

SEEK CONTENTMENT THROUGH GOD

I know indeed how to live in humble circumstances; I know also how to live with abundance. In every circumstance and in all things I have learned the secret of being well fed and of going hungry, of living in abundance and of being in need. I have the strength for everything through him who empowers me (Philippians 4:11–13).

Parenthood teaches us how to be content. Sometimes, you have to be satisfied with whatever snippets you get, even if it's not exactly what you want. Case in point: when my daughters were little, I longed to dine in restaurants. Occasionally my husband indulged me in this guilty pleasure. While we ate, I spent most of the night making repeated trips to the bathroom, cutting the kid's food, cleaning up messes, or helping them eat. It was not the dining experience I had in mind.

In today's Bible passage, I am reminded of having jubilant dining experiences alone with my husband or hanging out with friends, and food fights with my kids. I have experienced living in abundance and times of need around the dinner table. Because one daughter had an eating disorder, mealtime could be enormously stressful. I learned to be content with what I had on any given day. Some were better than others, but I remained thankful for each day with my family.

We can only be truly content when we seek comfort in God's love. God knows what we need and don't need. It doesn't matter if you're flat broke or filthy rich, unless you let God satisfy you, you'll never be content. Contentment is not based on your possessions (or dining experiences), but on who possesses your heart.

REFLECT

Consider that when you're at peace with God, thankful for your many blessings, you bask in the serenity of contentment.

✠ PRAY ✠

Dear Heavenly Father,

My heart belongs to you. Amen.

february 10

REST IN GOD'S LOVE

He said to them, "Come away by yourselves to a deserted place and rest a while (Mark 6:31).

Every year my sister runs in the Boston Marathon and each time she crosses the finish line totally exhausted. This is perfectly normal for someone who has put all of their physical and mental energy into one thing: a race. Her husband guides her to their hotel, where she gets rest and relaxation, plenty of food, and a massage to help her body recover.

What kind of a race are you running with your teenager? Perhaps you are racing one kid to an orthodontist appointment and another kid to an extracurricular event. It's taxing on you physically, mentally, and emotionally. While it might not seem feasible, it's important for you to take care of your own needs, too. Reflect on ways you might be able to replenish your body and soul. Could you take an extra-long bath or shower, slip into a comfy robe, and sip your favorite hot tea? Maybe all you can do is pop in ear buds and listen to your favorite playlist while you make dinner.

Although it's critical to reenergize yourself physically, it's also essential to revitalize your spiritual needs. Maybe you had to skip Mass to care for your sick youngster. Make the time to sit with God in adoration. Go away with the Lord to connect with him and rest in his love.

REFLECT

What is sacred to you? If you can't get to a church, find a quiet spot in your home where you can light a candle and dwell on Jesus' face.

✠ PRAY ✠

Dear Heavenly Father,

Scoop up my exhausted body in your sturdy hands and breathe life back into me. Revitalize me with your loving embrace and point me in the right direction so that every step I take is in your light. Amen.

february 11

WORDS ARE GIFTS

A word can be better than a gift.
Indeed does not a word count more than a good gift?
...Both are offered by a kind person (Sirach 18:16–17).

When my daughter was five years old, she wrote, "I love you, Mommy," on a heart-shaped piece of paper. I loved it so much that I stuck it in my wallet and it's been there ever since. During troubling times, I pull it out and reread it, which always makes me smile. When my daughter was a teenager she said, "You give the best advice!" Those words made my heart sing. Words can be great gifts, and they're free and abundant. Think about this: your kid can say, "I love you" over and over and you will never get tired of hearing it. But you can only get so many dish towels and coffee mugs before you eventually get tired of them.

Reflect on the last time someone said something nice to you that made you smile. You have the ability to shower people around you with the gift of words. Imagine how happy your teenager's doctor or teacher would feel if you complimented him or her. Some medical professionals or educators are never thanked. and maybe your simple words of appreciation would go a long way. You just never know the impact of your words can have on someone. Praising people sincerely is more beneficial than handing out free dollar bills to strangers. What would you rather have, a dollar or a genuine, heartfelt compliment?

REFLECT

Who do you need to say "thank you" or "I love you" to today?

✠ PRAY ✠

Dear Heavenly Father,

You have been a mighty sword in battle for me, and a healing touch in times of trouble. You have wiped away my tears and brought me to new places, presented new beginnings with newfound hope and enjoyment. You have transformed my life in glorious ways. I am so thankful for it all. I love you. Amen.

february 12

BE SOMEBODY

God, you know my folly; my faults are not hidden from you
(Psalm 69:6).

Abraham Lincoln's mother told him on her deathbed, "Be somebody." He lost eight elections, had two businesses fail, and suffered a nervous breakdown. Thankfully, he never quit. In life, it's difficult to rise above failure; yet if Abraham Lincoln didn't forge onward, he never would have become one of the greatest presidents our nation has ever known.

Consider the difficulties you and your teenager are struggling with. No matter how burdensome they are, don't quit. Teach your kid to be somebody and make something wonderful of his life because each day is a gift; what you do with it is your gift to God. Why not do something wonderful because anything is possible with God. The Lord knows your flaws and loves you regardless of them.

In one religion class I taught, I allowed each student to take an orange and "get to know it." Then, I collected the oranges in a large basket. At the end of class I allowed the students to find their original orange; they were all surprised when they found them. Each orange was unique, with identifying marks on the skin, flaws, and imperfections. God knows each one of us by our flaws and imperfections, too, and he loves us despite them.

REFLECT

Regardless of what your adolescent is struggling with, teach him to be happy with the way God made him; perfect in God's eyes. Despite his mistakes in life, encourage him to keep moving forward, like Abe Lincoln. Inspire him to make the most of what he has and to *be* somebody.

✠ PRAY ✠

Dear Heavenly Father,

Thank you for loving me despite my failures, my weaknesses, my flaws, imperfections, and fears. Thank you for creating in me the person you wanted me to be. Thank you for keeping me strong while I battle through (name's) issues. I love you, Lord, for all you have done and continue to do. Amen.

february 13

BE VIGILANT

For the love of God is this, that we keep his commandments.
And his commandments are not burdensome,
for whoever is begotten by God conquers the world.
And the victory that conquers the world is our faith (1 John 5:3–4).

One of Satan's strategies is to turn your mind away from God's assistance with your struggles against evil and tell you that you need to fight your battles alone. God knows you need his help. You aren't supposed to be able to do it all alone.

When evil temptations strike at you, scream forcefully at Satan, "Be gone!" Run from his grasp and use every device you can think of to drive him away. God will provide every tool you need to drive the devil away. Call out to the Lord in your time of desperation. Remember that the Holy Spirit dwells within you, and he will empower you. God doesn't want you to take on the troubles of the world alone. He wants to help you. All you need to do is ask.

REFLECT

A band of angels safeguard every step you take. When was the last time you've prayed for your guardian angel to keep watch and lead you in the right direction?

✠ PRAY ✠

Dear Heavenly Father,

If the thoughts in my head are not from you, take them away.
Empower me, Lord, to fight the evil that surrounds me now.
Calm me, Lord, and carry this burden so that I don't have to.
The troubles of the world have worn me down and I need you more now than ever before. Don't let Satan make a mess of my life.
Keep me vigilant in your love now and forever. Amen.

february 14

VALENTINE'S DAY

Love is patient, love is kind. It is not jealous, is not pompous, it is not inflated, it is not rude, it does not seek its own interests, it is not quick-tempered, it does not brood over injury, it does not rejoice over wrongdoing but rejoices with the truth. It bears all things, believes all things, hopes all things, endures all things. Love never fails. If there are prophecies, they will be brought to nothing; if tongues, they will cease; if knowledge, it will be brought to nothing (1 Corinthians 13:4–8).

On Valentine's Day you might be thinking about red roses or heart-shaped boxes of candy, but that is not what love is. Paul wrote the best description of love. Consider the amount of patience necessary to be a parent. The minute you learn you'll be a parent, the first thing you must do is be patient while you wait for the baby to be born. Then you must be patient while he learns to talk, and walk, and so on.

If your kid struggles, your love toward him is kind and compassionate while you help him overcome the obstacles in his path. In what ways do you demonstrate compassion toward your youngster? Most parents have their kid's back by defending, protecting, and supporting him.

If you haven't had an opportunity to fully live your own life before becoming a parent, you could feel resentment toward your offspring. Invoke God's help to remember that it's not your child's fault you feel you are putting your life on hold while parenting him. Caring for your child must be your top priority.

REFLECT

Parenting is a humbling job filled with sacrifices, giving over getting, and obligation over feelings. The rewards of parenthood are many, even on days when you can't see them. Love makes the picture clearer.

✠ PRAY ✠

Dear Heavenly Father,

Love is an essential aspect of parenting.
We need it just as much as our kids need it.
Help me to always be there for them, as you are always there for me.
Amen.

february 15

GOD KNOWS THE WAY

Then she prayed to the Lord, the God of Israel, saying:
"My Lord, you alone are God. Help me, who am
alone and have no help but you" (Esther C:14).

Several years ago, my mother and I attended a papal Mass at the Vatican. Saint Peter's Square was mobbed with people. During the service I left Mom to find a restroom. Working my way through the throng of worshipers, it became challenging to find her afterward. When I realized I was lost, I prayed to God to help me find her. Relief and comfort filled me as a path opened up before me and I walked straight to her. Have you ever felt lost? Reflect on the feelings that accompanied the isolation.

When you are alone in a quandary, call out to God. He will help you find your way. If you come to a fork in the road and you don't know which way to go, ask the Lord to guide your footsteps. He will not lead you astray. Pray about decisions before you make them and you'll find yourself making better choices with God leading the way.

REFLECT

Have you ever found yourself in a precarious position and can't fathom how you got there? Maybe you are considering a job transfer or relocating to another home or a different city. Invite God to journey with you in the direction he meant for you. Trust totally, completely, and absolutely in God.

✠ PRAY ✠

Dear Heavenly Father,

Please, help me, Lord. I feel so lost and alone. Rest your comforting hand on my weary shoulder and guide me down the path you mean for me to take. Be my reassurance that you know the way, even though I do not. Thank you for the desperation; for I have discovered the true depth of my faith. Amen.

february 16

REST IN JESUS' LOVE

"Come to me, all you who labor and are burdened, and I will give you rest. Take my yoke upon you and learn from me, for I am meek and humble of heart; and you will find rest for your selves. For my yoke is easy, and my burden light" (Matthew 11:28–30).

Do you ever feel like all you do is work? Maybe you have a job outside the home and you are dealing with a teenager who struggles with classwork or is overly committed to too many projects, functions, or extracurriculars. Let's not forget about the obligations you have running your home: laundry, grocery shopping, and meal preparation. Sometimes, you must feel tired or stressed out just thinking about all you have to do each day! That exhaustion and frazzled state might lead you to sin if you lose your temper, use foul language, or develop unfavorable attitudes. You are human. You're not expected to be a superhero.

Jesus invites you to leave sin behind and follow him and his glorious ways. Jesus cares about those who labor and are burdened by sin. He pardons, provides purity, and offers nourishment to those needing it. Jesus can lift your burdens. Slow down your pace and hand over your failure, neglect, and disappointment to the Lord. Accept rest in Jesus Christ; a rest of conscience, a rest of hope, and a rest of comfort and peace in your world.

REFLECT

Consider if you have embraced Jesus' teachings and the message concerning the kingdom of God. Truly Christ is the way, the truth, and the life; no one comes to the Father, except through the Son of God.

✠ PRAY ✠

Dear Heavenly Father,

In this fast-paced world that I live in, remind me to slow down and quiet myself to think of you. Take my worries and burdens and allow me to rest in your pure love. I ask this in Jesus' name. Amen.

february 17

BE STILL

Whoever conceals hatred has lying lips,and whoever spreads slander is a fool. Where words are many, sin is not wanting; but those who restrain their lips do well. Choice silver is the tongue of the just; the heart of the wicked is of little worth. The lips of the just nourish many, but fools die for want of sense (Proverbs 10:18–21).

Have you ever had a doctor, teacher, or therapist say something about your son that hurt you? Maybe you heard an unfortunate diagnosis or a poor evaluation. Did you feel like giving that individual a piece of your mind but refrained from doing so? Perhaps the stress of living with this problem is irritating and you snap at those around you. What you say and how you say it is important to maintaining a tranquil living environment. Instead of allowing the pressure of your circumstances to escalate, turn to Jesus. He is waiting for you.

Reflect on the quiet agony that Mary experienced as she watched her Son be led to his death. She was beside him each step of the way; her eyes never left him. Consider what you can do to act and think more like Mary. No mother wants to see her kid suffer. No one knows more than the Blessed Mother of God the depth of that despair. Turn to Mary in your misery. Ask for her help and strength as you walk with your child on her journey.

REFLECT

Have the courage to sit in silence and be still. Mary couldn't say anything to lessen Jesus' pain as he suffered on the cross. She never left his side. That was enough.

✠ PRAY ✠

Dear Heavenly Father,

Teach me to simply be still. My mind races with problems. Teach me to let it go and move on. I trust in you implicitly. Hold my hand and sit with me a while. I love you, Lord. Amen.

february 18

LIFE IS SHORT

LORD, let me know my end, the number of my days, that I may learn how frail I am. To be sure, you establish the expanse of my days; indeed, my life is as nothing before you. Every man is but a breath (Psalm 39:5–6).

When my daughter packed up the contents of her room and moved out to begin working at her first "real" job, I was amazed at how quickly the last twenty years had passed. It seemed like it was only yesterday she was a tiny baby snuggled sweetly in my arms, and now she was living in a bustling city managing her life on her own. Life flies by quickly for most people. We are all on this incredible journey, with peaks and valleys, migrating toward one place in particular: heaven.

Our true home is not here on this earthly plane, but in heaven with God. Therefore, don't get caught up in material things that weigh you down. Instead, wrap yourself in God's magnificent glory by performing acts of kindness and generosity toward your fellow man. You never know when your last day will be. Live each day as if it is the last. Live it fully and completely with abundant love for everyone.

REFLECT

The first place you can start this practice is by being caring within your own family. Sometimes family members can be difficult to love. Let every word you utter be a gift. Let your relatives see a tender smile. Do favors for them without expecting anything in return. Give as if you have an endless well to draw from.

✠ PRAY ✠

Dear Heavenly Father,

Empower me to become the very best version of myself. I want to do your will each day that I live. Each breath I take, I only want it to be of you. Each thought I have, I only want it to be of you. Each word I say and each deed I do, I only want it to be of you, for you, and by you. Amen.

february 19

THANK YOU, LORD

Blessed be the God and Father of our Lord Jesus Christ, who has blessed us in Christ with every spiritual blessing in the heavens, as he chose us in him, before the foundation of the world, to be holy and without blemish before him. In love he destined us for adoption to himself through Jesus Christ, in accord with the favor of his will, for the praise of the glory of his grace that he granted us in the beloved (Ephesians 1:3–6).

Don't drive yourself crazy by trying to obtain everything you need on your own. Remember that God provides all you really need. He calls you to respond by following his instructions, and he sanctifies your requests with every spiritual blessing. If there are earthly blessings you need or want, ask God for them and he will provide them according to his will. Remember, there are things better than material blessings. God desires that we have those better, everlasting things.

Knowing that all of your sins are forgiven is a spiritual blessing. Removing you from darkness and bringing you out into the light is a spiritual blessing. Consider the quality of life that is grounded in communion with God, who wants you to have the glorious spiritual blessings of heaven. How can you live closer to God amidst the chaos in your family right now? Try turning over your concerns and qualms to God and thank him for it all every day.

REFLECT

When praying to God, acknowledge his unwavering love for you and thank him for all he has done for you. Don't become obsessed with what you want or the "ideal" life and kids you thought you'd have. Don't focus on what God hasn't done. Consider what God's purpose for you and your family really is.

✠ PRAY ✠

Dear Heavenly Father,

Thank you for your steadfast love. I trust in your divine power to sustain, deliver, and bless me throughout this day. It is a gift, and I thank you for every second of it. What I do with this day will be my gift back to you. Amen.

february 20

HAVE HOPE

Not only that, but we even boast of our afflictions, knowing that affliction produces endurance, and endurance, proven character, and proven character, hope, and hope does not disappoint, because the love of God has been poured out into our hearts through the holy Spirit that has been given to us (Romans 5:3–6).

Optimistic people see a half-glass of water as completely filled with half liquid, half air. Optimism has taught me to look for the silver lining in unfavorable circumstances. Even if it cannot be seen, like the glass half full of air, it's there. It might not be easy to rejoice in the midst of a hardship, but allow your hopefulness to transport you through it. Hope enables you to forge onward. It enables you to climb the mountains that appear unclimbable, cross rivers full of torrents and undertows, walk through raging fires, and brave any storm. Hope comes from your faith in Jesus. How strong is your faith and where will it carry you?

REFLECT

Ponder what difficulty you are currently struggling with. Is it a financial difficulty that has you wondering if you'll be able to send your child to college? Is your teen slacking off and not taking his future seriously? Has a medical emergency turned your life upside down? As you endure these trials, rejoice in them because God is walking with you. The testing develops perseverance. Having faith produces hope, and hope gets you through difficulties.

✠ PRAY ✠

Dear Heavenly Father,

Help me to endure the pressures that have been weighing me down. Thank you for holding my hand and walking with me through the fiery furnace of life. Lift me up into your endless stream of love and compassion. I love you, kind and merciful Lord. Amen.

february 21

FLAVOR LIFE WITH LOVE

You are the salt of the earth. But if salt loses its taste, with what can it be seasoned? It is no longer good for anything but to be thrown out and trampled underfoot (Matthew 5:13).

During meal preparation, most cooks add salt to flavor or enhance their food. If you are the salt of the earth, how do you add flavor to the lives of those around you? Is it through kindness, love, and generosity?

Have you ever spent a lot of time fixing a meal and added too much salt by mistake? Too much of a good thing can be just as unappealing as insufficient seasonings. You need a perfect balance of spices. If you are overly generous to your teenagers, giving them everything they want, they may never learn how to work to achieve their goals on their own.

Try to find that balance between too much and too little. You are the seasoning in God's creation, but alone you'd make a poor meal. Be an example to your teens of what it looks like to be in balance with God's plan and his creation. Show them what it means to live as "the salt of the earth."

REFLECT

Preserve God's divinity by flavoring the world with love. Remember in everything you think, say, and do that God created you to be a precious preservative of his ways.

✠ PRAY ✠

Dear Heavenly Father,

When life seems difficult and I struggle to be everything to everyone, ease my burden, Lord. Thank you for making me the salt of the earth. I love you and trust in you. Amen.

february 22

EVERYTHING GOOD TAKES TIME

Those on rocky ground are the ones who, when they hear, receive the word with joy, but they have no root; they believe only for a time and fall away in time of trial. As for the seed that fell among thorns, they are the ones who have heard, but as they go along, they are choked by the anxieties and riches and pleasures of life, and they fail to produce mature fruit. But as for the seed that fell on rich soil, they are the ones who, when they have heard the word, embrace it with a generous and good heart, and bear fruit through perseverance (Luke 8:13–15).

This parable describes seeds that fall on rocky ground, thorns, or rich soil. During trials and tribulations, similar to those you are currently experiencing, it's important to remember not to fall away from God. Cling to the Lord during your strife. Strive to be the seed that falls on the rich soil.

We live in a society of button pushers and are conditioned to want immediate results. But all good things take time. Consider how long it takes a developing fetus to grow inside the mother's womb. God planned those nine months for a reason. Maybe you have spent many months or years watching your son work tirelessly whether in overcoming a disability, striving to become valedictorian, getting into his dream college, finding the right job, rising above bullying….Perhaps you are tired of watching and want to see the happy ending so he has time to rest and enjoy the fruits of his labors.

REFLECT

It's understandable to want to see fruit soon after you plant a berry bush; in life it's the same impatience when you want to see results. God knows this and understands. Simply be honest and accept that with time, patience, and perseverance you will reap positive results and bear much fruit.

✠ PRAY ✠

Dear Heavenly Father,

Help me to be patient as I watch (name) continue to grow.
Teach me patience, Lord, and bless my wait.
I have surrendered to you and put my faith in you, Lord Jesus. Amen.

february 23

SEEKING FORGIVENESS

We have sinned, been wicked and done evil; we have rebelled and turned from your commandments and your laws (Daniel 9:5).

I had an argument with a relative where hurtful words were said. The moment the cutting words were spoken, they were seared into our hearts like a brand that would never fade. Even though I was remorseful and deeply embarrassed, I knew those words could never be taken back. I was clearly wrong, but no amount of apologizing would be able to dissolve that pain. The words, "I'm sorry" would not suffice.

Sometimes in life we make mistakes and have trouble admitting we were wrong. We can make excuses for our bad behaviors, cast blame away from ourselves, or make up idiotic explanations to hide our blunders. In today's verse, Daniel admits sin. This authentic admission of guilt leads to conversion, the first essential step toward healing. God stands with open arms and an open heart ready, willing, and able to forgive completely. But first we must admit our sin, be truly sorry, and ask for forgiveness.

REFLECT

Even after God forgives us, it might take a while for us to forgive ourselves. It might take longer than we ever imagined. Remember that God will be with you as you work to overcome that sorrow.

✠ PRAY ✠

Dear Heavenly Father,

Take pity and have mercy on me, dear Lord.
For I am a lowly sinner begging for forgiveness.
Wash away my sins and remove the burdens that have crushed and derailed me. Shower me with your love, washing away my iniquities.
Fill my heart with compassion and let me dwell in your light again.
Amen.

february 24

BEING LOST

After three days they found him in the temple, sitting in the midst of the teachers, listening to them and asking them questions, and all who heard him were astounded at his understanding and his answers
(Luke 2:46–47).

When my daughters were little, one wandered away from me in a store. The panic I felt was paralyzing until I found her. Not knowing where your kid is can be nerve-racking. Perhaps your child is away at college and you aren't hearing from him as often as you'd like. Maybe your son is living in another location and it's unsettling, or maybe you have lost your teenager to drugs and alcohol. Whatever your fears are, remember that you are not the only parent to feel this way; Joseph and Mary felt anxious when Jesus was lost, too.

In this passage, Mary and Joseph didn't yell at Jesus, they didn't hit him, or punish him. We should work to imitate Mary and Joseph's parenting style. They were not overly strict with Jesus in the caravan. They gave him the freedom to walk with friends and be away from his parents. They did not overreact when they realized Jesus was missing but calmly searched for him and did not cease looking until he was found.

REFLECT

What reminders do you have in your home that help you remember to act like Mary and Joseph when parenting your teen? If you don't have any, considering hanging a picture of the Holy Family where you can see it.

✠ PRAY ✠

Dear Heavenly Father,

My heart aches when (name) is lost. Help guide him home, where we will welcome (name) back with open and loving arms. Amen.

february 25

BE HUMBLE

A leper came to him (and kneeling down) begged him and said, "If you wish, you can make me clean." Moved with pity, he stretched out his hand, touched him, and said to him, "I do will it. Be made clean." The leprosy left him immediately, and he was made clean (Mark 1:40–42).

After I felt my daughter had suffered long enough with an ailment, I demanded the doctor run more tests, change the current course of action, or make a referral. I didn't ask and I wasn't humble; I was infuriated and tired of being brushed aside. In today's passage, the leper humbly approaches Jesus asking to be healed, "if you wish." He doesn't demand to be cured. It was for God to decide.

I should have been more humble in the doctor's office. And I should have remembered to present my dilemmas meekly to God. Often with our kids' issues, we think of ways to solve the problems or right the wrong ourselves. How often do you think to ask humbly for God's intersession? How often do we ask by saying "if you wish?"

REFLECT

Remember to come humbly before God as the leper did. Remember to be compassionate to others who are hurting and have been shunned from society. It is not for us to decide who is worthy of healing. We are all children of God, brothers and sisters in Christ.

✠ PRAY ✠

Dear Heavenly Father,

Have mercy on us. I beseech you to hear my prayer.
Please, Lord, if it is your will, I humbly ask in Jesus' name
that (name) be granted this intention.
I will sing your praises each day of my life.
I love you, sweet Jesus. Amen.

february 26

APPREHENSIVE SUBMISSION

The Lord said to him, "Get up and go to the street called Straight and ask at the house of Judas for a man from Tarsus named Saul. He is there praying, and (in a vision) he has seen a man named Ananias come in and lay (his) hands on him, that he may regain his sight." But Ananias replied, "Lord, I have heard from many sources about this man, what evil things he has done to your holy ones in Jerusalem. And here he has authority from the chief priests to imprison all who call upon your name" (Acts 9:11–14).

I know when God is calling me to do his work because I am apprehensive. It's usually out of my comfort zone and I fear failure. I become fixated on the task while I discover methods to overcome obstacles. This happened when my husband and I felt called to adopt our daughters. God wanted us to spend our life savings, fly halfway around the world to a country we knew nothing about, to a place where we didn't speak the language, to a community where we didn't know anyone. The idea seemed impossible.

After submitting to God's will, he enabled us to succeed. God brought the right people into our lives at all of the right moments and, miraculously, we knew what to do. All we had to do was listen, trust, and obey.

REFLECT

I understand how Ananias must have felt when God came to him in a vision and requested an inconceivable task of him. He didn't want to approach someone who persecuted Christians. And yet, God was about to transform Saul's sinful heart by curing his blindness. But first, Ananias had to have faith by obeying God. Because Ananias conformed to God's will, Saul regained his vision and converted. When you surrender to God's will, you will be amply blessed. Allow God to use you to accomplish the unimaginable with your son.

✠ PRAY ✠

Dear Heavenly Father,

Help me to discern your call, your work, and your will.
Tell me what you want me to do. I will obey.
I trust you and love you. Amen.

february 27

YOU ARE NOT ALONE

The Lord, your God, who goes before you, is the one who will fight for you, just as he acted with you before your very eyes in Egypt, as well as in the wilderness, where you saw how the Lord, your God, carried you, as one carries his own child, all along your journey until you arrived at this place (Deuteronomy 1:30–31).

Before you had children, do you remember imagining what kind of parent you would be? You probably vowed to be the best caregiver, 24/7, no question about it! You would walk through fire for your kid if need be. All of your promises would be believable.

Just like a parent, God makes a commitment to us as his children. God promises protection against enemies, which is believable until life becomes difficult. In the midst of turmoil and struggle, it's understandable to forget God's promises (just like our teen sometimes forgets our promises as her parent when things don't go her way). You might try to solve your own problems using only the resources available to you, forgetting about what's available to us through God.

When life becomes complicated raising a teenager, take a moment to catch your breath and talk to God before you do anything else. Trust in God's plan; he knows what is best. Don't question God's judgment. You might not be able to see the big picture now, but maybe later you will understand it.

REFLECT

Is there an ongoing battle you've been fighting with your teen? Does your teenager want to stop attending religious education? Is she set on a plan for the future that you know won't end well? Whatever your struggles are, remember that God is with you. Remind yourself of your promise as a parent and stand firm for what's best for your teen.

✠ PRAY ✠

Dear Heavenly Father,

Thank you for staying at my side through the darkness
and for providing everlasting love when I need it the most.
Thank you for keeping me on course and carrying me when I tire.
I rest sweetly in your abundant love. I adore you, Lord. Amen.

february 28

DO GOOD DEEDS

Let us not grow tired of doing good, for in due time we shall reap our harvest, if we do not give up. So then, while we have the opportunity, let us do good to all, but especially to those who belong to the family of the faith (Galatians 6:9–10).

Sometimes it can be exhausting to continually do good deeds. God wants us to extend acts of kindnesses to others. He encourages us to stay on course because we might not see results now, but the seeds have been planted; the results will eventually show. Trials and tribulations are part of life. The difficulties of raising a teen can be spiritually and emotionally draining. Some trials are brief while others persist without ceasing (or possibly increase in intensity). Persevering in a loving manner in the midst of hardships is not easy.

One thing that might help you during this time is reading the Bible and reflecting on it throughout the day; try to incorporate the message in your routine. Strive to be the best version of yourself by imitating Jesus. It takes humility to endure what feels unfair. It always bothered me when my daughters were young and missed so much time from school due to illness. At the end of the year classmates were rewarded with perfect attendance records. It was unfair that my children were often sick. Rather than finding ways to take away the accomplishment of their classmates, I celebrated my daughters' academic success at home. In doing this, I taught my daughters to do good deeds despite our own circumstances. I was planting the seed.

REFLECT

How can you plant seeds in your life?

✠ PRAY ✠

Dear Heavenly Father,

Give me energy to keep going long after a rest is due.
Give me strength to continue onward
when the road seems exceptionally long.
Give me the patience to overlook my own tribulations
and help those around me who are much worse off than I am.
Amen.

february 29

PRAY IN ALL CIRCUMSTANCES

Rejoice in hope, endure in affliction, persevere in prayer
(Romans 12:12).

I cannot think of one circumstance where prayer is not warranted. The moment you open your eyes each morning, thank God that you are alive. When you get dressed, thank God that you have clothes to wear and the ability to dress yourself. When you walk into the kitchen to make breakfast, be thankful that you have food to eat. When you wash yourself, be thankful for clean and warm water. When you start work, give thanks that you are employed. Thank God for your home, electricity, and the abundance of gifts easily taken for granted.

When you walk outside, thank God for your legs that they can carry you to amazing places; lands that God created for you to enjoy. Give thanks for your ability to hear the joyful songs of birds that fill your ears. Thank God for the warm sunshine and gentle breezes. Maybe you have torrential rain, dark, gloomy clouds, or snow. Give thanks for that, too. God wants you to sing praises for everything, not just for what seems good. Many days of gloomy weather teach you how to hope for the sunshine.

REFLECT

In life, our days might not unfold effortlessly with everything rosy and bright. There are bound to be complications, mishaps, and troubles. Consider the difficulties you are grappling with as a parent. Does your teenager constantly bring drama into your family? Thank God for all of your teen's problems because they will draw you closer to her, they will make you stronger, and God will walk with you and help you through them.

✠ PRAY ✠

Dear Heavenly Father,

Help me through this frustration with (name).
I'm not sure why she is doing what she does,
and sometimes I feel she isn't taking the rest of the family
into consideration. Give me the strength to endure.
I adore you, kind and merciful Lord. Amen.

march 1

TESTS ARE NECESSARY

In this you rejoice, although now for a little while you may have to suffer through various trials, so that the genuineness of your faith, more precious than gold that is perishable even though tested by fire, may prove to be for praise, glory, and honor at the revelation of Jesus Christ (1 Peter 1:6, 7).

Imagine attending school and never taking a test. Without putting your new skills to work, how can you know that you retained the knowledge necessary to build on, function, and grow? Imagine no driving tests! Streets would be chaotic. Imagine having surgery knowing your doctor's skills were never tested. Tests are essential. They give you peace of mind that you understand something and are ready to move on to something bigger, better, and brighter.

Inevitably everyone endures tests of life through various trials. Consider the assessments you are currently undergoing in your family. Perhaps your teenager is acting out, rebelling, or struggling with something you cannot grasp. Try to be patient as you endure; don't give up on all that is good and sound. When stressed, draw strength from the understanding that your faithfulness will eventually be a cause for praise, magnificence, and honor.

REFLECT

Trust in God no matter how frazzled you get. The Lord will never abandon you during your time of need.

✠ PRAY ✠

Dear Heavenly Father,

In my weariness, lift me up to a better place.
Let me rest in your loving arms as I plod along this path
filled with roadblocks. Show me the light at the end of the tunnel.
Bring me out of the darkness into your bright light.
I ask this in Jesus' name. Amen.

march 2

HAVE CONFIDENCE

What then shall we say to this?
If God is for us, who can be against us?
No, in all these things we conquer overwhelmingly
through him who loved us (Romans 8:31, 37).

In our younger days, my husband and I would ski the Adirondack Mountains in upstate New York. At the top we would scrutinize a triple black diamond slope and ask, "Should we?" I had the confidence to do it, but lacked the ability. Being confident is good, but in this case it was not enough. The real issue is in whom, or in what, is our confidence. Dubious confidence, like skiing down a treacherous trail without the ability, could be deadly. Logical confidence is what we should aspire to.

Some Christians lack confidence in faith. They might agonize over it throughout their life, fearful that they won't go to heaven, even after repentance, confession, and absolution. These people need the confidence found in today's passage. Others have overconfidence in the wrong thing, believing they are invincible. Paul shows us that logical confidence is not found in ourselves but in our salvation and in God. This kind of confidence should offer hope and sureness in the midst of a crumbled world.

In his words, "If God is for us, who can be against us," Paul recognizes that we will have conflict in life. The question was designed to emphasize the smallness of any struggle knowing that God is our greatest advocate. We can do anything with God if it is his will.

REFLECT

What are the issues you're going through with your teen that seem larger than life? How can they become small in the Lord?

✠ PRAY ✠

Dear Heavenly Father,

My troubles seem monstrous; please rescue me from them.
Teach me to have confidence in you and grow in my faith.
I love you, Lord. Amen.

march 3

THY WILL BE DONE

And we have this confidence in him, that if we ask anything according to his will, he hears us. And if we know that he hears us in regard to whatever we ask, we know that what we have asked him for is ours (1 John 5:14–15).

No matter what you ask of God, he listens. It doesn't mean that if you ask for a million dollars he will give it to you, but he does hear your request. God also knows what's in your heart. If you ask in accordance to God's will, he hears and provides accordingly. Consider what petitions you have been making of God. Are your prayers an intercession for your teen?

Trust that God's will is right and good even if you don't know or understand what it is. God knows his plan for your teenager—you can only surmise and lead accordingly. As parents we often have our own plans for our teenagers and pray for things to work out according to our will for our teens. But that decision isn't up to us. Just like when we pray for ourselves, when we pray for our teens we should still submit to God's will, embrace it, and align with it even if it is uncomfortable to do so.

REFLECT

How flexible are you when it comes to submitting to God's will?

✠ PRAY ✠

Dear Heavenly Father,

I seek your direction for my life. I am ready, willing, and able to follow you and do your will—whatever it is. Please, Lord, help (name) overcome his difficulties. I accept whatever it is you want. I adore you. Amen.

march 4

GIVE SINS TO GOD

Who is there like you, the God who removes guilt and pardons sin for the remnant of his inheritance; Who does not persist in anger forever, but delights rather in clemency, And will again have compassion on us, treading underfoot our guilt? You will cast into the depths of the sea all our sins (Micah 7:18–19).

When one of my daughters was diagnosed with an incurable disease, I became angry at God. I blamed him for my daughter's illness. It took a while to work through that misdirected anger. No parent wants to see her child suffer. As a child of God, our Lord recognized that I was suffering, and he did something about it: My daughter recovered. More importantly, God allowed my broken heart to heal.

God accepts our sins, regardless of how big or small they are, and he forgives them completely. Consider how easily you forgive your daughter when she does something wrong. Give your sinfulness to the Lord. Jesus came into the world to take our sins and throw them into the depths of the sea. God takes the burden and frees us from the weight, guilt, and shame.

REFLECT

Do you accept God's forgiveness, or do you take it for granted? To clear your conscience, spend quiet time in contemplation. Make an act of contrition and accept the divine graces that come with the sacrament of reconciliation. Don't put it off another day.

✠ PRAY ✠

Dear Heavenly Father,

Take my sins from me, Lord, and wash me clean.
I bow before you, humbly, mercifully, and respectfully.
I love you, divine Creator. Take pity on me and save my soul.
Point me in the right direction to build a stronger,
more vibrant relationship with you today and always.
I humbly ask this in Jesus' name. Amen.

march 5

UNWANTED FAVORITISM

Israel loved Joseph best of all his sons, for he was the child of his old age; and he had made him a long ornamented tunic. When his brothers saw that their father loved him best of all his brothers, they hated him so much that they could not say a kind word to him (Genesis 37:3–4).

As a parent, it's hard not to play favorites when one child is suffering or struggling. I am guilty of this: my heart always goes out to the underdog. If one kid was recovering from surgery, she received special attention in every shape and form. It required double duty to step away with the left-out child to pay attention to her needs as well. Sometimes it required hiring extra help or including grandparents and extended family members to pick up balls that were mistakenly dropped. It required extra effort to ensure everyone's needs were met, and then some. We did want both of our children to feel loved, cherished, and adored. They both had to be favored even when it required extra effort.

Favoritism is more common during stressful times in a family. Failure to recognize and address it can cause longstanding problems and ruin relationships. Most parents know this and strive to avoid playing favorites, but some parents are unaware that it is happening in their homes. When you feel all your time is going toward one child, step back, say a prayer, and let God refocus your energy where it needs to be.

REFLECT

Consider if you have in the past or currently play favorites with your children. Was there a stressful incident or a major life event that caused you to devote all your time and attention to one child?

✠ PRAY ✠

Dear Heavenly Father,

Take my troubled heart into your mighty hands and sift through the problems that have accumulated there.
Help me to hold my family together through these stressful periods.
You created us for a reason; help us now to fulfill that purpose with your loving touch. I trust you, Lord. Amen.

march 6

SEEK REFUGE IN THE LORD

For six days you may do your work, but on the seventh day you must rest, that your ox and your donkey may have rest, and that the son of your maidservant...may be refreshed (Exodus 23:12).

Raising a family is exhausting. Raising teens with issues is even more demanding. It's a job that doesn't give days off for rest and relaxation, but the Bible says to take a day of rest anyway. It doesn't say take an hour of rest, it says a day is needed in order to be refreshed. When was the last time you took an entire day to rest? If you think rest isn't necessary, ask the marathon runner if he needs rest before running another race. Raising children is akin to running marathons back to back.

When you have a family depending on you for daily needs, you have to be creative to incorporate rest into your day. Maybe you could play cards or board games with your kids or have a day dedicated to movies. Instead of fussing over preparing meals, have one day be sandwich day or picnic day eating on the living-room floor. Use your imagination to create fun and rest. It's not a wasted day; it's a day where you build lasting memories with your family while teaching them the importance of taking time off. When I was growing up, Sunday was the day of rest in my home. I carried that tradition into my own home and hope my daughters do the same.

REFLECT

If you don't teach your children how important rest is, how will they know? If you don't have a day off "scheduled" soon, make that day today.

✠ PRAY ✠

Dear Heavenly Father,

Thank you for creating my body in such a miraculous way; it tells me when I need rest. Help me to carve out extra rest days so I can spend prayerful, quiet, and reflective time alone with you. I love you, Lord. Amen.

march 7

GOD'S MIGHTY FORCE

The Lord goes forth like a warrior, like a man of war he stirs up his fury; He shouts out his battle cry, against his enemies he shows his might (Isaiah 42:13).

The muscle of the United States military reassures us of our nation's security. The education and years of experience of your kid's doctors and teachers help you feel confident about the care they receive. So why do you still worry? The anxiety that you wrestle with can wear you down; nothing good will come from it.

When you start to worry about the bad things waiting for your kids in the world, remember God marches forward like a mighty combatant roaring against the enemy. Put your trust in the God you love and serve. He is the one who can defeat any enemy in battle. Call to God to help you fight your battles, whatever they might be. Is your adolescent battling: a disorder? difficulty in school? adjusting to college? bullies? toxic friendships or relationships? Your kid is not the enemy. Fight the problem. In your darkest hour, remember that God will help you.

Perhaps you are clashing against evil forces. The Bible tells us how Jesus outsmarted Satan. Use your intelligence to outwit the devil. God empowered you with intellect. Invoke the Holy Spirit to enable you to outthink the wicked ones who might be testing you. When it comes to battles fought, God is undefeated. Put your faith in God's mighty force.

REFLECT

Does it feel like you and your teen are going head to head? Is there an underlying problem you could be fighting against instead of your teen?

✠ PRAY ✠

Dear Heavenly Father,

As I prepare to advocate for (name), let me feel your strong arms around me, protecting and empowering me. I need you, Lord! Amen.

march 8

BE STRONG AND COURAGEOUS

Do not let this book of the law depart from your lips. Recite it by day and by night, that you may carefully observe all that is written in it; then you will attain your goal; then you will succeed. I command you: be strong and steadfast! Do not fear nor be dismayed, for the LORD, your God, is with you wherever you go (Joshua 1:8–9).

When the rein of leadership was passed from Moses to Joshua, God spoke encouragingly to Joshua before he began leading the people to the Promised Land. God told him to be strong and courageous. He told him not to be frightened or dismayed because God is beside him wherever he goes. God doesn't say, "Ease into it," or, "Slow and steady wins the race." God doesn't even tell him to pray over every decision. He tells him to "be strong and steadfast."

How have you had to be strong and courageous in order to keep your parenting skills on track in the midst of hardships? In times of crises, your fight or flight mechanisms kick in. Chances are good you will fight for the sake of your kid, no matter how strenuous the battle may seem. Whether you're facing a medical diagnosis, addiction, bad influences, college rejections, or classroom bullies, there is something you can do. When officials tell you there's no hope, look for someone else who will listen. Find communities online and research the situation. And, most importantly, pray and stay positive. There are many things you can do.

REFLECT

Are you doing the right thing by devoting so much time parenting your teenager, or is it time to take a few steps back and focus on yourself? How much time do you spend patiently waiting to hear God's voice?

✠ PRAY ✠

Dear Heavenly Father,

Help me to walk in greater boldness with you. I trust in your ways. Amen.

march 9

FORGIVENESS IS THE ANSWER

Then Peter approaching asked him, "Lord, if my brother sins against me, how often must I forgive him? As many as seven times?" Jesus answered, "I say to you, not seven times but seventy-seven times" (Matthew 18:21–22).

Throughout the Bible are stories on forgiveness. Jesus wants us to be all forgiving, which sounds doable until we are actually in a situation that requires it. Then it becomes tricky, especially if our kids are involved. In my house, before forgiveness happened an apology was required with a plan describing how the offense wouldn't reoccur. But Jesus doesn't say anything about a plan or an apology. He simply says to forgive as many times as necessary. He doesn't say to mull it over for a few days, or three strikes and you're out. He says you might have to forgive seventy-seven times!

When siblings bicker or your teen is fighting with a friend, it creates havoc at home. Sometimes you need to carefully intervene to bring peace back without being a referee for every battle. How do you let your teenagers untangle their problems while promoting forgiveness?

Forgiveness is intentionally releasing negative feelings and embracing positive ones for the offender. Reflect over a past occurrence where you needed to forgive someone. Did you first want to seek revenge or teach him a lesson? Forgiving someone doesn't mean you condone his behavior or excuse his action, but it does mean that you continue to love him.

REFLECT

Consider if you have ever struggled to forgive yourself. Have you sought divine pardoning for your own shortcomings or transgressions? Jesus is ready and willing to forgive us as soon as we sincerely repent.

✠ PRAY ✠

Dear Heavenly Father,

I humbly bow before you, baring my soul, and begging your forgiveness for all of the harm I have caused. Take away my inconsiderate thoughts and desires; replace them with only loving opinions, feelings, and emotions. Teach me to be more like you, Lord. Buff out my rough edges and make me shine like the brilliant star you created me to be. I love you, Lord. Amen.

march 10

TEACH YOUR CHILDREN

However, be on your guard and be very careful not to forget the things your own eyes have seen, nor let them slip from your heart as long as you live, but make them known to your children and to your children's children (Deuteronomy 4:9).

Parents try to offer sage advice to their progenies. Regardless of what I feel for my daughters, I always safeguard their best interest and try to provide all that is good, true, and wise. I wouldn't intentionally hurt them. There are myriad aspects of parenting, but the most important is not the things we provide, but the love of God we share with each other.

My mother had a rule in her house when I was growing up: We couldn't snack on anything an hour before dinner. She didn't want us to fill up on junk when a nutritious meal was in the making. What are your own kids "filling up" with? Mindless sitcoms? Time on phones, video games, or computers? In our desire to give them what they want, have we given them wholesome values to emulate?

Whenever my husband and I did community service, our teens came with us and learned through our example. We were planting the seeds that we hoped would take root later in life. There were many opportunities to dote over them with trips to Walt Disney World, the shopping mall, and dining out. What else was I teaching my daughters?

REFLECT

When was the last time you read from the Bible as a family, discussing passages that piqued your family's interest? Faith is a wonderful gift. Foster it by teaching your teen to pray.

✠ PRAY ✠

Dear Heavenly Father,

Help me to "fill" my offspring with stories and teachings of you. Let me be mindful of what they need and not just give into wants. I love you. Amen.

march 11

ATTITUDE ADJUSTMENTS

Ah, could my anguish but be measured and my calamity laid with it in the scales, They would now outweigh the sands of the sea! Because of this I speak without restraint. For the arrows of the Almighty pierce me, and my spirit drinks in their poison; the terrors of God are arrayed against me (Job 6:2–4).

I felt the rug pulled out beneath me when doctors delivered my daughter's medical diagnosis. I was despondent and grief-stricken to the point where I was like Job: my anguish could "outweigh the sands of the sea." I wondered if God was punishing me and I wallowed in self-pity. After heartfelt reflection, I realized my attitude needed a readjustment. I couldn't do anything to change my daughter's illness; however, I could change my attitude about it. Once I did that, I felt better, my daughter was happier, my entire family was better off.

God never said life would be easy, but it's still good. Everyone has a cross to carry. In elementary school a teacher said that if people traded their life crosses for something better, they might end up wishing for the old cross back. Other people's crosses might appear easier to carry, but looks can be deceiving.

In the midst of overwhelming suffering, we have the power to amend our attitudes. We can choose to be people of doom and gloom or people of peace, love, and joy. Succumbing to negativity in the face of adversity does no good to anyone. To uphold your conviction in God joyously requires grace when you must deal with anguish and disillusionments. This can be accomplished by remembering that you are not alone in your struggles. God is with you through it all.

REFLECT

What cross are you carrying?

✠ PRAY ✠

Dear Heavenly Father,

Thank you for providing me with abundant joy at a time when I need it the most. Thank you for difficulties; for it teaches me endurance, patience, and fortitude. With you beside me, I can withstand any force. You alone are my source of inspiration and strength. Amen.

march 12

DON'T GOSSIP

They said this to test him, so that they could have some charge to bring against him. Jesus bent down and began to write on the ground with his finger. But when they continued asking him, he straightened up and said to them, "Let the one among you who is without sin be the first to throw a stone at her" (John 8:6–7).

At a neighborhood playground, I overheard mothers commiserating with each other about how unruly, disobedient, and difficult their children were. When they were finished bad-mouthing their children, they moved on to verbally bashing their husbands, then their in-laws. Why do people gossip? Maybe they need to point out other's faults to feel a sense of superiority, or perhaps they need to vent.

If you have the desire to speak poorly about your teenager to friends, neighbors, or family members, imagine how she would feel if she were there listening. If it would make your daughter feel degraded, maybe you should keep your thoughts to yourself, or discuss them privately with your spouse, priest, or counselor.

In today's Bible passage, Jesus challenges us to mind our own business. Instead of being judgmental and condemning others, we should use that energy to reflect on ourselves and our own sins.

REFLECT

When people ask how your kids are doing, do you find yourself gossiping about them? Anticipate questions with polite responses that won't belittle or degrade your teen. Plan to build up your kids, not tear them down, regardless of how disparaging you may feel about the situation you are in.

✠ PRAY ✠

Dear Heavenly Father,

Enable me to better appreciate your love for me so that I constantly build up my kids. Teach me how to speak lovingly about them. Fill my head with positive thoughts, fill my heart with abundant love. Amen.

march 13

COUNT YOUR BLESSINGS

From Mount Hor they set out on the Red Sea road, to bypass the land of Edom, but the people's patience was worn out by the journey; so the people complained against God and Moses, "Why have you brought us up from Egypt to die in the wilderness, where there is no food or water? We are disgusted with this wretched food!" (Numbers 21:4–6).

Have you ever spent hours preparing a big meal for your family only to have them complain about it? Maybe the meat was too tough or no one liked the vegetables. With so many starving people in the world, I want my family to appreciate their food. In today's Bible verses, the Israelites, finally freed from centuries of enslavement, complain about the food. Why couldn't they be happy with their freedom? Do your kids complain about one thing or another? How do you deal with that?

In everyday life, I sometimes overlook my blessings when problems seem to rise up and grab me. Sometimes, it's easy to forget all of the wonderful gifts God has provided. Do you ever get overwhelmed with your problems and forget about the blessings God has showered you with? Just for today try to shift the focus away from your struggles. You have issues, you are addressing them. Don't dwell on them. Give them to God.

REFLECT

Spend your day in thanksgiving, singing praises to the Lord for all he has given: good and bad. Thank God for the problems, even though it's hard to do. There's a reason for everything he does.

✠ PRAY ✠

Dear Heavenly Father,

Thank you, Lord for blessings and the hardships.
Together, they make me a better person and a stronger,
more congenial parent. Help me through it all, Lord.
The journey is long and I am so tired. Take my hand and lead me.
I will follow you to the ends of the earth. Amen.

march 14

SERVE CHRIST

Whatever you do, do from the heart, as for the Lord and not for others, knowing that you will receive from the Lord the due payment of the inheritance; be slaves of the Lord Christ (Colossians 3:23–24).

As a stay-at-home mom, I felt overworked and underpaid. I rarely got time off, there were no paychecks or bonuses, there was little praise or recognition, and sometimes I didn't feel appreciated. Do you ever feel like that? I had to remind myself constantly that I was doing God's work. Being a mom is what God wanted me to do. Therefore, I took pride in it. Pride enabled me to work heartily because I was serving my Lord. I didn't need God to give me a paycheck or vacation time. My rewards would come to me in heaven.

In today's verses, the slaves are being lectured to work from the heart because they are not working for others; they are slaves of the Lord. And their due payment will come to them in heaven. This sounds good, but it's not easy to live day in and day out, especially if you have a difficult job where you have an unreasonable boss who has unrealistic expectations. Just remember that above that boss is your true boss: God in heaven. Regardless of your job title, your main job is serving the Lord. Do you work outside the home? Offer those labors to God because he is your true master.

REFLECT

When your job seems overwhelming, remember today's verses. Reflect on them and pray that God will help you through the tasks you must accomplish today. Remember that you are exactly where God wants you to be. Reflect on your role as a parent remembering that you are doing God's work as you raise your teenagers.

✠ PRAY ✠

Dear Heavenly Father,

Remind me, Lord that you govern over all. Remind me that I am doing your work and need to take pride in that. I love you, Lord, creator of heaven and earth. Amen.

march 15

GOD IS IN CONTROL

In my distress I called out: LORD! I cried out to my God.
From his temple he heard my voice; my cry to him reached his ears
(Psalm 18:7).

Tired of rejection letters, I decided to stop writing. I started to believe my words didn't matter. Before Mass, my parish priest spoke with me about an article I had written. He told me never to stop writing. How could he have known what I felt? God works miracles through ordinary people, as he did with my priest that day.

In your struggles, call out to God. No one likes being distressed, however during those times it can bring out the best in you. My priest didn't know me when he praised my writing one Sunday morning. That compliment kept me on track, and I wrote three consecutive devotionals.

Whenever life runs smoothly, we sometimes forget to thank God for all he does. Perhaps you hit green lights all the way to an appointment you were running late for. Maybe you found an ideal parking spot with time left on the meter. Thank God for the little things. Don't be too busy to pray when life is good. We think we are in control of our good fortune, but we are not: God is.

REFLECT

Allow God to work through you by offering random acts of kindness to strangers who might need their spirits lifted. Be the pencil in God's hand.

✠ PRAY ✠

Dear Heavenly Father,

I cry out to you in my time of need. Help me carry my burdens, Lord. The load is heavy; still I thank you for it. The suffering makes me a stronger, kinder, and gentler person. I love you, Lord! Amen.

march 16

TIME WITH GOD

For thus said the Lord God, the Holy One of Israel: By waiting and by calm you shall be saved, in quiet and in trust shall be your strength. But this you did not will (Isaiah 30:16).

When my daughters were young, I seemed to be racing everywhere: to the grocery store, drugstore, gas station, church, school, and friends' homes. I needed more time; there wasn't enough to accomplish all I needed to do each day. I also needed time to connect with God. It's not easy to squeeze in one more thing, especially when the plate is already full. However, it's critical to be calm and rest in God's love because in that restful period with the Lord we will be saved! Quietness and trust will be our strength.

As a multitask master, I found my quiet each morning in the shower. I allowed God to fill me up with his love and positive energy to begin my day. But prayer in the shower wasn't always possible if there was an asthma attack, upset stomach, earache, or sore throat. I needed prayer more when trouble was brewing, but it wasn't always easy to do.

Do you ever feel as if life is pitching too many fastballs and you're exhausted from batting them out of the park? Perhaps you get through one kid's problem and there's another one waiting for you with no time to rest.

REFLECT

Are you spending too much time trying to keep your life organized and on track but forgetting to take time out for God? The first thing you can do each day when you open your eyes is thank God for another day. Even before you climb out of bed, take a few minutes to talk to the Lord. Make it your new routine.

✠ PRAY ✠

Dear Heavenly Father,

Everything I have comes from you.
Thank you for it all.
You are my loving Lord and I am truly blessed
to have so many wonderful and exciting things to do today.
Thank you for helping me through it. Amen.

march 17

TRAIN YOUR CHILDREN

Train the young in the way they should go;
even when old, they will not swerve from it (Proverbs 22:6).

It's our job as parents to teach our kids right from wrong. If they don't learn morals and values at home, they could end up with a spiritual void in their lives that could leave them unfulfilled, searching endlessly for direction, with a sense of not belonging.

It isn't easy to instill discipline; it takes energy to make, implement, and enforce rules. Kids need boundaries and crave routines. They want their parents to be firm with them because it sends the message that they are loved and cared for. Begin setting limitations early in their lives and be consistent. If you let things slip, it sends the message that rules can be broken and you don't mean what you say. You want your teenagers to believe you when you say you love them.

Kids are like inquisitive sponges soaking up and questioning everything: your reasons for establishing such rules, your motives for your values, and purpose for obeying God's laws. Are your kids embracing your instructions or rebelling now that they're teenagers? My mother used to say to me, "Don't do as I do; do as I say." But I taught my daughters to do as I do. They learned by watching me succeed and fail. How will you train your kids?

REFLECT

Teach your teen by leading a good life and setting honorable examples. How have you been doing so far? Is there room for improvement in your own life?

✠ PRAY ✠

Dear Heavenly Father,

Thank you for putting ideas into my head to train (name) to learn and grow in your infinite love and wisdom. Thank you for prompting me to read to him from the Bible. Thank you for reminding me to sing praises to you and pointing out sage actions to emulate.
Thank you for lifting me up when I feel like letting something slide.
I love you, Lord. Amen.

march 18

TRUST AND OBEY

Many shall look on in awe and they shall trust in the LORD. Blessed the man who sets his security in the LORD, who turns not to the arrogant or to those who stray after falsehood (Psalm 40:4–5).

When my daughter was in high school, I gave her my sapphire ring. My parents gave this special ring to me when I was a teenager. She only wore it to church under my watchful eye until one day she decided to wear it to school, confident that she could take care of it on her own. On that day she lost it and cried out for help to find it.

When was the last time you thought you could handle something on your own only to cry out to God for his help when it proved more than you could handle? Perhaps you were frustrated with your kid's behavior or a condition that is troublesome to you. Maybe you tried to rectify it on your own and weren't successful. Give it totally and completely to God and then trust and obey him. When you give God your problems, trust that his will shall be done. You might not like what his will is, but it is what God wants for you right now. Maybe God wants you to wait a while longer. Perhaps there is a lesson to be learned in waiting. Trust in God's ways, for those who do will be blessed.

REFLECT

How often do you trust your burdens to God and then don't trust him to take care of them? How often do you take matters into your own hands and then when it goes wrong cry out for his help? Do you want to trust your life in God's hands or your own?

✠ PRAY ✠

Dear Heavenly Father,

Teach me how to give you my problems and then not take them back. Teach me to trust implicitly in you. Guide me down the path you mean for me to take. Let me find peacefulness in the journey as I wait for resolve. You are always with me, and so I have nothing to fear. I love you and trust you. Amen.

march 19

ST. JOSEPH'S DAY

Oh, that you would be altogether silent;
that for you would be wisdom! (Job 13:5).

My doorstop is a metal plaque depicting a mother bear safeguarding her cubs. If you encountered mama bear in the wild, you would avoid her. You don't have to hear her growl; the bear guards in silence. Parents protect their kids in a similar fashion. God chose the very best guardian to care for Jesus and Mary: Joseph. While Joseph is mentioned in the Bible, there are limited accounts of him, and we never hear him speak. Yet we know he had to be a wonderful foster father.

During the passion when the apostles were questioned about Jesus, God protected Mary, ensuring no harm came to her. Mary didn't speak during the passion; yet, we know by her presence how troubled her heart was. Mary was extraordinarily special to God; he showed tremendous care choosing a spouse to look after her. God picked a spouse proportional to her in order to create the perfect family.

God chose you to parent your offspring carefully, too. He didn't pick just anyone, he chose you for a reason. At times you might feel overwhelmed that the job is too complicated. When this happens, reach out to God because he is your heavenly father, safeguarding you. God, like the mighty bear in the woods, won't let a hair on your head be harmed.

REFLECT

Listen to the silences in your life while seeking their significance.

✠ PRAY ✠

Dear Heavenly Father,

I once thought silence meant that you had forgotten me.
Now, I know you are always with me
and I trust in the silence that fills the air.
I trust in your ways, even though
I don't always understand them. Amen.

march 20

GOD'S DIRECTIONS ARE DIVINE

The human heart plans the way, but the L*ORD directs the steps*
(Proverbs 16:9).

I make lists each day to remind me of all I must do regardless of how much I actually accomplish. I recently began prioritizing and achieving the two most crucial things on the list every day. Then I have a sense of accomplishment that something of importance was completed. I like making plans because it offers a feeling of control over my life. Yet God is the only one in control of my life. He guides my steps, which is wonderful because my human reasoning isn't as wise as the Lord's. His insight and judgment are far superior to mine.

Reflect on all you must do today. What major tasks are essential? Maybe you have a doctor's appointment or a parent-teacher conference to attend. Do your kid's activities conflict with any of them? It's difficult to juggle multiple tasks. Seek the Lord's wisdom in planning your day and deciding what will stay and what will be eliminated.

God overrules the plans of people to fulfill his purposes. Therefore, contemplate what your true purposes are. If you're trying to work through an issue, consider what you are hoping to accomplish and how happy that action will make God. If you are doing God's work, then you are delighting the Lord. If you are doing God's work but doing it begrudgingly, you are doing it with the wrong spirit. Imagine God standing beside you while you toil. Would you complain about it, or smile and do it lovingly?

REFLECT

The next time you feel irritable about an appointment you must make, a phone call you have to take, or a task you must do, imagine God beside you as you work.

✠ PRAY ✠

Dear Heavenly Father,

I want to please you in my actions, the errands I run,
the people I encounter, and the obligations that I have.
Teach me how to do them happily.
Where you lead, I will follow. Amen.

march 21

GOD'S PURPOSE FOR YOU

The Lord called me from birth, from my mother's womb he gave me my name (Isaiah 49:1).

Prior to our birth God had a purpose for us. God knew what our name would be, he knew our talents, our weaknesses, and he had a marvelous plan for our life. We might think of our life as ordinary, but to God it's quite special. I once thought of myself as "just a mom." However, I realize that God chose me because he thought I was capable of adopting and raising two children. While I was going through it, I didn't think I was capable. In fact, I thought I was failing miserably. Nonetheless, I was doing what God intended for me.

Have you felt like your role in life is inconsequential? Perhaps you cannot see the significance of it because you are too close to it. Trust in God that you are doing what he designed you to do. Sometimes God asks us to wait for a specific task. Pray during that waiting period. God will enlighten you. Ask him to bless the time you spend preparing for an important job. Maybe that job is to parent a needy youngster. Remember that God will give you the tools and talents you need. He will bring the right people into your life to help you.

REFLECT

Don't compare yourself to your neighbor; just focus your energy on the plan God chose especially for you. Take pride in it and do the best you can with it. You might not realize that you are making a difference in someone's life, and that could be a part of the role God decided for you.

✠ PRAY ✠

Dear Heavenly Father,

Help me embrace the work you chose for me.
Bless me while I do each task that you set before me.
Don't let me hurt anyone as I toil and keep the devil away from me.
I offer my works and sufferings of this day to you, Lord. Amen.

march 22

GOD IS WITH YOU

May the L*ORD give might to his people;*
may the L*ORD bless his people with peace!* (Psalm 29:11).

There are many times when the troubles of my day keep me up all night. I relive them, try to solve them differently, opting for brighter outcomes. I feel the weight of the world on my shoulders as I try to untangle every web of disparity. Those are evenings I forget to call upon the Lord for help. God wants us to call out to him! No problem is too big or too small for God. He wants our difficulties; he knows what to do with them.

What problems are keeping you up at night? Are you struggling to be nice to people who are unpleasant to you? Have you ever gone to an appointment and were confronted with an ornery receptionist? Or perhaps you missed an appointment by being overcommitted. Have you met resistance from insurance companies? Maybe your teenager is having issues with driving or parking the car. Whatever your woes are, give them to God. He will give you the strength to work through every situation. Maybe he will ask you to wait because the problems will fizzle away.

REFLECT

Remember to invoke the Holy Spirit within you. When you talk to God every day, capturing his love, you will begin to sleep better each night.

✠ PRAY ✠

Dear Heavenly Father,

Thank you for never leaving me in times of trouble.
Thank you for strengthening me when I feel myself falter.
Thank you for putting the perfect people in my path, the perfect ideas in my head, and the perfect feelings in my heart to enable me to get through every day in your love and peacefulness. Amen.

march 23

LEARNING CONTENTMENT

Indeed, religion with contentment is a great gain. For we brought nothing into the world, just as we shall not be able to take anything out of it. If we have food and clothing, we shall be content with that (1Timothy 6:6–8).

In preparing to adopt our second child, funds were earmarked for the adoption process, including paperwork, airline tickets, visas, and passports. With no money to spend on a nursery, we repurposed a display case from an old store, transforming it into a diaper-changing table. After a thorough cleaning and painting, I learned to be satisfied with what I had. God gave me a beautiful child to raise and love. The furniture didn't matter; the baby did.

In our society, people don't appear content with what they have; they always want more, bigger, or better. They want a bigger house, a better car, more vacations, nicer clothes, a more prestigious job, you name it and they want it. Consider your own circumstances and the things you want. If you get the things you desire, will it finally bring you happiness, or eventually will you want even more?

Is your teenager hoping stuff will make him happy? Acquiring more possessions won't be fulfilling. Contentment can't be found in stuff. Contentment is a state of satisfaction. If we truly want to find the contentment Paul wrote about we must build a personal relationship with Christ.

REFLECT

Do you feel satisfied with your life and what you have, not desiring anything else? In this passage, Paul learned to be content with what God gave him. Consider what it would take for you to become satisfied with what you have been given.

✠ PRAY ✠

Dear Heavenly Father,

Enable me to focus on you, Lord: your love, your security, your mercy, your divine tranquility. I surrender to you. Take me and do what you will with me. I am yours, and I long to do your will. Amen.

march 24

HOPE FOR WHAT WE CANNOT SEE

For in hope we were saved. Now hope that sees for itself is not hope. For who hopes for what one sees? But if we hope for what we do not see, we wait with endurance (Romans 8:24–25).

When I was a young girl, I bought kitchen wares and household items for a hope chest. I acquired these things for the family I hoped to have some day. There were anxious moments when I watched girlfriends marry and have children while I remained single. But I waited patiently for the person God meant for me to spend my life with. And I waited even longer for the children God meant for me to have. It's not easy to wait, but it's essential to trust in God's plan for us and hope for what we cannot see.

We cannot see the kingdom of heaven either; yet we hope it exists. We are saved by hope. We hope for future glory; we experience an attitude of waiting for an impending state of acceptance. Perhaps we are sustained in our trials, by hope. Some of our trials are so intolerable that only the possibility of future deliverance can sustain us. The prospect is sufficient to enable us to bear those sufferings with patience.

Hope gives us something to cling to and enables us to bear trials without complaining. Remember that in hope we are saved.

REFLECT

Reflect on the trials you are struggling with. Maybe your teen has annoying habits or deplorable behaviors. Call out to God to reinforce your fortitude.

✠ PRAY ✠

Dear Heavenly Father,

When my burden is too heavy to bear, take it from me.
Whisper in my ear the promise of what is yet to be.
Reinforce my hopefulness.
Strengthen me, Lord, while I trust in you. Amen.

march 25

IS YOUR OXYGEN MASK ON?

But when (God), who from my mother's womb had set me apart and called me through his grace, was pleased to reveal his Son to me, so that I might proclaim him to the Gentiles, I did not immediately consult flesh and blood, nor did I go up to Jerusalem to those who were apostles before me; rather, I went into Arabia and then returned to Damascus. Then after three years I went up to Jerusalem to confer with Cephas and remained with him for fifteen days (Galatians 1:15–18).

Before departures, airline stewardesses advise passengers to put on oxygen masks prior to assisting children if there is a loss of cabin pressure. The only way to ensure that you can help others around you is to help yourself first. Consider all you have been doing: household chores, job, child rearing, activities, and more. When you add on top of everything a complicated teenager, he could be the straw that breaks the camel's back. You must take care of yourself if you are to be any good to anyone else.

Paul "put on his oxygen mask" before he began helping others. In fact, he spent three years adjusting it, working out any kinks, before spreading the word of Jesus Christ. He traveled to Damascus to immerse himself in the word of God, and then he journeyed to Jerusalem to spend several weeks with Peter to make sure they were all on the same page. Once he had his mask fitted properly, he began helping people in the Gentile world.

REFLECT

How can you do this in your own home? Perhaps you could set aside quiet time to meditate. Maybe you could climb into a hot tub of bathwater, light a candle, and ruminate ways to be a productive parent in your home.

✠ PRAY ✠

Dear Heavenly Father,

Don't let me wear myself ragged. Remind me to stop and care for myself with proper nourishment, rest, and prayerfulness. I accept the hints you give to me in the form of snags in the road. They make me notice what I have neglected. I love you, kind and merciful Lord. Amen.

march 26

REDEMPTION THROUGH JESUS

All have sinned and are deprived of the glory of God. They are justified freely by his grace through the redemption in Christ Jesus, whom God set forth as an expiation, through faith, by his blood, to prove his righteousness because of the forgiveness of sins previously committed, through the forbearance of God—to prove his righteousness in the present time, that he might be righteous and justify the one who has faith in Jesus (Romans 3:23–26).

There were many times that I climbed into bed thinking that I was the world's worst mother. I might have yelled undeservingly at my daughters, been short with them, or acted aloof when they needed my attention. I would peek at them asleep and wonder how I could lose my patience with those angelic faces. Has this ever happened to you? Maybe you said "no" too many times to your kids or they were grounded needlessly.

We are human; therefore, we're imperfect and make mistakes. This sentiment stems from the reality that sin is part of human life. However, God lifts us up from a point of condemnation to a place of acceptance, forgiveness, and merciful love. We are free to go.

REFLECT

The next time you sin, look at the cross and remember that Jesus died for your sins. Embrace your redemption through Jesus today, allowing his kindness to lead you to repentance. When you make a mistake with your teenager, apologize to him and to God. To err is human, forgiveness is always divine.

✠ PRAY ✠

Dear Heavenly Father,

Thank you for the divine sacrifices that you made for me.
Forgive me, Lord, for my trespasses.
Allow me to make amends. Amen.

march 27

LETTING GO

Now a man of the house of Levi married a Levite woman, and the woman conceived and bore a son. Seeing what a fine child he was, she hid him for three months. But when she could no longer hide him, she took a papyrus basket, daubed it with bitumen and pitch, and putting the child in it, placed it among the reeds on the bank of the Nile (Exodus 2:1–3).

I carried my daughter home in a wicker basket, all the while thinking about Moses floating down the river in something similar. I vowed then never to let her go. But as time marched on, it became necessary to let her go for her to grow. She thrived in nursery school once I walked out the door. When she learned how to ride a bike without training wheels, I eventually had to let go of her then also. It was important to let her go to sleep-away camp. They were milestones that prepared me to let go of her when she went to college. Letting go is critical for all parents.

Perhaps your teenager is transitioning from adolescence to adulthood. It's a bumpy road to maneuver, so be prepared to offer encouragement, praise, and support. Hopefully your kid will return home a friend. Just as Moses left his people, climbed Mount Sinai, received the Ten Commandments, and returned to his people; your teen will leave home, seek adventure, and return an adult.

REFLECT

After years of parenting, it's not easy to stop, but this is when your kid needs a friend. It's challenging not to give unsolicited advice. If you intervene too much in their lives, they might resent and avoid you. It's not easy to stand by and watch them make mistakes, but sometimes that's the only way they will learn. Remember that God is with them during this time.

✠ PRAY ✠

Dear Heavenly Father,

Give me the stamina to watch (name) make one mistake after another. Let me put my faith and trust in you that there is a reason for it all. Keep me strong, Lord. Amen.

march 28

LOOK FOR JESUS

After they had completed its days, as they were returning, the boy Jesus remained behind in Jerusalem, but his parents did not know it. Thinking that he was in the caravan, they journeyed for a day and looked for him among their relatives and acquaintances, but not finding him, they returned to Jerusalem to look for him
(Luke 2:43:46).

Having a child wander off course is frightening. Parents want to protect and safeguard their kids at any cost. Has your teenager ever wandered away from you? Maybe you knew where your daughter was, but you didn't know who she was with, or what she was doing, which could also be alarming.

It's difficult to stand by while your teenager wanders off course. Perhaps you did everything right during her childhood, but watching her make mistakes in her teenage years can be heartbreaking. Adolescents desire independence, but you may question if she's mature enough to make decisions on her own. What are your doubts with your teen? Does she appear to be lost?

In today's passage, Mary and Joseph thought they knew where their twelve-year-old son was. Imagine their fear when they realized Jesus was missing. Mary and Joseph assumed Jesus would do as they wished and adjust to their way of thinking. When Passover had ended, it was time to go home. However, Jesus wasn't ready to leave; he chose to stay behind.

REFLECT

Have you ever moved on, leaving God behind? If you have done this inadvertently, stop what you are doing and look for him, the way Joseph and Mary did. It might be necessary to go back to the place where you lost him in order to find him again.

✠ PRAY ✠

Dear Heavenly Father,

When something is missing in my life, I will first look for you because you are the answer to everything. Amen.

march 29

PRAY ON IT

When his parents saw him, they were astonished, and his mother said to him, "Son, why have you done this to us? Your father and I have been looking for you with great anxiety" (Luke 2:48).

Have you ever wondered what it was like to raise Jesus? Surely he would never make mistakes; not like the blunders your kid makes—right? But Jesus did know when Passover was over that everyone would leave to go home, and yet he chose to stay behind without telling his parents. If your adolescent did that, you would be angry, too! What recent mistakes has your teenager made that caused you heartache and what did you do about it? Perhaps you don't agree with something he has done. Maybe your kid has been running with the wrong crowd or acting out. Has he been lying, stealing, or cheating?

Joseph and Mary explained their worry to Jesus. Have you explained your aggravation to your teen? Perhaps your son doesn't understand your annoyance. Sometimes an explanation is all that's necessary. Jesus explained to his parents, but they couldn't comprehend it. Even if you cannot understand your teen's reasons for his actions, can you keep him close to you and give him to God?

REFLECT

During this difficulty, don't rely on your own understanding. Turn to God in prayer. God will enlighten you and guide you in the right direction. Remember that God loves you the way you love your kid.

✠ PRAY ✠

Dear Heavenly Father,

Take my woes and make sense of them because I am unable.
Guide me, Lord, in the direction you have chosen for me to walk.
I am here, ready to serve, even if I don't understand.
I trust in you always. Amen.

march 30

IT'S OK TO BE ANGRY

How long, O people, will you be hard of heart? Why do you love what is worthless, chase after lies? Selah know that the Lord *works wonders for his faithful one; the* Lord *hears when I call out to him. Tremble and sin no more; weep bitterly within your hearts, wail upon your beds, offer fitting sacrifices and trust in the* Lord (Psalm 4:3–6).

This passage reminds us that it's OK to be angry but not to sin. Anger is an emotion we all feel. It's what we do with anger that matters. We are told to ponder in our heart when we go to bed at night or in the silence of our heart when we are still and to trust in the Lord. What circumstance has caused you to be angry recently?

When you feel anger, it might be cause for reflection, not instantaneous action. My father's advice about anger was to sleep on it, mull it over, determine how you felt the next day, then pray on it for a solution. Can you learn to tolerate your angry feelings while learning from them? Allow your irritations to rest until you can figure out what to do.

Perhaps you're dealing with your teenager's anger. A parent's job is to survive in the face of her daughter's anger, not to retaliate or abandon her. Anger signals that something could be wrong or that something needs to change. Help your teen understand that anger is good for identifying problems but not for solving them. Enable her to identify early-warning signs of anger and then to step away and contemplate an appropriate response to the situation. Even if you're dealing with a teenager ranting, don't get drawn in. Wait until after your teen has calmed down to talk about it.

REFLECT

Examine what brings you anger and test it against Scripture.

✠ PRAY ✠

Dear Heavenly Father,

Help me to handle anger constructively.
Thank you for giving me this emotion, but don't let it consume me.
Teach me to learn from it and live wisely while I serve you.
I ask this in Jesus' name. Amen.

march 31

WALK AWAY

I urge you, brothers, to watch out for those who create dissensions and obstacles, in opposition to the teaching that you learned; avoid them (Romans 16:17).

Some parents think their kids can do no wrong. I didn't actually believe this until my daughter was bullied on the school bus. When I approached the bully's parents, I was dismayed that they believed their youngster was innocent of any wrongdoing. Like today's Scripture, I told my daughter to avoid the bully. Have you experienced a situation like this?

Perhaps you fear that your teenager might be going in the wrong direction with his beliefs or friends. Maybe his views seemed acceptable, but you knew something about them was off. These opinions can cause divisions in your relationship with him. Discussions might turn into heated arguments, creating wider gaps between you. Paul doesn't endorse accepting any doctrine, but sometimes it's better to avoid those topics you know will lead to a fight. Arguing brings out the worst in us and usually nothing good gets accomplished. It's better to walk away, pray, lead through example, and invoke the Holy Spirit to shine through us.

It's complicated when your teen is the one with false beliefs. It's not easy to turn your back on your kid. Implore the Holy Spirit to enlighten you. Speak lovingly with heartfelt concern. Lead by example and pray unceasingly.

REFLECT

Think of ways you can invite your teen to experience God's love today. Is there volunteer work you can have him do with you? A community rosary or novena you can have him attend with you?

✠ PRAY ✠

Dear Heavenly Father,

My heavy heart aches because I fear (name) is falling away from you.
Don't abandon us, even though he might be deserting you.
I beg for mercy, Lord. Inspire me to speak words you place on my tongue. With you all is right in the world. Amen.

april 1

SEASON OF LENT

Who among you is wise and understanding? Let him show his works by a good life in the humility that comes from wisdom (James 3:13).

As we enter the season of Lent, reflect on this passage to select what you could be doing to make life better for others. As a child, I always gave up candy for Lent. As an adult, I embraced works of service. Inevitably, by the time Easter approached, a transformation occurred in me; the charitable acts were truly satisfying. I was the true benefactor because, once Lent was over, I wanted to keep doing the work.

In our busy lives it's difficult to include one more thing, even if it is Lent. If you cannot tackle one more thing, recall how Jesus felt when he was being whipped, beaten, and nailed to a cross. He could've said, "I've had enough of this. I'm outta here." Yet he endured, and we should, too.

When people go on diets, they are more successful when they have a buddy: someone to commiserate with, exercise with, and count calories with. Lent offers an opportunity to involve your entire family. You will be more effective as a unit and experience a tight-knit bond overflowing with love and joy during a time of fasting, penance, and service.

Contact Catholic Charities or your local parish to learn ways to help those in need. Perhaps you could begin by cleaning out your closets and donating half to the poor. Include your teenagers in selecting a bag of food to donate then spend the afternoon organizing it on the shelves at the food pantry. Make it a family tradition!

REFLECT

James wrote that our wisdom and understanding are not exhibited by our words but by our deeds done in humility. Any time we see the need and do nothing, we are responsible.

✠ PRAY ✠

Dear Heavenly Father,

Let me roll up my sleeves and dig into the ministry that you are calling my family to work in. I am here, ready to lead by example, Lord. Amen.

april 2

SUFFERING DURING LENT

Therefore, since Christ suffered in the flesh, arm yourselves also with the same attitude (for whoever suffers in the flesh has broken with sin), so as not to spend what remains of one's life in the flesh on human desires, but on the will of God (1 Peter 4:1–2).

Peter's encouraging words inspire us to turn away from sin, even if it will cause suffering. He recommends living not for human passions, but for the will of God. Jesus suffered in the flesh and lived free from sin. We are called to do the same thing. Consider if you drink too much, overeat, spend too much time on the internet, are unfaithful, carry grudges, or are unforgiving.

Lent is the perfect time to reflect on negative attributes that you can rid yourself of. Perhaps you can trim your family's waistline and make desserts for a Ronald McDonald House or domestic-violence shelter. Instead of buying wine during Lent, you could increase your church contributions. Maybe you could limit computer time and pray the rosary as a family. While we are on earth, God expects us to suffer. In time, the sufferings will begin to feel good when you see how happy you made someone by providing a chocolate cake you wanted to eat yourself.

REFLECT

Choosing to refrain from sin is difficult, God knows. Have you walked away from friends who were making sinful choices? It isn't easy taking a stand, but when you do, God is elated. What choice will you make today to please God?

✠ PRAY ✠

Dear Heavenly Father,

Help me make the right choices.
I want to please you here on earth and in the next life as well.
I offer to you to fruits of my labors, the joy from my experiences,
and the pain found in any suffering. I love you, Lord. Amen.

april 3

GOD IS NEAR

Where can I hide from your spirit? From your presence, where can I flee? If I ascend to the heavens, you are there; if I lie down in Sheol, there you are. If I take the wings of dawn and dwell beyond the sea, Even there your hand guides, me your right hand holds me fast (Psalm 139:7–10).

Before a job interview, I sat for a few moments in my car and prayed. I never thought of my car as a sanctuary, but I realized I had rosary beads, a holy medal, and a prayer card with me. When I closed my eyes holding these objects, God was right there with me and I no longer felt alone or scared. It was the last place in the world I expected to connect with God but I did, and I have used my car as a safe haven for prayer since then.

What's amazing is that God can be wherever you are; just be still and quiet. Think of the last time you felt anxious or scared. Perhaps you had to speak to your daughter's teachers or counselors and you feared a confrontation. Maybe you were waiting to pick up your teenager after detention. While you wait, invoke the Holy Spirit to invigorate you and bless the solitude you have together. Ask God to help you deliver a heartfelt message to your daughter instead of ranting about the things she did wrong. Resist the urge to preach, teach, or lecture.

REFLECT

The next time you are in a precarious situation, remember that all you have to do is close your eyes and envision Jesus. No matter the place or situation, God is there, ready, willing, and able to be gracious toward us.

✠ PRAY ✠

Dear Heavenly Father,

Thank you for always being there whenever I need you.
I call out, and you answer me regardless
of where I am or what I am doing.
I will sing your praises every day of my life.
I love you, Lord. Amen.

april 4

YOUR BODY IS A TEMPLE

Do you not know that your body is a temple of the Holy Spirit within you, whom you have from God, and that you are not your own? For you have been purchased at a price. Therefore, glorify God in your body (1 Corinthians 6:19–20).

Imagine walking into God's palace in heaven and it was dusty, messy, and unkempt. Because the Holy Spirit dwells within you, your body is God's sacred temple. Think of that the next time you scarf down a bag of potato chips. Especially during Lent, try to fuel your body with nutritious meals and healthy snacks. You might prefer candy bars over carrot sticks, but the sacrifice you are making is pleasing to the Lord.

When was the last time you exercised? Do you have a piece of exercise equipment in your home that you haven't used in ages? Consider giving your body periodic workouts to keep you strong and physically fit. If your son is exercising, join in making it a family affair.

When was the last time you got eight hours of sleep at night? Your body will function much better if you are well-rested. Instead of staying up late to watch something on TV or peruse the internet, go to bed and get some much-needed rest. Don't fill your head with junk; read a religious book instead. Numerous saints have penned books that would make an interesting read before bedtime. Share what you learned with your teens each day.

While building your body into the temple it should be for the Lord, remember spiritual enrichment. Set aside some quiet time for reflection, reading the Bible, and prayer. Imagine presenting God with a beautifully wrapped gift: yourself. When you take good care of yourself, you are presenting God with a gift that he dearly desires of you. He made you and wants you take care of the body he gave to you.

REFLECT

When you have taken care of yourself both physically and spiritually, you are better able to resolve issues that surface with your teenagers.

✠ PRAY ✠

Dear Heavenly Father,

Thank you for creating me in your image.
Thank you for giving me the tools to be strong
and grow in your indelible love. Amen.

april 5

ALLOWING FOR HUMANNESS

And as they reclined at table and were eating, Jesus said, "Amen, I say to you, one of you will betray me, one who is eating with me." They began to be distressed and to say to him, one by one, "Surely it is not I?" (Mark 14:18–19).

God created us imperfect. Everyone on earth struggles with sin from time to time. Each one of us has a particular downfall we are trying to overcome. It could be overreacting, yelling, using foul language, lying, the list is endless. We confess our sins, make penance, and try to improve. We pray, read holy Scripture, give alms to the poor, love our family, and life seems good once more. Until we fall again.

Ruminate on how long the disciples followed Jesus, how devoted they were to him, how much they learned from him, and how much they loved him. With such sincere dedication, it's hard to fathom them asking who among them would actually betray Jesus. Their statement to Jesus, "Surely it is not I" shows their humanness revealing their vulnerability to sinfulness. Peter, founder of the Church, betrayed Jesus three times! If these holy men can mess up their lives, it's understandable that you and I and everyone else will, too. It's not an excuse to make mistakes; it's the ability to forgive yourself or your kids for being susceptible to sin. Knowing that you sin, allow some slack for your teenager.

REFLECT

Consider in the silence of your heart what sins you are guilty of. Are you overreacting to something your teenager did that upset you or did you handle it improperly? Maybe you are so angry at your son that you failed to think about your role in it. Perhaps you are angry at a teacher who doesn't seem to understand your child. Is your anger misdirected? What can you do to be more like the disciples who questioned Jesus if they were the one to betray him?

✠ PRAY ✠

Dear Heavenly Father,

Take my humble heart into your mighty hands and breathe your mercy into it. Shelter it from sinfulness and all that could derail me. Enlighten me to be a better parent: more forgiving, more loving, and more generous. I ask this in Jesus' name. Amen.

april 6

SAFEGUARD YOUR TREASURES

A man had two sons, and the younger son said to his father, "Father, give me the share of your estate that should come to me." So the father divided the property between them (Luke 15:11–12).

Consider if you are saving an heirloom for your daughter: a special piece of jewelry, a set of dishes handed down from one generation to another, a favored musical instrument, or a family Bible. What item in your home would you like to pass down? If you received a family treasure, you know the importance of safekeeping an invaluable, irreplaceable item. It's an honor to receive such a gift; taking good care of it is expected.

What valuables will you pass down to your kids? If you have several children, how will you decide who gets what? At some point you could have a discussion with your youngsters about what items they might want you to leave them in a will. If you don't have a will, this might be a good time to consider getting one. Planning a family will might enable you to take a proper perspective of your life to ensure you don't lose sight of what's really important.

REFLECT

Take a few minutes to reflect over items in your home that you have a strong attachment to, and then decide what you can and cannot live without.

✠ PRAY ✠

Dear Heavenly Father,

Thank you for showering me with countless blessings. You gave me the perfect family and I am most grateful for them. Help me to appreciate the good and bad in everything and not to overlook the beauty and value of my children for they really are treasures. Amen.

april 7

CHILDREN MAKE MISTAKES

After a few days, the younger son collected all his belongings and set off to a distant country where he squandered his inheritance on a life of dissipation. When he had freely spent everything, a severe famine struck that country, and he found himself in dire need. His son said to him, "Father, I have sinned against heaven and against you; I no longer deserve to be called your son" (Luke 15:13–14, 21).

Parents worldwide send teenagers to college, hoping they will not squander the opportunities presented to them. Yet each year, students decide to party instead of attending class. Many parents' dreams are dashed when their kids go into debt only to flunk out. The reality is that the teenage brain is inadequately developed when they are set free on college campuses. They are expected to make wise decisions with an underdeveloped brain.

All kids will make mistakes in their lifetime. It's our job to help them when they fail, regardless of where they are in their life: college, summer camp, studying abroad, or at home. Your child might experiment with drugs, drink and drive, lose her new phone or laptop, come home with a tattoo, or worse, because she is still learning. Help her learn from her mistakes so they're not repeated. Some kids learn at a faster pace than their peers. Everyone is different.

REFLECT

Give your kids room to flap their wings and pray that they soar and succeed. If they fail, don't rub it in. But be there for them when they come to their senses. Whatever heartbreak you feel over an injury caused from your teens' faults, they feel that pain, too.

✠ PRAY ✠

Dear Heavenly Father,

Take the crumbled pieces of my heart and put it back together again. Heal the pain that aches throughout my entire body, Lord. Lift me to a wiser level of understanding so that I can love (name) unconditionally, the way you love me when I mess up. Help us on our journey to reach you. Amen.

april 8

THE PRODIGAL CHILD

But his father ordered his servants, "Quickly bring the finest robe and put it on him; put a ring on his finger and sandals on his feet. Take the fattened calf and slaughter it. Then let us celebrate with a feast, because this son of mine was dead, and has come to life again; he was lost, and has been found." Then the celebration began (Luke 15:22–24).

This father knows unconditional love entwined with an impeccable style of forgiveness. Imagine having a kid who blows through your hard-earned money to party, live recklessly, and turn his back on siblings, friends, and God. This kind of living causes broken hearts. The father in this story experiences true unconditional love. Excited to embrace his son, he is not judgmental of his son's past nor does he question the future.

This kind of parental devotion is just a fragment of God's love for us. God calls us to be near and dear to him regardless of what is happening in our lives. Forgiveness is woven throughout the Bible. God constantly pardons us and accepts us into his graces. While Jesus socializes with sinners, he doesn't mask the message he tries to convey—God seeks the fallen and is merciful on their souls. At some point we have all fallen. How marvelous is God to accept us, faults and all, and love us totally and completely? Can you love your teenager with that kind of love?

REFLECT

What has your teenager done recently to break your heart? Has he left home to stay with a friend? Once your teenager returns home, the joy of the homecoming is immeasurable.

✠ PRAY ✠

Dear Heavenly Father,

Thank you for teaching me to stop dragging baggage and adoring material things. I appreciate what is really important: the need to forgive and love unconditionally. Thank you for your unending stream of mercy. I adore you. Amen.

april 9

PURE TRUST

When you pass through the water, I will be with you; in the rivers you shall not drown. When you walk through fire, you shall not be burned; the flames shall not consume you (Isaiah 43:2).

There have been occasions where I felt overwhelmed by problems that could have consumed me. Hearing a foreboding diagnosis was one such time. Instead of succumbing to grief and misery, I remembered that God would remain beside me protecting me and keeping me strong. Everyone experiences heartache and loss at some point throughout their lives. Our faith can keep us afloat during our worst moments.

When we encounter trials and tribulations, we need to persevere so that the problems don't take over our lives. If problems take us down and we can't get through on our own, reach out for Jesus. If you don't lean on God, bitterness and depression have room to grow and take over. God may not remove us immediately from our situation; there may be a reason for it. However, God won't leave us in our time of need.

As difficult as it may seem, trust completely in God's way. If you can give into totally trusting God, even during the worst times of your life, he will help you through it. God will walk beside you through a raging fire and you will not be burned. When God brings you through to the other side, you will be truly amazed. You will be so enriched and strengthened in your deepened faith that God will not ever abandon you. This unshakable faith allows you to reach out to others, helping them.

REFLECT

Consider a time when you needed comfort and God brought someone to you.

✠ PRAY ✠

Dear Heavenly Father,

I pray I experience this kind of intimacy with you, my divine Savior. You are everything to me. Amen.

april 10

PRAY PERSISTENTLY

"Ask and it will be given to you; seek and you will find; knock and the door will be opened to you. For everyone who asks, receives; and the one who seeks, finds; and to the one who knocks, the door will be opened" (Matthew 7:7–8).

I read this passage to my daughter when she was younger and she said, "I'm going to ask God for a million dollars!" I explained that the Almighty isn't giving us a blank check to get whatever our hearts desire. God isn't a magic genie in a bottle. We also must live by God's word where our faith is strengthened and nourished by the sacraments. These verses remind us to strive for wisdom through prayer. Prayer is a powerful means through which the Lord carries out his will.

Often we don't go to God as persistently as he wants us to. Jesus invites us three times to come to God. He says ask, seek, and knock. God loves it when we pray constantly, especially for the same thing. He tells us he will answer; that it will be given, we will find, and it will be opened. Sometimes it takes a lot longer to get what we need than we are willing to wait. We might give up on prayer. But God wants us to pray persistently. Sometimes what we want is not in God's plan for us, or he might give us something else. In all things, we need to trust in God's plan for us and pray fervently to do his will, not ours. Don't give up on God; pray until something happens.

REFLECT

How frequently do you get frustrated and abandon prayer only to pick it up again in a time of crisis? Don't forget God can come to us in both the storm and the calm.

✠ PRAY ✠

Dear Heavenly Father,

I pray that you bless my family and me with peacefulness, love, and good health so that we can all live long lives doing your will, whatever that is. I trust in your ways, Lord, even though I do not completely understand. I ask this in Jesus' name. Amen.

april 11

FORGIVE

Then Judas, his betrayer, seeing that Jesus had been condemned, deeply regretted what he had done. He returned the thirty pieces of silver to the chief priests and elders, saying, "I have sinned in betraying innocent blood" (Matthew 27:3–4).

Because we are human, we all make mistakes. Some are worse than others. One of the great gifts you can give to others is forgiveness. If your daughter has done something upsetting, offer forgiveness the way Jesus sought forgiveness for those who were crucifying him. Remember there have been times in your life when you needed to be forgiven.

One of the best things we implemented in our home was the "do over." It reminds us that because we are human, we will make mistakes. A "do over" allows for another chance, to stop bad behaviors, and to seek improvement. Wipe the slate clean and start over with a new approach. It's important to devise a plan so the problem won't be repeated. When my daughter got a speeding ticket, she agreed to use the cruise control to drive slower and safer. Mistakes have consequences. My daughter also had to pay a fine for her ticket and get her own car insurance. Because of the "do over," she is a better driver today.

REFLECT

When something goes wrong, it's understandable to become overly cautious. Use it as fuel to ignite your passion for keeping your daughter safe and well by staying on top of things. Make sure your teen understands forgiveness is not the same as condoning actions.

✠ PRAY ✠

Dear Heavenly Father,

Increase my watchfulness so that I know and understand what is going on with (name). Help me to appreciate the delicate nature of these problems. Touch my heart with your warmth and teach me to be more forgiving. I love you, Lord. Amen.

april 12

GOOD FRIENDS

There are friends who bring ruin, but there are true friends more loyal than a brother (Proverbs 18:24).

Teenagers are affected by friends more than anyone or anything else. Sometimes they will listen to a friend before a parent. A true friend is a gift, but the wrong kind of friend can be detrimental to your teen and your family. A true friend is loyal and brings out the best in your teenager, possibly even inspires him to become the best possible person he can be. Help your kids choose their friends wisely. Do this by listening to the music they like, getting involved in their activities, and inviting your kid's friends to your home. Really get to know them.

We transformed our basement into a warm and cozy room where our kids' friends felt welcome. Every weekend they were greeted with a safe place to chat or play games, eat snacks, listen to music, or watch movies. I wanted them to "hang out" in my house so I could see what they were like and know what they were up to.

REFLECT

Remind your teenagers that the best friend they will ever have is the Lord. Teach them to get to know God the way they get to know their friends. God is the one who will help them understand all their other friendships, and he will guide them to the right friendships.

✠ PRAY ✠

Dear Heavenly Father,

Keep me strong, Lord, as I embrace my kid's friends. Parenting is the hardest job I've ever done; please, Lord, give me the strength to do it well. Don't let me falter. I ask this in your sweet name, Jesus. Amen.

april 13

HIGHWAY TO HEAVEN

A highway will be there, called the holy way; No one unclean may pass over it, but it will be for his people; no traveler, not even fools, shall go astray on it (Isaiah 35:8).

An exceptionally cold winter destroyed the roads, creating an enormous number of potholes—the kind that wreak havoc on the suspension and undercarriage of the car when hit. A driver might end up with a flat tire on the spot. In April, road crews were out in force trying to repair the damage.

Consider the road you have been navigating during lent. Is it full of divots and pitfalls? What is causing potholes to occur in your life and how can you stop them from forming in the first place? Are you experiencing a harsh season with your teenager? Perhaps the closing days of the end of the school year are weighing on your teen's heart. Have a talk with your daughter about her fears and apprehensions. Really listen without judging or trying to fix her problems. Listen with the goal to simply understand her.

Remember that your kids are developing physically, socially, and emotionally. They are experiencing frequent growth spurts while undergoing sexual maturation and psychological changes. A lot is happening to them, which could lead to issues with their personal identity, sense of self, or emotional independence. Notice, praise, and celebrate even a hint of positive progress because it will ensure a healthier transition into adulthood. Don't let negativity create holes in the relationship you have with your teens.

REFLECT

If there are holes in the relationship between you and your teens, how can you work to repair them this spring?

✠ PRAY ✠

Dear Heavenly Father,

I am overwhelmed by all of my parenting responsibilities.
Sometimes I feel as if I am not making any progress at all.
Help me, Lord, to do the job you created me to do.
I ask this in Jesus' name. Amen.

april 14

ABANDON DENIAL

Everyone who acknowledges me before others I will acknowledge before my heavenly Father. But whoever denies me before others, I will deny before my heavenly Father (Matthew 10:32–33).

Twenty-five years ago, Pat and I traveled from Northern Ireland down the coast where we encountered military guards securing a border surrounded by a chainlink fence covered with thick coils of barbed wire. One soldier, carrying a gun, asked for passports while the other questioned my husband. "Patrick is a fine Irish name. Canale is an Italian name. Are you a Catholic Italian or a Protestant Irishman?" he quizzed. Patrick swallowed hard before answering, "I'm whatever you want me to be as long as you remember I'm American!"

I remember that story each year at this time when I think of Peter betraying Jesus, hearing the cock crow after each time. Now I have the courage to declare that I'm proud to be Catholic. It's imperative to stand up for what I believe and not worry about the waves I make while doing it. If I'm not making waves in my life, then I'm doing something wrong.

It might be uncool for your teenager to say grace before meals, attend the Stations of the Cross, go to confession, or be present at Mass, but it's your responsibility to stay true to your core values. Is your teenager embarrassed by your religion? Encourage your son to participate in youth programs at church. God is the most important element in your kid's life. You might need to remind him of that from time to time.

REFLECT

Are you making waves in your teenager's life by standing up for what you believe?

✠ PRAY ✠

Dear Heavenly Father,

Empower me to keep you as the focal point of our family life.
I am proud of my faith and spirituality.
Help me ignite the fire in my son's life so he is proud, too. Amen.

april 15

DON'T DENY THE LORD

But Peter stood at the gate outside. So the other disciple, the acquaintance of the high priest, went out and spoke to the gatekeeper and brought Peter in. Then the maid who was the gatekeeper said to Peter, "You are not one of this man's disciples, are you?" He said, "I am not" (John 18:16–17).

Many years ago, I awoke in the middle of the night to the sound of burglars attempting to break into my home. I broke off the bedpost and swung it like a Ninja warrior trying to protect my family. I never imagined I would react like that during a break-in, but we never really know for sure how we will act until we're in that situation.

If we were Christ's disciples, walking with him every day, witnessing his miracles, and listening to his word, would we deny him like Peter in his time of need? We don't know how we would react. We deny Jesus for less some days.

These awe-inspiring moments give a hint of the fear that settles over our hearts as we realize that we can deny Jesus, too. This fear is different from the panic I felt when my life was endangered; it's an anxiety that impacts my character. Pray about the sustenance of your heart and all it possesses so that the next time an opportunity knocks, you respond by embracing Jesus.

REFLECT

When neighbors gossip, do you join in? When an elderly shopper struggles, do you look the other way? Have you walked away from your teenager wondering if an "I love you" might make a difference? Have you felt the Holy Spirit nudge you? Don't ignore the divine prods.

✠ PRAY ✠

Dear Heavenly Father,

Thank you for the cognizance to examine my heart and act favorably when I am needed. Don't let my words, thoughts, or actions deny you. I seek your mercy on my soul for all of the times I looked the other way. I am committed to you, Lord. Please, let me show you how much I love you in all I think, say, and do. Amen.

april 16

BLESS MY WAIT

But if we hope for what we do not see, we wait with endurance. In the same way, the Spirit too comes to the aid of our weakness; for we do not know how to pray as we ought, but the Spirit itself intercedes with inexpressible groanings. And the one who searches hearts knows what is the intention of the Spirit, because it intercedes for the holy ones according to God's will (Romans 8:25–27).

Have you ever browsed through a library admiring the different titles that catch your eye? You might spend hours looking around. Then the librarian shows you an intriguing book with an alluring title, a captivating cover, and a famous author. The minute you see it, you realize it's what you wanted.

Occasionally we can feel lost while meandering through life, knowing we need something but aren't exactly sure what it is until God directs us to the very thing we needed most. Waiting can be difficult. Emily, a recent college graduate, waited an agonizing seven months for a job to open up in her field. The new position was in a picture-postcard town where homes were framed with white picket fences with gorgeous flowers spilling over them. God blessed her wait as she landed in this lovely community where her contribution mattered.

Believe that God's purpose for you counts. Parenting a teenager can sometimes make you question its value. Perhaps you are waiting for an attitude to change or a condition to improve. Maybe you are waiting for your teenager to decide what she desires for her future. Perhaps she is considering joining the armed services or Peace Corps. Trust in God's plan for your teen's future even if that means waiting a while for it to be revealed. God's ultimate plan is for us to imitate Christ. If your teen stays focused on God, no matter how things look now, it will be OK.

REFLECT

Don't be overly anxious for God to reveal his plan for your child. Let it be revealed in God's time. If you feel you have to do something, pray.

✠ PRAY ✠

Dear Heavenly Father,

Bless my wait and lift me up so I can continue onward,
doing whatever it is that you ask of me.
I trust in your plan and seek you in all I see and do. Amen.

april 17

OVERCOME TEMPTATIONS

At this, Jesus said to him, "Get away, Satan! It is written: 'The Lord, your God, shall you worship and him alone shall you serve.'" Then the devil left him and, behold, angels came and ministered to him (Matthew 4:10–11).

Each year when I give up cookies, cakes, and candy for Lent, I falter a week into the observance. Temptations gnaw at me as I question if an animal cracker is a cookie or a cracker as the name suggests, because then I can eat it. And what exactly is a doughnut? Can I eat that? I normally abstain from sweets until I hear Satan questioning my endurance. I should tell Satan to "get away!" It's nearly impossible when I'm weak, hungry, have animal crackers and doughnuts, and no one is looking. But the glory I give to God through my suffering is a humble gift. It's the least I can do for all God has done for me.

What is the devil luring you to do? Perhaps you feel tired and worn down by your teenager and want to give in to temptations because it's easier than standing firm. When other parents are doing something, it's challenging to stand alone and say, "No, you can't go to that party or to the mall all afternoon." It's tough to be the only parent to say, "You have to work, do chores, and homework." It's tempting to look the other way and say, "What's the harm with one party?" Let your model during Lent be Jesus in the desert overcoming temptation. The other option is sin. When we sin, we hurt Jesus.

REFLECT

If you are struggling with temptation, consider all of the gifts God has given to you. Reflect on the unconditional love God has showered you with. A temptation is a trick, a deception, a lie. God's truth will show you the right path.

✠ PRAY ✠

Dear Heavenly Father,

Strengthen me, Lord, to be steadfast during Lent. If the thoughts in my mind are not from you, take them from me. Replace them with loving thoughts and examples I should follow. I only want to please you, Lord. Help me to be obedient. I ask this in Jesus' name. Amen.

april 18

WHERE ARE YOUR NAMES WRITTEN?

Jesus said, "I have observed Satan fall like lightning from the sky. Behold, I have given you the power 'to tread upon serpents' and scorpions and upon the full force of the enemy and nothing will harm you. Nevertheless, do not rejoice because the spirits are subject to you, but rejoice because your names are written in heaven" (Luke 10:18–20).

My daughter spent years taking practice SAT tests hoping to ace the real exam. When she saw her score, she was elated, not because of the number but because it meant she would most likely be accepted into her preferred university. She was focused on seeing her name on the acceptance list.

In today's passage, Jesus tells us our "names are written in heaven." This is good news for everyone because it implies that God has a book in heaven where he writes the names of his true followers. I want my name to be on that list, don't you?

Have your kids asked to go on a church mission trip? Each year the church I attend sends youth-group members to El Salvador on spring break. The teenagers return energized and transformed from witnessing God's love on a basic level or on a grand scale. In this Scripture, Jesus speaks to people who were on their own kind of mission trip. They were elated with all they had done and experienced, but Jesus instructs his workers to suppress their enthusiasm over their work. Instead, they should rejoice that their names are written in heaven. When God provides us with the tools and opportunities to do good, we need to remember the thanks still goes to God. Our good works mean nothing without him.

REFLECT

In heartfelt reflection, we can recognize God's blessings in our lives and thank him for them. What are your blessings? Do you consider your teenager one of them?

✠ PRAY ✠

Dear Heavenly Father,

Let me rejoice in the salvation through Jesus Christ's life, death, and resurrection. Please, Lord, let my name be inscribed in heaven. Amen.

april 19

BE CONTENT

The riffraff among them were so greedy for meat that even the Israelites lamented again, "If only we had meat for food! We remember the fish we used to eat without cost in Egypt, and the cucumbers, the melons, the leeks, the onions, and the garlic. But now we are famished; we have nothing to look forward to but this manna (Numbers 11:4–6).

After saving for years, we took our daughters to Walt Disney World on vacation. The thrill waned when they returned to school to learn some of their classmates went to Europe. One daughter cried because we didn't take her there. I felt unappreciated. Have you felt the good you do has been unacknowledged because of your teenager's thanklessness?

In today's Scripture, God provided manna each day so that the Israelites wouldn't starve to death. Every morning it miraculously appeared, but instead of giving thanks for it, the people complained! Have you ever complained over what God has provided to you? The next time you feel like complaining about your teenager, remember the infertile couples who would give anything just to have a child to nurture and love. If you want to lament about the difficulties of your job, remember how many unemployed people would love to be in your position. Whenever you feel like bemoaning the confines of your home, think of the homeless who feel blessed to sleep under a roof in inclement weather.

REFLECT

God has showered your life with countless blessings. Examine them in the light of his divine provisions so you can be truly thankful for them. Don't take God's gifts for granted. Be joyful for what he has given you.

✠ PRAY ✠

Dear Heavenly Father,

I'm sorry that I have taken your love for granted. I'm sorry that I haven't thanked you for all you have given to me and continue to provide. You are so kind and generous to my family and me. I truly appreciate the good and the bad that you have given us, even though I don't understand some of it. I trust in you and love you. Amen.

april 20

KEEPING CONFIDENCES

As they were coming down from the mountain,
Jesus charged them, "Do not tell the vision to anyone
until the Son of Man has been raised from the dead" (Matthew 17:9).

After we adopted our daughters, people would ask us personal information about the girls' birth history. We safeguarded this information, allowing our daughters to be the ones to reveal it to whomever they chose. There were close friends who we wanted to discuss this information with, but we remained silent because we respected our daughters' privacy.

Jesus allowed Peter, James, and John to witness the miracle of the transfiguration, but then he informed them not to tell anyone. After seeing something so magnificent, it's hard to imagine the three apostles keeping quiet. Imagine going on a hike with one of your favorite teachers and he begins to glow like the sun. Then you hear God say he is pleased. Wouldn't you want to tell someone about it?

Have you ever entrusted your teenager with a family secret only to learn later that your private information was revealed? How did you handle that breach of trust? Maybe you broke a promise to keep your teen's personal information within your family unit. How did you gain your son's trust back? In these instances, it's difficult to be loving and merciful, but that is exactly what God wants you to do.

REFLECT

Even though Peter was chosen to experience this glorious sight, he still went on to deny Jesus three times at his passion. If Peter can break God's trust and be forgiven, you and your teenager can find forgiveness for each other.

✠ PRAY ✠

Dear Heavenly Father,

You have spoken and I have listened, but it is so hard
to act responsibly. Wash away my sinfulness and help me
to be strong in your loving embrace so I can
fulfill your promise on earth and in heaven. Amen.

april 21

JESUS LOVES YOU

For Christ, while we were still helpless,...died at the appointed time for the ungodly. Indeed, only with difficulty does one die for a just person, though perhaps for a good person one might even find courage to die. But God proves his love for us in that while we were still sinners Christ died for us (Romans 5:6–8).

Rarely would anyone die for an unrighteous person. A parent might put his own life on the line for a child. Would you run into a burning building or jump into dangerous waters to save your teen? What if your child started the fire or purposely jumped into that raging river? Would you trade places with your teenager if he faced a firing squad? What if your teenager deserved a harsh punishment by living immorally, sinning constantly, and breaking the commandments? Would you still spare your child's life and die for him?

God demonstrates his love for us by dying on the cross when we didn't deserve the sacrifice. Jesus died for us while we were helpless and ungodly. What a gift! Even though we are less than worthy, God sees our potential. Knowing God can give up his precious life for us, sinners, should enable us to look past our teenagers' sins to their potential and love them unconditionally as God loves us. We are all sinners.

REFLECT

Consider, "What would Jesus do?" He is merciful, kind, and loving. And he died willingly for our sins. If your teenager has done something horrendous and you are finding it challenging to forgive, think of Jesus and how limitless his love is. He was willing to die for you. What will you do for your child?

✠ PRAY ✠

Dear Heavenly Father,

Thank you for your infinite stream of affection.
In you I will find rest. In you I will find the truth.
You illuminate my path. I will follow you always. Amen.

april 22

SIMPLIFY

Mary took a liter of costly perfumed oil made from genuine aromatic nard and anointed the feet of Jesus and dried them with her hair; the house was filled with the fragrance of the oil (John 12:3).

With the threat of an impending tornado, I took my most valuable possessions to the basement: my family. During such circumstances we can reevaluate what's really important. My house is cluttered with stuff that doesn't really matter. Often we also hang on to things both physical and emotional, like guilt, pain, or anxiety.

Consider decluttering your home and your life. Start by cleaning out closets. Donate superfluous items to refugee resettlement groups or homeless shelters. After you remove clutter from your home, simplify your heart by eradicating unhealthy behaviors and bad habits. Consider what addictions you can eliminate. Is your heart filled with gossip, profanity, complaints, or lies? Sometimes parents gossip or complain about their teenagers to other parents, friends, or family members. Before you speak harshly about your teen, think how she would feel if she could hear you. You are supposed to be her lifeline, her safe haven, her supportive safety net. How can you be these things to your daughter when you speak poorly about her? If you were talking to Jesus about your teenager, what would you say?

REFLECT

Don't lose sight of what's really the most important thing in your life. Set your priorities straight as Mary did in today's Bible verse. She anointed Jesus' feet with her most valuable perfumed oil, then used her hair to dry his feet. What would you do?

✠ PRAY ✠

Dear Heavenly Father,

Teach me how to simplify my life and let go of the baggage that holds me back and drags me down. Release me from the grasp of stuff that I don't need cluttering my life so that I lose sight of what's really important. Remove the blinders from my eyes. Let me focus on you, and the rest of my life will become clear. Amen.

april 23

BE BOASTFUL ABOUT GOD

But rather, let those who boast, boast of this, that in their prudence they know me, Know that I, the Lord, act with fidelity, justice, and integrity on earth. How I take delight in these—oracle of the Lord (Jeremiah 9:23).

I wasn't a boastful person until I became a mom. When my daughter was six months old, I told everyone she could blow a toy horn. As she grew up, I was boastful of all of her accomplishments. When I was bursting with pride, I wish I had commended my daughter and praised God for it.

Just because other parents brag about their kids doesn't mean I should. Some families have bumper stickers on their car exclaiming that their kids take karate, Irish step dancing, or are members of honor societies. Teenagers boast by wearing in-style fashions, having the latest and greatest phones, and by driving their parent's car. Reflect on whether or not your teen, or even yourself, is conceited.

This kind of boastfulness usually points toward what our society values. You won't see teens mimicking Joan of Arc. Instead, teens today enjoy their vanity rather than celebrating that goodness comes from God. This sort of boastfulness is disrespectful of God. Not all boastfulness is bad though. The kind of boasting that is glorious is boasting in the Lord. Boasting about God isn't being conceited when done in a praiseworthy fashion. For example, if you buy a new outfit for Easter and you admire the way you look in it, thank God that you are healthy and look and feel good. Praise God that he has blessed you with the ability to afford a new outfit. Try to thank God after everything he gives. Strive to be less self-centered during Lent.

REFLECT

Acknowledge God for all of the blessings he has bestowed on you. God loves to be thanked, just as you appreciate receiving a thank-you note from someone you gave a gift to.

✠ PRAY ✠

Dear Heavenly Father,

Thank you for granting me another day to live with my family.
Thank you for the love you pour over us throughout this day.
Thank you, Lord, for the birds that sing.
Thank you, Lord, for everything. Amen.

april 24

LOVE LIKE GOD DOES

When he returned to his disciples he found them asleep.
He said to Peter, "So you could not keep watch with me for one hour?"
(Matthew 26:40).

After a large extended-family dinner, I asked my daughters to do the dishes because I was exhausted from preparing the meal. Several hours later, with the girls nowhere to be found and the dishes still on the table, I did them myself. As I worked, I recalled this passage where Jesus' humble request of Peter, despite being so simple, was left unheeded. Peter had good intentions and thought he could stay awake, but his humanity befell him.

I would hope that if Jesus asked me to stay awake in Gethsemane, I would do whatever it took to keep my eyes open. I would also like to believe if Jesus asked me to do something, some meager task, that I would do it. In retrospect, there have been times when I saw a homeless man on the street and did nothing. There have been occasions when the phone rang but I didn't answer it. There have been opportunities where God was asking me to do something, but I used my free will and said "no." I cannot throw stones at Peter and chastise him for not staying awake when I have turned a blind eye to the Lord in the midst of my own life.

Because of this revelation, I can be disappointed but I can't condemn my daughters for "forgetting" to do the dishes. For, even though God might be frustrated with me when I don't do as he asks, he never stops loving me. God doesn't yell at me and tell me I was thoughtless and unappreciative. He doesn't call me lazy or swear. He doesn't give up on me.

REFLECT

The next time your teenager "forgets" to do something, remember Peter in Gethsemane.

✠ PRAY ✠

Dear Heavenly Father,

Thank you for giving me another chance to serve you.
Thank you for opening my eyes to those around me who need a friend, for you are in each one of them. Keep me strong, ever-loving, Lord, so that I can best serve you. Amen.

april 25

SHOWING RESPECT

While he was still speaking, Judas, one of the Twelve, arrived, accompanied by a large crowd, with swords and clubs, who had come from the chief priests and the elders of the people. His betrayer had arranged a sign with them, saying, "The man I shall kiss is the one; arrest him" (Matthew 26:47–48).

It's shocking every time I read that one of the twelve disciples betrayed Jesus. They were close, personal friends; they loved each other. How in the world could someone deceive his friend? Consider what kind of betrayal has happened within your family. Has your relationship with your teenager gone sour? Maybe she is struggling with the loss of a friendship. Try to find comfort that even Jesus had to deal with this sort of thing. For Christ, it ended with his arrest, imprisonment, and crucifixion.

If your relationship with your teenager needs repairing, begin the process of reconciling today. Set a good example by resuming respectful treatment. Ask yourself, "What would Jesus do and say?" Then, do that. If Jesus is forgiving and loving, emulate him.

If your teenager is experiencing difficulties with a friend at school, be a sounding board and allow her to talk it out with you. Often when someone talks about her circumstances, she can see the convolutedness of her friendship and resolve it on her own. Ask your loved one if she wants your advice or if she just wants you to listen. You gave years of advice and you modulated for them between right and wrong. With prayer and divine guidance, they can do anything they put their mind to.

REFLECT

The next time your teenager starts to talk about a problem, make sure you're really listening. Don't just jump in and start giving advice.

✠ PRAY ✠

Dear Heavenly Father,

Thank you for becoming fully human so I can relate to your experiences as I walk my life journey. When I don't know what to do, I read your word and you smile. With you I am at ease. With you, I am complete. With you, I am everything you want me to be. I love you. Amen.

april 26

CONQUER ANGER

And behold, one of those who accompanied Jesus put his hand to his sword, drew it, and struck the high priest's servant, cutting off his ear. Then Jesus said to him, "Put your sword back into its sheath, for all who take the sword will perish by the sword (Matthew 26:51–52).

When my kids were little, one daughter drew all over her face with a permanent marker. In frustration I grounded this poor kid for a million years. Afterward *I* sat in the time-out chair, which worked wonderfully. After I got out of it, I realized it was my fault for leaving the marker within my daughter's reach. It's hard to stop myself from swinging the sword in the heat of the moment, but Jesus tells us that if we use it, we will die by it.

It isn't easy to bite your tongue when you want to ground your teenager, but do it anyway. Give yourself a time out. Decide what chair in your home would make a good prayer chair. Define this spot as a place you can retreat to during difficult moments and call out to God for enlightenment. The Holy Spirit who dwells within you can calm you so you can think clearly and rationally. Begin by reciting the Our Father slowly. Let it sink into your soul, focusing only on the Lord. God can calm your wrath.

REFLECT

When you teenager disappoints you, try to be more Christlike, even if you have to sit in the time-out chair longer than you expected.

✠ PRAY ✠

Dear Heavenly Father,

Help me, Lord, to sort through the scrambled messages in my head.
Fill my heart with the knowledge to devise a sound plan for (name).
Enrich my thoughts, infusing them with your love
and infinite wisdom. Bless me with every kindness
that will help me to become a better parent. Amen.

april 27

MISTAKES HAPPEN

A little later the bystanders came over and said to Peter, "Surely you too are one of them; even your speech gives you away." At that he began to curse and to swear, "I do not know the man." And immediately a cock crowed. Then Peter remembered the word that Jesus had spoken: "Before the cock crows you will deny me three times." He went out and began to weep bitterly (Matthew 26:73–76).

Even Peter—who loved, admired, and respected Jesus—sinned by denying him. He cursed and swore that he didn't know Jesus when only a few hours before they had shared an intimate Passover meal. The best of people make mistakes. We are all human; we all will make mistakes.

When Peter realized his, he wept bitterly. After a slip-up, it's important to learn from it. If your teenager has made a blunder, coach her to find a lesson from the experience. Remind your daughter that after Peter's sin, he went on to be the rock of the Church. Teach your teenager that she can grow from a mistake and become a better person by not repeating that negative action. Don't allow your teen to wallow in self-pity because that could be an excuse to continue being sinful. With God, your daughter can move forward, seek forgiveness, and blossom into the person God intended for her to be. God knew Peter was going to deny him and he loved him anyway.

REFLECT

Have you made a parenting mistake? Teach your teen how to apologize by example.

✠ PRAY ✠

Dear Heavenly Father,

How glorious you are. I live for you, sweet and merciful, Lord. Teach me how to be a better parent and embrace (name) despite her sinful behaviors. Teach me to let go of past hurts and move to future endeavors with her. Build me up, Lord, so I can help (name) to follow you and your marvelous ways. I ask this in Jesus' name. Amen.

april 28

EXPERIENCING SHOCK

But Jesus cried out again in a loud voice, and gave up his spirit. The centurion and the men with him who were keeping watch over Jesus feared greatly when they saw the earthquake and all that was happening, and they said, "Truly, this was the Son of God!"
(Matthew 27:50, 54).

The centurion and other men who kept watch realized Jesus was the Son of God, but it was too late. They had witnessed him being beaten and nailed him to a cross, and now he was dead. Imagine the realization zip through them like a bolt of lightning rendering them paralyzed with panic and fear. What had they done?

I experienced a similar feeling a while back when I opened an email that contained a virus. The second I clicked on it, I knew it was a horrendous mistake. I was about to lose everything on my computer and I would be in a pile of hurt trying to bail myself out of the mess I had just created. Has something similar happened to you?

After we lose something important to us, we then truly appreciate it. If you have lost a job, a friend, or good health, it can be befuddling. Perhaps you have discovered something shocking about your teenager. Maybe he got a tattoo that you didn't approve of, or you learned he was using drugs. The awful blow can literally take your breath away. Like the centurion, our realization came too late; the damage has been done. Now what?

REFLECT

Whatever has happened in your teen's life, don't allow it to paralyze you. Give the shock, hurt, or frustration to God and ask him to help you find a way to work toward a solution.

✠ PRAY ✠

Dear Heavenly Father,

God of mercy, God of love, hear my cry!
Save me, Lord, from the depths of despair.
Tell me what to do. Tell me what to say. Move through me, Lord.
Let me rest in your warm and gentle embrace. Amen.

april 29

WAIT THREE DAYS

So they set out at once and returned to Jerusalem where they found gathered together the eleven and those with them who were saying, "The Lord has truly been raised and has appeared to Simon"
(Luke 24:33–34).

When I was a teenager, my dad told me not to mail a letter I wrote in anger until after three days had passed. He implied that a lot can happen in three days. He was right. Many times my feelings changed and I ended up destroying the letter.

It isn't easy for teenagers to manage anger. Writing out anger can be a cathartic process, but not everyone can do that. Some kids are more physical and might need to exercise their anger away. Perhaps they could hop on a treadmill or go for a long walk in a nearby park. Encourage your teen to keep up the process. In three days, whatever angered your teenager might resolve itself.

Three days after Jesus' crucifixion, something magnificent happened: He rose from the dead! Can you imagine what the apostles were feeling once they realized this? Jesus made the impossible possible. If Jesus can do this, he can do anything, including providing divine intervention and guidance to your teen.

REFLECT

Encourage your teen to reach out to the Lord during difficulties. God is only a heartbeat away.

✠ PRAY ✠

Dear Heavenly Father,

I praise your sweet name night and day.
Thank you for dying on the cross for my sins.
Thank you for suffering so I won't have to.
Thank you for rising from the dead and providing the hope I need to spend eternity with you. For now, fill my heart with your love so I can parent (name) lovingly, kindly, and peacefully.
I ask this in Jesus' name. Amen.

april 30

EASTER MIRACLES

But they were startled and terrified and thought that they were seeing a ghost. Then he said to them, "Why are you troubled? And why do questions arise in your hearts? Look at my hands and my feet, that it is I myself. Touch me and see, because a ghost does not have flesh and bones as you can see I have." And as he said this, he showed them his hands and his feet (Luke 24:37–40).

Years ago, my parents tried to climb Apparition Hill in Medjugorje in Bosnia and Herzegovina. The ascent challenged them to navigate over countless boulders that peppered the mountainside. It was too much for Mom, so they prayed the rosary at a halfway point. When a beautiful woman dressed in white approached, Dad invited her to pray with them. When Dad turned to thank the lovely woman for her prayers, she vanished. One side of the mountain was a cliff; the other was hazardous rock terrain. There was no fathomable explanation for her disappearance. Later, they concluded they were visited by an angel.

In today's Bible passage, the disciples needed a miracle or proof of Christ's resurrection. When Jesus appeared, there was pandemonium. Jesus had to show them his hands and feet, encourage them to touch him and even share a meal with them. Why didn't the disciples recognize Jesus immediately? They probably struggled to comprehend what was unfolding before their very eyes similar to the way my parents couldn't immediately understand that a heavenly angel prayed beside them on that mountain.

REFLECT

What miracles does your teen need in order to believe? What is he struggling to overcome? God is in our midst, but first we must recognize him. Look for him in the eyes of the homeless, the indigent, the lonely and sick, the depressed, and the hungry. He is everywhere.

✠ PRAY ✠

Dear Heavenly Father,

Touch my heart with the Easter joy that you want me to experience in your unending stream of love. Amen.

may 1

FRUIT LOOPS OR COCOA PUFFS?

When they had finished breakfast, Jesus said to Simon Peter,
"Simon, son of John, do you love me more than these?"
He said to him, "Yes, Lord, you know that I love you."
He said to him, "Feed my lambs" (John 21:15).

I tried to ensure that my daughters ate breakfast each day. When they were little, I made oatmeal for them during the winter and let them watch their favorite TV show while they ate. During the summer, they enjoyed selecting their favorite boxes of cereals at the grocery store. As adults, they often skip that most important meal despite my constant urging, nagging, and rebuking.

After Christ's resurrection, Peter returned to what he knew: fishing. He wasn't successful until Jesus told him to fish on the other side of the boat. Then his nets filled with fish. On the shore, Jesus didn't chastise him for returning to his fishing job. Instead, they shared breakfast and simple conversation. "Do you love me?" Jesus asked three times, one for each of Peter's rejections. Each response was a resounding yes!

Jesus knows how we really are, what we really need, and how to get us back on track. Peter needed this gentle nudging. In our own lives we might need to be like Jesus, gently prodding our teenagers. Perhaps they are tumbling down from the burdens of school, sports, or activities. Because you love your kids, offer helpful suggestions like Jesus did for Peter when he said, "Cast your net on the other side of the boat."

REFLECT

Allow God to help by working through you. Be his finest tool. Choose to let Jesus' enduring love and easygoing nature guide your interactions with your teens.

✠ PRAY ✠

Dear Heavenly Father,

How glorious is your name! You lead me through darkness
and I don't have anything to fear because I trust in your divine power.
Fill me with a smidgen of your wisdom to help my struggling child.
Tell me what to say and do. I trust and love you, Lord.
Your way is my way. Amen.

may 2

RECOGNIZE HIM

*And it happened that while they were conversing and debating,
Jesus himself drew near and walked with them,
but their eyes were prevented from recognizing him* (Luke 24:15–16).

When my husband and I least expected it, we spotted a bald eagle soaring overhead. Initially, we wondered if our eyes deceived us. Then, we tried to etch the scene permanently in our minds. It took a while to digest what we just saw and we talked about it for hours. Have you ever witnessed something amazing when you weren't trying? Maybe you saw your teenager acting more maturely than usual or you saw him in a different light.

The message of surprise in Luke's passage reminded me of my astonishment when I spotted the eagle. The confused apostles must have wondered if their eyes were misleading them when they stumbled upon the risen Christ en route to Emmaus. The disciples admitted that they doubted Jesus was alive. When they brought the "stranger" home, they recognized Jesus when he broke and blessed the bread they shared. With that realization, Jesus vanished from their sight. Luke wants us to recognize Christ in the strangers we meet every day. Do you recognize Jesus in your teenager?

REFLECT

The risen Christ is in our midst. He is everywhere if we look using eyes of faithfulness. Every now and then you might get a glimpse of the adult your child is transforming into. Perhaps you get a glint of God and a glimmer of hope. That brief serendipitous encounter will be perfect.

✠ PRAY ✠

Dear Heavenly Father,

*Thank you for returning to us and walking among us,
kind and generous Lord. Thank you for reminding me
to look for you in the smile on the face of my dear child. Amen.*

may 3

WINDY WORDS

I have heard this sort of thing many times.
Troublesome comforters, all of you! Is there no end to windy words?
What sickness makes you rattle on? (Job 16:2–3).

When we traveled to Romania to adopt Andrea, Juliana stayed home with my parents. The moment we returned home, Juliana fell into my arms and cried herself to sleep. Nothing I could say could comfort her. All I could do was hold her while she cried. The best thing for her was for me simply to be there. Have you ever experienced something similar with your child? Perhaps your teenager has recently encountered a difficulty and you were unsure of how to comfort her.

As a parent, we tend to want to fix it and make the hurt magically disappear. We grasp at comforting words hoping to make our child feel better. We seek explanations and pray for resolution. We remind her that God has a reason for everything he does and we need to trust in his plan.

Job's friends were similar. They explain why his children have died, his livestock have disappeared, and sores cover his body. The explanations that Job's friends offer aren't the reasons Job encountered the hardships. Sometimes, comforting words can cause anxiety, awkwardness, and embarrassment. There will be times when words will fail us. There will be times when we are stumped and cannot find an explanation that will suffice. In these situations, God wants us to simply be there; like the time when Juliana needed to be held while she cried it out.

REFLECT

The next time your dear child is brokenhearted and you don't know what to say, remember that sometimes "windy words" are not what's needed. Occasionally, all you have to do is be there with open arms.

✠ PRAY ✠

Dear Heavenly Father,

I imagine you standing with your arms stretched out to me,
waiting to embrace me and to bring me comfort when I am down.
Remind me to do the same to (name) when she is melancholy.
You are always there for me. I love you, Lord. Amen.

may 4

COMPLETE JOY

We are writing this so that our joy may be complete (1 John 1:4).

Mr. Coty was a favorite teacher in high school because he taught me to tap into my creative side to write amazing stories. An awesome story is only as good as the paper it's written on until it's read by people. Once a story is published and read by others, that's when the true happiness comes. For many writers, sharing stories is the reason we write. When my daughters were little, I told them, "Sharing is caring." Today whenever we share something, no matter how small or insignificant we think it is, we always repeat that mantra.

John was one of Jesus' dearest friends. He spent time with him and heard him speak, yet that didn't complete his joy. How could it be that knowing Jesus and hearing his messages weren't enough? Like other writers, John composed this letter to complete his joy. From a writer's perspective, I totally understand that his joy came after sharing Jesus with others because "sharing is caring."

Jesus is the source of our joy, and what a wonderful joy it is. It's the type of ecstasy that can split seams open as it bubbles out all over the place. If your joy isn't complete, perhaps you need to start sharing Christ with those around you. The joy God grants you isn't intended for you to keep locked up in a special vault for only you; it's meant to be shared.

REFLECT

Start today by sharing the joy of Jesus with your kids. Remind them of the times when Jesus was there for you, how he lifted you out of a bad place or showered you with abundant blessings. Your kids will thank you for sharing this gift.

✠ PRAY ✠

Dear Heavenly Father,

Glorious God, creator of heaven and earth, I bow before you grateful and satiated with your overflowing joy. Remind me to share it with others around me, for you will constantly fill me up. Amen.

may 5

CONSTRUCTIVE CRITICISM

Do not reprove the arrogant, lest they hate you; reprove the wise, and they will love you. Instruct the wise, and they become still wiser; teach the just, and they advance in learning (Proverbs 9:8–9).

When I was learning how to be an x-ray tech, I despised hearing about all of the techniques or procedures I did wrong. I wondered why the instructors couldn't point out the things I did right. Embracing the criticism was difficult but necessary because I learned through my mistakes. Students generally don't like their blunders pointed out, especially if they think they're right. The wise student accepts criticism diplomatically because she knows she doesn't know it all.

There isn't a soul on earth who knows everything. Does your teenager think she knows it all? This is a common phase that some teens experience since they don't want to believe they have faults or room for improvement. When your youth becomes a "know-it-all," sometimes it's best not to engage with her and allow her to goof up. Eventually, your teen will learn how to listen graciously by observing others. Can you modulate this for your teen? When she sees friends or family members changing, she might, too.

REFLECT

Are you a good role model for your teen when it comes to handling criticism? Just because you think you know best doesn't mean you do. How open are you to suggestions for self-improvement?

✠ PRAY ✠

Dear Heavenly Father,

Teach me, Lord, how to handle criticism better so that (name) can learn from me how to embrace it, learn from it, and grow. Touch my soul, Lord, to make it a richer dwelling place for you. Amen.

may 6

INVITE GOD IN

"Father, if you are willing, take this cup away from me; still, not my will but yours be done." And to strengthen him an angel from heaven appeared to him (Luke 22:42–43).

Jesus prayed in Gethsemane with an anguished heart, knowing he would suffer greatly before being put to death. He chose to do God's will knowing it meant an excruciatingly painful path. Sometimes we are called to walk a trail filled with problems and roadblocks, but we traverse it anyway, knowing we are obeying God's plans for us. Have you ever chosen to take on a more complicated role because you thought it was what God wanted of you? Reflect on it and the blessings you received along the way. Each time you do God's work, he provides solutions to your problems, supplies encouragement through rough patches, and illuminates the darkness that engulfs you.

I felt God calling me to teach religion to middle-school kids. It wasn't exactly what I wanted to do with my time at that point in my life, but I accepted that God was charging me with an important task that he felt I could do. Without any teaching experience, I placed all of my faith in God, believing he would help me, and he did. I overcame my shyness and found the time to prepare lesson plans. Ideas gushed out of me. I engaged the students and left them thinking about the lessons after class. It turned out to be one of the best years of my life, and I was immensely glad I decided to follow God's mission.

REFLECT

Has God been calling you to do something you'd rather not do? If you ignore his request, he will stop whispering and start knocking louder than ever on your heart. Open the door and invite him in. You will be so glad you did, for he has countless blessings he is aching to give you.

✠ PRAY ✠

Dear Heavenly Father,

Thank you, Lord, for building me into the person you want me to be.
Mold me, kind and merciful, Lord, into the creature you desire.
I am here, Lord, waiting to serve. Do whatever you may. I am yours.
Amen.

may 7

AVERT SIN

We know that our old self was crucified with him, so that our sinful body might be done away with, that we might no longer be in slavery to sin (Romans 6:6).

A while ago, a woodpecker chipped a gaping hole in the cedar siding of our home. I was surprised how such a tiny thing could cause so much trouble! The bird was so destructive that it took a lot of time and money to repair the damage. I eventually hung tinfoil pie plates from a nearby tree to keep the bird away.

Like a woodpecker, sin destroys, too. It might begin harmlessly fluttering in and out without much notice. It could start slowly with a few meager taps here and there. But before you know it, there could be a huge hole in your once- perfect life. Many lives have been destroyed by giving into selfish and sinful desires. You might be tempted to look the other way and pretend a little sin isn't a problem. Over time, though, that little sin could lead to much worse behaviors and real destruction. Stop it now by bringing Jesus into your family life.

Jesus' death conquered our sin. He died so we could have eternal life in heaven. Because of his death and resurrection, we don't have to fear our own death. If we can handle death, surely we should be able to manage our life. Even though there are times when life seems incredibly challenging, it can't possibly be as bad as Christ's death.

REFLECT

Has something malicious worked its way into your life? Maybe your teenager has brought foul language or unsavory friends into your home. Perhaps your teenager is showing signs of an eating disorder or spending too much time playing violent video games. What steps can you take to keep those little sins from growing into hard-to-fix problems?

✠ PRAY ✠

Dear Heavenly Father,

Thank you for dying on the cross for my sins.
Thank you for the hope I have for my future with you in heaven and my life here on earth. Help me through my difficulties, Lord.
At times the stress is overwhelming and I don't know what to do.
It could always be worse, but for today, it is wearing me down.
Please build me up today to be the best parent I can be. Amen.

may 8

BE LIKE A FLOWER

Learn from the way the wild flowers grow (Matthew 6:28).

My dad's backyard garden has a lovely assortment of roses and perennials. He claims gardening is like raising children. The roses can be temperamental and high maintenance, requiring much daily care such as primping and fertilizing and having optimal sun and soil conditions. After the perennials are transplanted in the ground, they barely require any work. In fact, many just want to be occasionally watered. The wildflowers that grow require even less; they take whatever God gives them.

What kind of flowers are your children like? Do you have one child who needs a lot of coaching and guidance, but another who does fine on his own? If one adolescent requires more of your attention, that can be exhausting. Parenting a demanding teen is challenging and frustrating, especially when nothing you do seems to be satisfying.

Talk to your teenager about what's really important: their intelligence, compassion, integrity, and ability to be Christlike. Some teens delineate their worth centered on computer skills, their cell phones, the car they drive, fashion, or their ability to be cool among peers. Help them realign what's really important. Perhaps you can plan one day a month where your entire family helps those in the community who are less fortunate. Maybe he will learn something new or meet new people. Volunteering can make your teenager feel connected and part of something big. Also, there is a link between volunteering and living a happier, healthier, longer life.

REFLECT

Spend time reflecting with your teen after doing service projects because you will get the most out of your experience. Bring each experience full circle, back to God. While this may take effort now, your teen will blossom like flowers in a garden.

✠ PRAY ✠

Dear Heavenly Father,

Teach me to be more like the flowers, bending when the wind blows.
Help me, Lord, to redefine (name)'s moral compass
and teach him how to be more giving and kind, like you. Amen.

may 9

LAUGH PROBLEMS AWAY

Sarah then said, "God has given me cause to laugh, and all who hear of it will laugh with me (Genesis 21:6).

After Andrea spent nearly a year in an orphanage, the first thing we tried to teach her was to laugh. She sat on a pile of freshly laundered, crisp white pillows in a classy hotel in Switzerland and laughed her head off until she fell asleep.

Laughter really can be the best medicine for whatever ails you. Life is so serious, compounded with problems that are no joking matter. It's almost undignified to laugh out in public, but it's important that we do it anyway. I laugh at the squirrels that appear like trapeze artists swinging from one tree branch to another. What do you smile about? Laughter can't solve our problems, but it can quell the pain of a broken heart.

Listening to roaring laughter is contagious and triggers healthy changes in the body by strengthening your immune system, increasing your energy, and it's an antidote to stress, pain, and conflict. Humor can inspire hopefulness while connecting you to others, as it did with Andrea on her first night with us. With the power to heal and revitalize, the knack to laugh easily and frequently is a marvelous way to enhance your relationships while improving your emotional health.

REFLECT

Can you do more activities with your teenagers that would promote laughter, such as playing board games, skating or biking together? Maybe you could watch funny movies together knowing how good laughter makes you feel. How will you incorporate laughter into your family life today?

✠ PRAY ✠

Dear Heavenly Father,

Thank you for creating me with a funny bone. You are so awesome to build in so many health benefits to something that is so enjoyable. Lighten my heart, my sweet Lord, so that I can laugh more freely and love thee more dearly. Amen.

may 10

MOTHER'S DAY

He went down with them and came to Nazareth, and was obedient to them; and his mother kept all these things in her heart (Luke 2:51).

I love this passage because it's the only time in holy Scripture that Jesus did something to upset his parents. Jesus was obedient and didn't put up a fuss or act out in any way. Mary and Joseph handled the situation remarkably well when they found Jesus in the Temple. And Mary's heart preserved it all.

Mary didn't have an easy job raising the Son of God. Most mothers can guess what motherhood will be like. But what did Mary have as a reference? Her kid was God! I imagine Jesus was a nice little boy. However, when he became a teenager, he thought, spoke, acted, and behaved differently. Mary had to be afraid when he would go off alone to pray or when he preached about the kingdom of God in large gatherings. Yet she remained stoic in the background.

At the passion, Mary stood by while the crowd taunted her son and spit at him. She watched him be beaten and carry the cross he would be nailed to. She never left him. What do you think her heart was like then? Mary remained beside Jesus until he died, then cradled his crumpled body at the foot of the cross before he was laid in a tomb. That must have been extremely difficult to endure. She didn't go home and write a journal about it, she didn't belabor it at the well to her friends; instead, she kept it all in her heart. How brave Mary was!

REFLECT

On Mother's Day, instead of recollecting how difficult or convoluted your journey of motherhood has been, focus your thoughts on Mary, the true queen of Mother's Day. Try to emulate her actions, her thoughts, her desires. For today, try to think, speak, act, and love the way Mary would. Then, try to do it again tomorrow and the day after that.

✠ PRAY ✠

Dear Heavenly Father,

Thank you for giving me a true queen in heaven to emulate.
Let her bring me closer to her Son through her loving heart. Amen.

may 11

DO GOD'S WILL

Your kingdom come, your will be done, on earth as in heaven (Matthew 6:10).

The first thing I do each morning is thank God for giving me another day. Then I tell God I am here to do his will, whatever it is. I hope his will for me is to eat a big bowl of corn flakes, drink hot coffee, and enjoy a long shower. I hope his will includes me writing devotions, but he could say, "Not today. I want you to do something else." As hard as that is, I force myself to do it. When I obey God's call, mysteriously, everything gets done. Somehow my devotions get written and his ideas get carried out.

When I turn on the TV and see the devastation caused by a twister touching down overnight in tornado alley, I wonder what the heaven-bound prayers were like amidst that chaos. It's easy to thank God when everything is going well, but when it isn't, how difficult it must be to walk through the wreckage and say, "I'm here to do your will." God teaches us these times are when we need to call out to him the most. He hears every word we cry.

REFLECT

Maybe the chaos is caused by your teenager who whips through your home with the destruction of a cyclone. Or perhaps her language is damaging to your family life. Has your daughter visited unscrupulous websites recently? Whatever the bedlam is in your life, ask God to help you deal with it. Wherever you are in your life, pick up your cross and let God know that you are ready, willing, and able to do his will, whatever it is.

✠ PRAY ✠

Dear Heavenly Father,

Help me to remember that nothing will happen today that you and I can't handle together. Remind me, my sweet Lord, that you are with me throughout my turmoil and you can help me sort through it and make sense of it. I am here, Lord. Let me do your will. Amen.

may 12

TRANSFORM ENVY

When his brothers saw that their father loved him best of all his brothers, they hated him so much that they could not say a kind word to him. Once Joseph had a dream, and when he told his brothers, they hated him even more (Genesis 37:4–5).

When Patrick and I were planning our family size, we hoped for two girls so they would have each other as lifelong friends. While some kids have a tight-knit bond with their siblings, it's also common for brothers and sisters to quarrel. My daughters didn't always see eye to eye on everything. If they weren't envious of each other, they may have been jealous of classmates who took fancy vacations, bought designer-brand clothes, drove luxury cars, and lived in mansions. Who wouldn't be green with envy? Do you have sibling rivalry in your family or are you dealing with issues of jealousy?

Perhaps you could encourage your teenager to use envy as a springboard for change. For example, when two friends lost a ton of weight, I used that envy to go on a diet and lose weight. If your son wants to travel, encourage him to get a job and save for it. Perhaps he could take a mission trip and do God's work overseas. See if there is a solution for the envy that has been growing in your home. Try to shift envy away from someone else's life and turn it into a positive change in your own.

REFLECT

If you're having trouble finding a solution to your teen's envy (or even your own) ask God to help you see it. With God's help, you can find a solution to any problem.

✠ PRAY ✠

Dear Heavenly Father,

Thank you for the blessings you have given to my family.
You are such a generous and loving king of all nations.
I feel honored that you would give so much for the little I do for you.
Teach me, Lord, how to transform envy into thankfulness.
I want to always have a grateful heart. Amen.

may 13

SHARE WHAT YOU HAVE

Abraham replied, "My child, remember that you received what was good during your lifetime while Lazarus likewise received what was bad; but now he is comforted here, whereas you are tormented" (Luke 16:25).

In this passage, both men receive differently. The story describes the rich man's clothing and sumptuous feasting, with Lazarus famished, sickly, and incapable of fending off dogs. Only the gate divides them. Misery was God's gift to Lazarus. Lazarus didn't ask for it or cause it. However, he endured it. The wealthy man descends from luxury to suffering, while Lazarus rises from pain to sacredness.

This is the time of year when garage sales pop up. People clean out their garages, basements, or attics in hopes of making some money off the small enterprise. Some folks collect an odd assortment of stuff thinking it will bring them happiness. When it doesn't, some hold yard sales to get rid of it.

Problems can mount up with a growing pile of stuff. Some people buy home-security systems, window blinds, or stockade fences. Others hire lawyers and financial planners to help deal with it. Society tells us we need to have stuff in order to be happy. Open the newspaper and notice how many ads fill the pages. Just because we have a lot of stuff doesn't mean we're happier or even more blessed than those who have less.

REFLECT

Consider having your family clean out the closets and donate some of what you find. How many different coats or pairs of shoes do you really need? Why not give some to charity? Simplify. Share what you have.

✠ PRAY ✠

Dear Heavenly Father,

You have blessed me ten times over with much goodness and bounty. Teach me how to share it with those who have nothing. When I get bored, don't let me shop. Remind me to pray. There are so many sickly people in the world who need my prayer. Let me pray for each one of them. They are my brethren. I adore you, Lord. Amen.

may 14

WE'RE APPLES AND ORANGES

Not all flesh is the same, but there is one kind for human beings, another kind of flesh for animals, another kind of flesh for birds, and another for fish. There are both heavenly bodies and earthly bodies, but the brightness of the heavenly is one kind and that of the earthly another (1 Corinthians 15:39–40).

God created us in his image, and yet we are all different. We might have different personalities, talents, likes, and desires. While my daughters Juliana and Andrea have similarities, their unique personalities set them apart. Juliana is serious, Andrea is playful. As kids growing up together, they balanced each other socially. Juliana inspired Andrea to be more studious; Andrea encouraged Juliana to play more.

In our family, we celebrated and embraced differences, probably because we are all vastly different. Those differences made us love, respect, and appreciate each other. Is an orange the same as an apple? Sure. Both are nutritious round fruits that grow on trees. They can be easily transported and eaten just about anywhere. They're juicy and tasty. Apples and oranges can be the same, depending on how you view them.

REFLECT

Think of a time when you wanted your teenager to conform to be like everyone else instead of celebrating his differences. What particular uniqueness makes your teenager special? Is your son a risk taker or does he like to play it safe? Is your teenager outgoing or a loner? Does your son plan everything methodically on spreadsheets, or does he wing it? Whatever attributes make your teen unique, celebrate them. Don't try to change them.

✠ PRAY ✠

Dear Heavenly Father,

I belong to you, O Lord, my Creator.
Thank you for making me in your glorious image.
Teach me how to be respectful of (name)'s differences that seem to rub me the wrong way. How shall I overcome them, Lord?
Show me the way. Amen.

may 15

PATIENCE

Be still before the LORD; wait for him. Do not be provoked by the prosperous, nor by malicious schemers (Psalm 37:7).

When my daughters were applying to colleges, the wait to find out what school they would go to was unbearable. As acceptance letters started filling their friends' mailboxes, their anxiety skyrocketed. It's never been easy to be patient. Patience wasn't a highly valued virtue in biblical times, either. For really important matters, it's hard to wait.

Perhaps your teenager is experiencing anxiety over a relationship. If the ideal person and greatly desired relationship doesn't materialize on her time frame, that frustration could lead to a premature sabotage of it, overlooking that it takes a while to cultivate a bond. Being aware of impatience gives your teen a chance to learn from it and discern a circumstance that isn't healthy, giving her the opportunity to change it. Have your teen think about her problem, and if impatience isn't warranted she can fix it by getting to the root of the problem instead of feeling stressed.

REFLECT

What is your daughter impatient for? Could she benefit from a to-do list or help with time management? When those moments of impatience arise, encourage your teen to pray. Prayer ranks high among the best stress busters.

✠ PRAY ✠

Dear Heavenly Father,

How glorious you are to me! Fill (name) with the inspiration and love she needs to overcome stress. Teach us patience so we can grow closer to each other and to you. Amen.

may 16

WAITING

Wait for the Lord, *take courage; be stouthearted, wait for the* Lord
(Psalm 27:14).

We are told to wait for the Lord when waiting doesn't come naturally. While I loved holding my daughters when they were little, I couldn't wait for them to walk. Once they got into everything, I couldn't wait for them to know better. After they understood between right and wrong, I couldn't wait to see the adults they would grow into. My inclination was to speed up their growing process; God wants us to slow down. When life decelerates, we can relish the good we have on our journey. We can appreciate and be thankful for the little things in life, like teaching our son how to ride a bike or watching him attend his first prom.

Instead of being fixated on waiting as a period of not accomplishing anything, live in the moment and be thankful for the blessings God is providing. Transform the wait from inactivity to one of hopefulness. It's exciting wondering what God is going to do, how he will work through you, or others around you, and what the final outcome will hold for you. During the wait, maybe he is building you up for some monumental task. Maybe God is restoring your body the way your cell phone needs recharging. We cannot view our waiting period with the same perspective as God's because he sees all and knows all. Lean into his love during this time. He has carved out a special place for you to rest while you wait.

REFLECT

Have you been doing a lot of waiting? God might be energizing you for some greater purpose. Maybe he wants you to spend more quiet time meditating or praying to listen to him. Trust in God during this waiting period.

✠ PRAY ✠

Dear Heavenly Father,

Bless my wait. Let me fill the idle time with prayer
and rejoicing in your marvelous ways.
Even though I don't understand it,
I trust and hope in you, sweet Lord. Amen.

may 17

READ HOLY SCRIPTURE

Now Jesus did many other signs in the presence of [his] disciples that are not written in this book. But these are written that you may [come to] believe that Jesus is the Messiah, the Son of God, and that through this belief you may have life in his name (John 20:30–31).

My daughters liked visiting the library because they loved to read. It made them feel special to bring their own tote bags and library cards. To make it interesting, we traveled to neighboring towns to explore libraries that offered a wider selection. What's interesting is that many Catholic homes possess Bibles, but few families read Scripture the way they read other material. Do you read the Bible, processing the messages individually, or do you read it together as a family? Or do you do both?

When you get a new car, do you read the manual first, or do you just hop in and drive without fully understanding what all of the buttons, knobs, and signals mean? When you first discovered that you were expecting a baby, did you read books about what to look for? The Bible is our operations manual; it guides us, advises us, and encourages us along our life's journey. Life can be complicated. So can raising teenagers. The Bible helps us to live fully and completely the way God intended.

REFLECT

Experience something truly amazing by opening the Bible randomly and reading whatever your eyes land on. Then ponder the passage you just read. Ask God to deliver a message to you about it. Read the same passage a second time and ponder it again. God will speak to you in your stillness.

✠ PRAY ✠

Dear Heavenly Father,

What do you want to tell me, Lord?
What message do you want me to hear?
I am listening with my heart, mind, and soul.
Speak to me, sweet Jesus. I am yours. Amen.

may 18

SPEAK GOD'S LANGUAGE

And they were all filled with the holy Spirit and began to speak in different tongues, as the Spirit enabled them to proclaim. At this sound, they gathered in a large crowd, but they were confused because each one heard them speaking in his own language
(Acts 2:4, 6).

I don't know when it happened or how it happened, but there is a new language that has evolved through the use of quickly advancing technologies. My daughters text me with messages like, "C U @ 4 2day." I don't like it, but I use it with my kids because I want to keep the communication lines open between us. I don't understand some of their texts: They're like riddles I have to solve or interpret.

Wherever you go it's important to learn to speak the language. When you vacation in Rome, do you try to learn Italian before you arrive? Perhaps you begin slowly by learning essential phrases like, "Where's the bathroom?" It's OK to begin slowly to learn God's language: intentional silence. It's his first language because it's where meditative prayer happens. It's the place where inner loquaciousness and noise end. Intentional silence is centering prayer, which is crucial to spiritual awakening. It's work to free your mind, then restrain it from wandering by impeding your thought process. Focus on God by looking at a picture of Jesus. Gaze into his loving eyes and dwell on his abundant love for you despite your problems. If your son's issues are consuming you, step away from them in silence to find the Lord. He is waiting for you.

REFLECT

Has God been sending you messages you don't understand? Spend time in silence trying to understand what he's saying.

✠ PRAY ✠

Dear Heavenly Father,

Remove the preoccupation I have with (name)'s goals, fears, desires, and issues. Take my hand and guide me as I walk blindly through a minefield of problems. Let me reach you through silence. I am here, patiently waiting for you, Lord. Amen.

may 19

DISAPPOINTMENT

A foolish son is vexation to his father,
and bitter sorrow to her who bore him (Proverbs 17:25).

I was disappointed when my daughter stopped wearing her retainer and her teeth fell out of perfect alignment. I saw all of the money I had spent on braces and years of frequent trips to the orthodontist's office go down the drain. Many parents, at one time or another, experience disappointment with their kids. When this happens, try to focus on the positive things your child has done and thank God for all of them. God even wants us to thank him for the disappointments. Even though we can't always see or understand his reasons, we still need to thank God.

The Bible says when dealing with disappointment we should keep our eyes on God. Forgive your daughter for the disappointment no matter how bad it was. If you made a mistake, God would forgive you. Forgiveness isn't easy, but it's liberating. Also, search for God's reasoning behind it. Deliberate if the disappointment came because something you wanted was not in line with God's plan. Turn your disappointment over to God. Stop trying to rely on yourself so much. Give it to God. He is much stronger than you are and can take on burdens when you can't.

REFLECT

How easy is it for you to forgive you child when she disappoints you? Does your family cultivate a culture of forgiveness or one of grudges and blame?

✠ PRAY ✠

Dear Heavenly Father,

Thank you for the disappointment I have recently felt with (name).
There is a reason for it, so thank you for your infinite wisdom.
I trust in your miraculous ways even though I cannot understand
them because I carry them in my tousled and broken heart.
Let your love transport me through this difficulty,
and for that I am eternally grateful. Amen.

may 20

IMPORTANCE OF PRAYER

But I will call upon God, and the LORD will save me.
At dusk, dawn, and noon I will grieve and complain,
and my prayer will be heard (Psalm 55:17–18).

Planting flowers is tricky because some require partial sun or direct sun. Some plants are particular about the type of soil, depth of soil, and drainage of the soil. Some like to be watered a lot and others hardly at all. You have to consider how tall the flowers will grow and when they will bloom. There is much to consider, but every gardener will tell you it's worth the effort.

Likewise, there are many things to consider when praying. You have to begin with the right attitude. Prayer is not like walking up to a vending machine and deciding how much to put in to get what you want. Prayer is a gift that feeds our life. It's like sunshine, water, and fertilizer to a plant.

Everything in your life will come together when you put God first, even if your life is in turmoil, complicated by raising teenagers. Make an appointment to speak with God today—and keep it! If you had an appointment with the dentist and you got busy, you wouldn't reschedule at the last minute because you had too much going on. If you had an appointment for a job interview, you would dress up and be on your best behavior. You wouldn't race in and say you only have five minutes. Therefore, don't do that with your appointments with God. Put him first on your list of things to do today.

REFLECT

Find a comfortable place where you can be quiet with the Lord, free from interruptions and the noise of your house. Give your undivided time to God, clearing your mind from every worry, and begin with adulation for the infinite stream of blessings God has given you. Let the words flow from you like water from a well. It will gladden your heart as much as it will God's.

✠ PRAY ✠

Dear Heavenly Father,

How glorious is your name. I belong to you O Lord,
rich in kindness and mercy. You are my loving Lord,
and my love for you will never die. Amen.

may 21

STRENGTHEN YOUR FAITH

The Lord said to Gideon: You have too many soldiers with you for me to deliver Midian into their power, lest Israel vaunt itself against me and say, "My own power saved me."
That night the Lord said to Gideon: Go, descend on the camp, for I have delivered it into your power (Judges 7:2, 9).

God tested Gideon's faith by asking him to trim down his soldiers to 300 men to fight against an army that far outnumbered his. Gideon's army defeated the enemy without any casualties because they knew that God was with them. Against all odds they were victorious. I always think about this battle when I am faced with conflict in my own life. What battles have you been fighting at home with your teenager? Do you ever feel like you are the only parent who won't allow your teenager to see R-rated movies? Are you the only parent who insists that a parent be home when your daughter visits her friends? Are you the only parent who prohibits co-ed sleepovers? It's OK if you are outnumbered. Gideon was outnumbered, too, and he won the war without a single casualty.

If you face a bleak situation that seems impossible to overcome, ask God to intervene on your behalf. Like Gideon, trust God that he will never leave your side, even if your problems have impossible odds. It's not easy to be the unpopular parent, the outspoken parent, or the one with all of the rules and regulations. If you begin to suspect you are overreacting, or being too harsh, ask the Holy Spirit to guide you through it. Don't consult with other parents, consult directly with God. These are the battles God will help you overcome.

REFLECT

What battle are you currently waging? Ask the Holy Spirit to guide your actions in the fight.

✠ PRAY ✠

Dear Heavenly Father,

Shield me with your armor as I wage war against a society with corrupt morals and pathetic values. When I feel unsure of myself, come to my rescue and flood me with your wisdom to make the right decisions for my family. Keep us out of harm's way even if it looks like there is no way out. Open a safe path for my family and me. Amen.

may 22

ANGER MANAGEMENT

When the people in the synagogue heard this,
they were all filled with fury (Luke 4:28).

Teenagers know how to push your buttons. If you have a teenager who is constantly testing your limits and wearing your patience thin, how do you handle your anger? There are many coping strategies: count to ten, listen to music, exercise, prayer, and more. Be mindful that you are modeling for your teen how to keep your cool when you feel like blowing a fuse.

Anger informs you that something is wrong. You might feel yourself getting tense with a clenched jaw, reddened face, or rising voice. Use these signals to keep your emotions in check by reminding yourself to relax, take a few deep breaths, invoke the Holy Spirit to calm and help you. Define the infuriating problem and ponder pragmatic ways to deal with it by devising a plan. Then see it through.

What if your teenager is being treated unfairly at school? The anger might enable him to stand up for his rights in a constructive manner. Teach your teen to mull it over a few hours so he doesn't overreact and thinks rationally. Encourage your adolescent to share his feelings while being mindful not to cast blame. Remind your son that the Holy Spirit dwells within him and can move him to resolve differences amicably.

REFLECT

Consider all of the physical changes your teen's body is going through in addition to hormonal surges that can cause mood swings and confused emotions. Maybe you are trying to fix his problems or faults, second-guess his decisions, or challenge his opinions.

✠ PRAY ✠

Dear Heavenly Father,

You are immensely wonderful; I wish I could be more like
you when things go wrong. Don't let anger control me.
Help me remain tranquil in your love and mercy.
Don't let me say anything I'll regret. Let every word that rolls off my
tongue be words you formed in my heart.
I love you and need you, Lord. Amen.

may 23

GOD'S UNBRIDLED CLEMENCY

If we acknowledge our sins, he is faithful and just and will forgive our sins and cleanse us from every wrongdoing (1 John 1:9).

My daughters attended a costume party in high school where Juliana colored her hair with pink glitter spray and Andrea painted her face silver. Their appearance was completely transformed, but thankfully it all washed off by the end of the night. By morning, my daughters were clean and happy, ready to begin another glorious day.

Today's Scripture reminds me of my daughters' costume party with the paint symbolic for sin. The warm water and soap in the shower represent God's infinite stream of mercy, washing their souls clean. No one is without sin. When we confess our sins with remorse, God forgives us, washing us clean, making us new again to keep enjoying the life God gave us.

Some people don't let go of their guilt; they can't put the past behind them and move on. The smallest mistakes weigh them down with an enormous amount of guilt. They might keep rethinking whatever they had done, believing God could never forgive them. But God is all-loving, kind, and merciful. Try to avoid getting caught up in negative thoughts because nothing good comes from that.

REFLECT

Talk to God in the silence of your heart about any guilty feelings you have been harboring. Repeat positive mantras like: "I love you, Lord"; or, "Jesus, help me." If you are still struggling to overcome guilt, perhaps you could consult with your local priest.

✠ PRAY ✠

Dear Heavenly Father,

Take my sins, Lord, and crumble them into the wind.
Wash me clean and help me to stay on the straight and narrow path.
Walk with me, Lord. I love you now and always. Amen.

may 24

STRENGTH FROM WEAKNESS

"My grace is sufficient for you, for power is made perfect in weakness." I will rather boast most gladly of my weaknesses, in order that the power of Christ may dwell with me. Therefore, I am content with weaknesses, insults, hardships, persecutions, and constraints, for the sake of Christ; for when I am weak, then I am strong
(2 Corinthians 12:9–10).

As a surprise to me, my daughters decided to bake a raspberry pie. I was recovering from surgery and was resting near the kitchen when I overheard them discussing the pie dough. I sensed their concern when I heard, "Mom's dough never looks like this." Thank goodness they asked for help. I discovered they added one cup of shortening instead of one cup of flour. After the recipe was corrected the pie was delicious.

Today's Bible passage is comforting during times of difficulty because God reassures us that when we are in a hot mess and can't see a way out, the Almighty strengthens us when we invite him in. When Paul admitted his weakness and stepped aside to allow God to take over, Paul was his strongest. When we allow God's strength to work through us, God gets the credit, not us. Repeatedly throughout the Old Testament, God instructed the leaders of Israel to decrease the size of their armies, or he told them how to win their battles so they would trust God instead of their own strength.

REFLECT

What difficulty have you been struggling through with your teen? Maybe you gave advice to your son but he didn't take it and now is in trouble. It's painful to stand by and watch your child hurt. Some of his lessons will be learned the hard way. Encourage your teenager to call upon the Lord for strength. God is waiting to be invited in.

✠ PRAY ✠

Dear Heavenly Father,

In my moments of weakness, please comfort me and tell me what to do. I cannot see a way out, but I trust in you and will do whatever you tell me to. You are my strength, my shining star, my world. I love you, Lord. Amen.

may 25

WHO DO YOU BELONG TO?

He said to them, "Whose image is this and whose inscription?" They replied, "Caesar's." At that he said to them, "Then repay to Caesar what belongs to Caesar and to God what belongs to God" (Matthew 22:20–22).

Each time I see a penny on the sidewalk, I pick it up because the word "God" is written on it. You can't buy anything with one cent, but I feel special, as if God is smiling on me to say, "I am thinking about you again! Here is a penny for your thoughts."

The Bible notes that the Pharisees were trying to stump Jesus by questioning the census tax. However, Jesus was aware of their malice. Jesus' brilliant response was to acknowledge that Caesar's image on the coin was an emblem of ownership. Jesus' retort to render to Caesar the things that are Caesar's answered and satisfied their deceitful question. Jesus made his point when he concluded his statement with "and to God the things that are God's." Ponder those thought-provoking words. Because God created all of us in his image (Genesis 1:26), we all belong to him.

It's easy to get distracted by money because society puts so much out there to tempt you. Teenagers take the bait because they want to conform to fashion trends, improvements or advancements in technology, and keep up with the Joneses. Get back to the basics: Don't allow money to control you or your teenager.

REFLECT

You have God's image stamped on you, therefore you belong to God. Render to him all that you do.

✠ PRAY ✠

Dear Heavenly Father,

I am yours, sweet Lord. Do with me what you may. I am putty in your hands; mold me how you want to. I will conform to your ways. Thank you for creating me in your image. I love you, Lord. Amen.

may 26

SPREAD THE WORD

The woman left her water jar and went into the town and said to the people, "Come see a man who told me everything I have done. Could he possibly be the Messiah?" (John 4:28–29).

The Samaritan woman was so enthralled by Jesus' revelations and secrets of her heart that she forgot her water at the well. She rushed back to town to tell everyone about this wonderful man she met: Jesus. She wanted everyone to know him. Has something so wonderful ever happened to you that you couldn't stop talking about it?

On a recent pilgrimage I made to Lourdes Shrine in France, I experienced a healing after being submerged in the miraculous baths. I had deteriorating vision that was completely resolved. After the healing occurred, I was like the Samaritan woman at the well. I wanted everyone to know and I couldn't stop talking about it. I retold the story so often that I can hardly remember who I haven't told! Sharing with others how Jesus touches our hearts and moves us to act, think, and speak is fascinating to those who don't know God or who haven't experienced God's love the way I have. God's revelation in our life is attractive to people who want to know him. God wants us to share our stories and to evangelize with the same bursting excitement that the Samaritan woman had when she realized Jesus knew her heart.

REFLECT

Perhaps your teenager would rather talk about rock bands, but maybe that's because he doesn't know it's OK to have conversations about how God touches his life each day. Consider if you should be evangelizing your own family members. Spread the word. Start talking about the wonders of the Lord today!

✠ PRAY ✠

Dear Heavenly Father,

Help me to start talking about you to those around me.
I want them to know you the way I do.
You are such an amazing presence in my life.
Thank you, Lord, for hearing me and answering me. Amen.

may 27

LISTEN WITH YOUR HEART

The Lord called Samuel again, for the third time. Getting up and going to Eli, he said, "Here I am. You called me." Then Eli understood that the Lord was calling the youth. So he said to Samuel, "Go to sleep, and if you are called, reply, 'Speak, Lord, for your servant is listening.'" When Samuel went to sleep in his place, the Lord came and stood there, calling out as before: Samuel, Samuel! Samuel answered, "Speak, for your servant is listening" (1 Samuel 3:8–10).

Listening is a complicated skill that takes work and time to master. Sometimes we don't often hear the same thing like in the telephone game when one person whispers to another a phrase he heard and then the phrase is passed on, mishearing and all. By the end, the phrase is often distorted. Or perhaps we heard correctly but interpreted it incorrectly. Sometimes when we hear sad news, we are in denial or disbelief that what we heard was in fact true. If we are stressed, we might hear incorrectly or not understand what we think we hear. Listening is not easy.

Do you think your teen doesn't listen to you? Teenagers listen differently than adults do. For teens, listening is like seeds sprinkled on a field after the soil has been tilled: It might take a while for the seed to sink in and grow, but it will. Don't stop talking to your kids just because you don't see any results; it takes a while for your words to take root.

REFLECT

In order to live by God's word, we must listen to him calling us. We have to understand what we are hearing, decipher the message, and act on it. God will bless your life with direction, meaning, and purpose as you hear his voice and follow him.

✠ PRAY ✠

Dear Heavenly Father,

My ears are open and my heart longs to hear your voice, Lord.
Speak to me. Let your words fall like raindrops on
the parched soil desperate for your nourishment.
I'm here, Lord, waiting, wondering, and wanting to do your will.
Amen.

may 28

BLESS OUR CHOICES

But Ruth said, "Do not press me to go back and abandon you! Wherever you go I will go, wherever you lodge I will lodge. Your people shall be my people and your God, my God" (Ruth 1:16).

God gave us the ability to make our own choices. At times we might feel like we don't have a choice, but if we scrutinize a particular situation carefully, there's always a choice, even if the only thing to decide is how we'll react to a circumstance. If your teenager has made a dreadful mistake, perhaps the only thing you can do is change the way you are reacting to it. If your teenager has landed in jail, used drugs, or is pregnant, you cannot change the events that led to the situation. The past has passed. But you can change the way you feel and react now and going forward.

Life is not easy. Each of us has a cross to bear, and some appear heavier or bigger than others. When Jesus carried his cross, he stumbled and fell three times. In times of extreme difficulty, we can choose our attitude. Little effort is needed to be negative about the hardships we might be enduring. Upholding faithfulness in joy requires grace in the midst of disillusionment, despair, and disaster.

God never promised us an easy life and happiness on earth. But he says we can call on him for help. The Lord will never leave us alone in our time of need. The situation may not be resolved the way we want, but at least God is beside us each step of the way. Remember that gold is tested in the fire. When the situation has resolved, know that you will be a stronger and better person for having gone through it.

REFLECT

Look for the silver lining in the dark clouds overhead and thank God even for the bad, because tucked inside is something good waiting to be discovered. Look for the good and be glad.

✠ PRAY ✠

Dear Heavenly Father,

Please, God, help me through this difficulty. Amen.

may 29

ASCENSION OF THE LORD

When he had said this, as they were looking on, he was lifted up, and a cloud took him from their sight. While they were looking intently at the sky as he was going, suddenly two men dressed in white garments stood beside them. They said, "Men of Galilee, why are you standing there looking at the sky? This Jesus who has been taken up from you into heaven will return in the same way as you have seen him going into heaven" (Acts 1:9–11).

This passage brings immense hope because it says Jesus will return to earth at some future point, possibly by descending from the clouds. It could be in our lifetime. Are you ready? If Jesus rang your doorbell today, what would that be like? Perhaps you could use this time to prepare your family for Jesus' arrival. Your mission as a parent is blossoming as your child matures into adulthood.

Jesus' ascension into heaven meant he accomplished God's mission and was successful with his human ministry on earth. He could now return to his heavenly home with God the Father. Has something run its course in your teen's life, and is she struggling now that it has ended? Perhaps your youth struggles with the end of the school year and must now make plans for the summer, one that doesn't include sleeping the day away. Has your teen just graduated from high school, with college a few short months away?

REFLECT

What can you do to ensure your teenager has a smooth transition from a rigorous class schedule into a relaxing yet productive summer? Will you plan to take a family vacation over the summer or will you encourage your youth to get a job? Ensure that your teen is involved in the planning process.

✠ PRAY ✠

Dear Heavenly Father,

Fill me with the wisdom I need to move (name) along on her life journey. Bless each step we take toward finding the right venue to spend her summer. Let us do your work, whatever that is. We concur and will abide in your ways, your love, your light. Amen.

may 30

MEMORIAL DAY

"Thus says the LORD: You must not go out to war against your kinsmen. Return home, each of you, for it is I who have brought this about." They obeyed the word of the LORD and turned back from going against Jeroboam (2 Chronicles 11:4).

If only there could be peace on earth, or at least no war. On Memorial Day, let us remember all of the men and women who died while serving our country. Let us ponder the sacrifices they and their families made to ensure our freedom and the freedom of others. If only we could achieve world peace. To begin, we must have peace within our own families. Consider how peaceful your home is living with a teenager.

Our homes are supposed to be a sanctuary. It isn't easy to create a tranquil environment with kids in the house. Teenagers tend to be synonymous with noise and mess. Quell the racket by listening to relaxing music. Clear out the clutter and some of the chaos might go, too. Close your teenager's bedroom doors if their rooms are messy. Get involved in a hobby or community service project. Sometimes too much togetherness or boredom creates tension in families. When there's a hobby, project, or place where you can seek asylum, it's easier to feel peaceful.

REFLECT

Be mindful of your family's daily stresses. It's easy to take our family for granted, but show respect for them and remember they have feelings, too. Pick your battles carefully with teenagers. Let the little things go. Instead, challenge the important issues.

✠ PRAY ✠

Dear Heavenly Father,

Thank you for blessing me with the ability to raise (name). As difficult as it can be at times, thank you for sticking with me through the good times and bad. Thank you for putting all of the perfect notions in my head and the love in my heart. Amen.

may 31

REJECT SIN

After this Jesus found him in the temple area and said to him, "Look, you are well; do not sin anymore, so that nothing worse may happen to you" (John 5:14).

When Andrea was young, she had surgery on her foot that required her to spend several months in a wheelchair. A bus equipped with a hydraulic lift transported her to and from school each day. She had to be carried up and down stairs and wasn't allowed to participate in gym or recreational time. When her cast was removed, Andrea was disheartened because she would miss out on all the special attention she'd been receiving. She wanted the cast back on even though she had completely recovered.

The man Jesus cured lingered at the Temple area even though he was well. We can speculate why he did that, but only Jesus knew for sure and encouraged him to get going or else something worse could happen to him. Does your teenager need reassurance to move along or else risk something worse happening? Maybe there was a skirmish at school that your teenager witnessed. Did something happen after class like bullying, name calling, or social media harassment that your adolescent was involved in? Sometimes, kids are involved just by being there even if they didn't do anything (guilt by association). Teach your daughter to reject sin or trouble will follow.

REFLECT

Deliberate sin destroys us or impedes us from becoming the person God created us to be. There is no compromising with sin. If sin has taken up residence in your youngster, now is the time to address it and make a change. Don't make excuses. Get rid of sin now.

✠ PRAY ✠

Dear Heavenly Father,

Give me the courage to address (name)'s sinful nature.
Put the right thoughts, ideas, and words into my head
so I may help to get her back on the right track.
Please, Lord, help me do the right thing. Amen.

june 1

EYES ON THE PRIZE

Brothers, I for my part do not consider myself to have taken possession. Just one thing: forgetting what lies behind but straining forward to what lies ahead, I continue my pursuit toward the goal, the prize of God's upward calling, in Christ Jesus (Philippians 3:13–14).

Andy and Judy Zatony fled Communist Hungary in the middle of the night in 1956 by sneaking across a heavily guarded border. When a frosty winter wind blew Andy's hat off, his wife told him to let it go and not take one step backward to retrieve it. She told him to focus on the prize: freedom. I recall this couple's clandestine escape whenever I backslide. It's so easy to do when parenting teenagers. Do you hesitate to hand over the car keys after a bad driving experience? Do you pause before leaving your teenager home alone after he invited friends over the last time when he knew not to?

It's easy to overlook our own shortcomings when we spend so much time looking backward at our kid's faults. It's important to remember that, because we are human, we will all make mistakes even if our eyes are fixed on the prize: God's upward calling in Jesus. This turns out to be a very good thing because our Lord is the God of second chances, third chances, and infinite chances. Paul encourages us to look forward, not behind, regardless of the regret we might hold or disguise. Every human being has experienced some form of regret. If given the chance to change something in our past, we all would want to fix something; but we can't. Don't keep looking in the past, stop kicking yourself over a mistake, and stop making excuses for it; learn from it and move on.

REFLECT

Is there an opportunity for you to show your teen you're willing to move forward with him? Does your teen need a reminder to keep moving forward after a bad grade, broken friendship, or other experience that has him distracted from the future?

✠ PRAY ✠

Dear Heavenly Father,

Please take my problems from me. Lighten my burden, dear Lord, and keep me fixed on you. Let me serve you, Lord, in spite of my shortcomings and mistakes. Take pity on me, O Lord, and let me feel your warm embrace. Amen.

june 2

SELF-CHANGE

But when they continued asking him, he straightened up and said to them, "Let the one among you who is without sin be the first to throw a stone at her" (John 8:7).

My mother-in-law used to say, "Just take care of yourself; that's an enormous job in itself." The words rolled off her tongue whenever quarrels erupted in the family. It was a good reminder for self-examination and self-improvement instead of focusing on trying to change others by pointing out their faults. Our teenagers' problems are blatantly obvious. Is it our "job" to point them out in order to help them grow? Maybe it's not what we say, but more how we say it. Were your words cutting to your teen when they didn't have to be? Sometimes we're the one who needs to change!

Teenagers are constantly judged at school by outside appearances: what they wear, the music they listen to, and the crowd they hang with. The last thing they need is to come home and be ridiculed and challenged by their parents. Sometimes it might be best to let the little things slide, refrain from nitpicking, and instead focus on making your kids feel loved, wanted, and appreciated. How can you overlook your kid's messy hair or the earrings you loathe? Try to envision Jesus in your child. Did Mary tell Jesus to comb his hair or get a haircut? Think about how Mary acted as the Mother of God. Then, do that.

REFLECT

In today's Scripture, Jesus challenges us to leave others alone. We are not to judge or criticize. However, we can improve our own dispositions and character flaws. You might not see your faults, but if you ask your teenager, she could tell you all about them!

✠ PRAY ✠

Dear Heavenly Father,

Enable me to be more appreciative of the abundance of love you give to me each day. Teach me how to focus on your love, your gifts, your blessings, so that I stop looking at (name)'s faults. Don't let me put her down. Teach me how to find the best in (name). Thank you for your patience with me. Amen.

june 3

ARDENT PRAYER

The fervent prayer of a righteous person is very powerful (James 5:16).

The night before exams, my daughters would cram and pray fervently. The morning of their tests, I would bless them with holy water and say a special prayer over them. Even though I advised them to study each night and pray every day, they still crammed the night before, praying frantically. This system worked for them, as it probably does for countless other teenagers.

Nearing the end of the school year, consider how your teen will pray before exams. If your son doesn't pray, maybe you could suggest praying with him for clarity or enlightenment. Make a Sign of the Cross on his forehead and place your hand firmly on his head while you ask the Holy Spirit to help him be the best he can be.

It is also wise to teach your son to pray every day, not just when he needs something. When your teen needs a recommendation for a job or college application, he wouldn't ask someone he rarely talks to. Advise your teen to talk to God daily. God will be the best friend he could possibly have.

REFLECT

Ardent prayer won't help those with lukewarm faith. Make sure you and your teen are on the right path. Don't be afraid to teach your teen how to act, even if it's not popular. When you are exhausted from repeating yourself, keep going. Never quit.

✠ PRAY ✠

Dear Heavenly Father,

Please, God, help me to keep (name) on the straight and narrow path.
I am reaching out to you for help, sweet Lord.
Tell me what to say. Tell me what to do. Amen.

june 4

MARY AND MARTHA

Mary [who] sat beside the Lord at his feet listening to him speak. Martha, burdened with much serving, came to him and said, "Lord, do you not care that my sister has left me by myself to do the serving? Tell her to help me." The Lord said to her in reply, "Martha, Martha, you are anxious and worried about many things. There is need of only one thing. Mary has chosen the better part and it will not be taken from her" (Luke 10:39–42).

Whenever my sister and I would visit our parents, I was always the one cooking the meal and doing dishes while my sister chatted away merrily. I constantly thought about today's passage, wishing the work was done magically so I could enjoy a carefree visit. If Jesus came to my home, I would order take-out so I could visit with him. He would be my number one priority. I would listen to his messages, hanging on each word. What if he asked me to make my special beef burgundy stew that takes hours to prepare? I wouldn't have to think twice about it: I would obey.

Today we become acquainted with Jesus through prayer, attending Mass, and Bible study. Some of us are like Mary in our Christian walk, while others resemble Martha. It's probable that the business of life keeps us from spending much time with God. We might have outside jobs, appointments, kid obligations, school projects, and community-service duties. The list is endless. But we can't let anything distract us from spending time with God.

REFLECT

Jesus softly chided Martha for being anxious and worried. While service is good, sitting at Jesus' feet is better. We must remember what is most important. When we give Jesus the attention he deserves, he empowers us to serve others. Who have you been serving?

✠ PRAY ✠

Dear Heavenly Father,

You strengthen me and provide everything I have.
I thank you for it all. Amen.

june 5

OBEY

They refused to obey and no longer remembered the wonders you had worked for them. They were obdurate and appointed a leader in order to return to their slavery in Egypt. But you are a forgiving God, gracious and merciful, slow to anger and rich in mercy; you did not forsake them (Nehemiah 9:17).

Scripture reminds me that I am not alone in my struggles. Throughout history, people have faced problems much greater than mine. With some people not obeying and forgetting the wonders of the Lord, I reflect on all of the good I have done for my kids, and then I wonder how could they not obey me? What is a parent to do?

Every parent has experienced one of those days when nothing went right: The kids misbehaved, their rooms were a wreck, their grades were abhorrent, you grounded them for life, someone felt sick, the refrigerator died, bills were high, and funds were low. What did you do? Life seems to run in cyclic patterns with good and bad balancing each other out. When it feels like you are at your lowest, perhaps the breaking point, don't flip your lid. Instead, call out to the Lord.

God knows our weaknesses, our troubles, and our sinfulness. When we humbly seek him, we'll see his goodness. It will stand out like a bright light against our dark transgressions. There isn't anything preventing God from pardoning us except our refusal to come to him through Jesus. He stands ready, willing, and able to pardon us, if we are ready to receive it.

REFLECT

Open your arms to the Lord and embrace his merciful love. Let him wash you clean and empower you to stand against the wickedness of the world that your teenager drags into the house. With God, you can overcome anything.

✠ PRAY ✠

Dear Heavenly Father,

Rain down on me your indelible love, Lord. Wash away the filth that has soiled my soul. I try to be a good parent, but I am challenged each step of the way. Lighten my burden, Lord. Make this path less tiresome. Walk with me, Lord. Take my hand. I need you. Amen.

june 6

MY SHIELD

How many are my foes, LORD! How many rise against me! How many say of me, "There is no salvation for him in God." But you, LORD, are a shield around me; my glory, you keep my head high (Psalm 3:2–4).

I was the unpopular parent who discontinued junk food in the school cafeteria. I was the only parent who kept an early curfew on school nights. I made my daughters attend religious education and Mass each Sunday. I made enemies. Other parents claimed I was unreasonable. I prayed as I stood alone to protect my family's values. But I wasn't really alone—God was with me, shielding me from the foes I wrestled against. Have you made enemies in your teen's world because you took a stand against something you deemed unacceptable?

In David's psalm, I feel his urgency as he was pursued by enemies. His prayer showed his confidence that God would protect him and allow him to hold his head up high. In the middle of hearing others tell David there was no salvation for him in God, he maintained hope. His faith didn't come from his own abilities to fight and win but from God. He believed God heard him and would help him. Why can't we have unwavering hope like that when we are in crises?

REFLECT

The last time you were in a precarious situation that required divine intervention, did you call out to God asking for his help? When God offers you a shield, perhaps you can use it to guard you while you pray. Sometimes, prayer can be the battle.

✠ PRAY ✠

Dear Heavenly Father,

Pluck me from the distress of the earthliness
and lift me into your waiting arms.
Save me while I gaze into your eyes
regaining the strength I need to forge on.
I will sing your praises every day of my life. Amen.

june 7

RESCUE ME

But you, LORD, are my Lord, deal kindly with me for your name's sake; in your great mercy rescue me. For I am poor and needy; my heart is pierced within me. Like a lengthening shadow I am gone, I am shaken off like the locust (Psalm 109:21–23).

Most parents want to be rescued from parenting teenagers. It's the hardest job I've ever done. I survived it and I'm here to tell you that you will, too, with the grace of God. You can accomplish anything if it is God's will. You just might not do it the way you imagined or on the time line you planned. Since God is wise, his way and outcome will be for the best if you place all of your hope, trust, and faith in him.

Perhaps God allows us to suffer through a particular trial so we will turn to him instead of trying to resolve it on our own. Each difficulty is another opportunity to depend on God and trust in his marvelous ways. I was heartbroken when my daughter was diagnosed with an incurable disease. I spoke to experts seeking a cure—but there wasn't one. After I turned the situation over to God, the disease went into remission and my child has been fine ever since. Even when all seems hopeless, remember to call out to God, for nothing is impossible to him.

REFLECT

When your heart is full of pain, give it to God. As you cry out to God in prayer, he will hear and rescue you from despair. Regardless of how dismal your situation is, God will rescue you.

✠ PRAY ✠

Dear Heavenly Father,

Hear me, O Lord, take this pain from my heart
and replace it with your goodness, mercy, and love.
Do what is best for (name).
I trust in your ways. Amen.

june 8

PENTECOST

And suddenly there came from the sky a noise like a strong driving wind, and it filled the entire house in which they were. Then there appeared to them tongues as of fire, which parted and came to rest on each one of them (Acts 2:2–3).

Jesus told the apostles to remain in Jerusalem until he sent the Holy Spirit. They stayed in seclusion for seven agonizing weeks, during which the citizens grew restless over anyone who followed Jesus. By remaining behind, their lives were in jeopardy, yet they waited obediently. They remained unified in the upper room in steadfast prayer.

Have you had an experience where you asked your teenager to do something important, but she "forgot?" Have you ever asked your daughter to return a library book or pay a bill for you, but it slipped her mind? Meanwhile, you incurred late fees because of her mistake. If you cannot depend on your teenager to handle a small task, how can you trust her with a larger one?

Jesus entrusted his apostles with a monumental undertaking because of its dangerous nature: They were to remain in place and pray fervently. Then they were blessed with the gift of the Holy Spirit. The apostles' prayers were the preparation for this outpouring of Spirit.

REFLECT

Prayer is the preparation for a powerful movement of the Holy Spirit. Is it possible to pray more intensely when you make a request of your adolescent?

✠ PRAY ✠

Dear Heavenly Father,

Grant me the unity with my family and fellow churchgoers as we pray more intently and wait to be filled with the power of the Holy Spirit. Let us do your will, Lord, on your time line, not ours. I ask this in Jesus' sweet name. Amen.

june 9

BIGGER PICTURE

As he passed by he saw a man blind from birth.
His disciples asked him, "Rabbi, who sinned,
this man or his parents, that he was born blind?"
Jesus answered, "Neither he nor his parents sinned; it is so that
the works of God might be made visible through him (John 9:1–3).

Viewing a Monet painting up close resembles random blobs of paint. However, from a distance you'll see a masterpiece. What you'll view depends on where you stand. This can also be true in our lives as we see the wickedness and brokenhearted surrounding us.

In today's passage, the disciples fixated on the disparity instead of seeing God working through it. We do this, too, when we say, "How could God let this terrible thing happen to me?" My daughters have wondered why God allowed so many children to be institutionalized in Romania. When they stand back and see how many thousands of people traveled overseas to adopt these children they begin to see the bigger picture. Sometimes if you can only see the pain in a situation, you might have to take a few steps back to recognize and value the masterpiece.

If I had fixated only on my infertility, it might have consumed me. Thankfully, God pulled me back to enable me to stop thinking about that tiny void in my life. God allowed me to experience brilliant artwork few get to see. It was an amazing gift, laced with miracles and countless blessings. Instead of focusing on your problems up close, step back and focus on the remedy: Jesus.

REFLECT

Don't waste time or energy dwelling on your problems or blaming God. Instead, step back and praise God. Even if you cannot see the bigger picture, eventually God will allow you to see it, feel it, and experience it in all its glory.

✠ PRAY ✠

Dear Heavenly Father,

I'm sorry that I have been focusing on the problems, anguish, and discontentment of my life. Don't let me miss the glory that you reserved for me. Take me back, Lord, so I can see the bigger picture. I love you. Amen.

june 10

TRUSTWORTHINESS

Roam the streets of Jerusalem, look about and observe, search through her squares, to find even one who acts justly and seeks honesty, and I will pardon her (Jeremiah 5:1).

No matter how deplorable the situations were that Jeremiah found people in, he continued searching for honest individuals. In raising teenagers, there were times I wanted to throw in the towel. We established a rule in our family requiring my daughters to call if they had to stay after school. They needed a good reason for it, possibly to make up a gym class, seek extra credit for additional assignments, or meet with a teacher. One afternoon, my daughter came home late but never called. She said she called, but without proof I didn't believe her. She received a harsh punishment for not calling and lying about it.

Has your teenager destroyed your trust in her? Trust is a vital aspect of a healthy relationship that materializes gradually over many years. Trust is earned; however, it can be damaged and rebuilt over time. It's best to resume respectful treatment and allow your adolescent to gradually climb back up the ladder of trust. Begin slowly and cautiously by trusting your teen with small responsibilities, a little at a time. As she shows a higher caliber of trustworthiness, you can depend more on her. It's not an easy process because risk and perseverance are involved. As you work through this process, invoke the Holy Spirit to strengthen you.

REFLECT

Has your teenager broken your trust recently and you find yourself reluctant to give her opportunities to earn it back? With the help of the Holy Spirit, allow your teen to begin that gradual climb back to trustworthiness.

✠ PRAY ✠

Dear Heavenly Father,

Help (name) to develop trustworthiness. Give me the strength I need to continue living with and loving her. It's difficult to do when lies fill my ears and crumble my heart. Fill me with your wellspring of love, Lord. I live to please, honor, and serve you all my days. Amen.

june 11

WEATHERING STORMS

Then he made the disciples get into the boat and precede him to the other side, while he dismissed the crowds....Meanwhile the boat, already a few miles offshore, was being tossed about by the waves, for the wind was against it (Matthew 14:22, 24).

My husband and I flew to Romania to adopt an orphan because we felt God calling us there. The day we arrived a moratorium was placed on all adoptions. We ran out of money, became ill, and the paperwork seemed impossible to complete. I wondered why God called us there with so many obstacles in our path. Did God know how difficult it would be?

Today's verses take place before Jesus walks on water. While this passage typically focuses on Peter's faith or Jesus calming the storm, it's important to note that Jesus sent the disciples across the lake knowing there would be a storm. The apostles didn't know it, but Jesus did; he knows everything.

Jesus never promised my husband and I an easy passage as we followed him to Romania. When we answer God's calling, we won't be spared from the storms of life. In John 15:20, Jesus says, "If they persecuted me, they will also persecute you." Followers of the Lord will not have it easy. But the rewards are worth it.

REFLECT

Maybe God has called you to teach a religion class or volunteer to chaperon your teen's class trip. Whatever endeavor you think God is calling you to do, know that he will never leave you in your time of need. Perhaps you feel like you are in the middle of a storm and question where God is leading you. Remember what Jesus says: "Take courage, it is I; do not be afraid."

✠ PRAY ✠

Dear Heavenly Father,

I will follow you to the ends of the earth,
if that is what you want.
I am yours, dear Lord. Amen.

june 12

LEAVING THE NEST

As an eagle incites its nestlings, hovering over its young, so he spread his wings, took them, bore them upon his pinions
(Deuteronomy 32:11).

Have you watched birds care for their young? The moment the eggs hatch, the parent bird spends practically every waking moment tending to their needs. Then, at precisely the right time, the chicks are nudged out of the nest. It's a part of nature.

Scripture uses a metaphor to reference the deliverance of the Israelites from Egypt and their training in the desert. I fixate on the figure of the parent bird training its inexperienced fledglings for flight exchanged for that of a parent teaching his child to walk, drive, or leave home. Are you trying to teach your teenager to drive or are you preparing your daughter for college? Do you feel like your kid has one foot out the door of your home already? Resembling the birds, it's a part of nature to equip your child with the skills necessary to thrive on her own.

It's physically, mentally, and emotionally exhausting raising a family today. There is so much you need to do. It requires patience and love while you do it. Sometimes it could feel like it is all work and very little fun. Be mindful of maintaining stability in your hectic life. Perhaps you could play a board game after a driving lesson. After researching colleges, maybe you could take a bike ride together or build a bonfire in your back yard to roast marshmallows. Balancing the stressful situations with amusing activities will create a more harmonious atmosphere in your home.

REFLECT

Ensure that your top priority is refueling your family's spirituality. By centering your family life on God, everything else will fall into perfect place, the way God intended.

✠ PRAY ✠

Dear Heavenly Father,

Bring me to your resting place where I can regain my composure in your love and fidelities. Teach me how to be a kinder parent to (name). Fill me with confidence and courage to nudge her out of the nest gently, sweetly, and lovingly. Amen.

june 13

DO AS YOU ARE TOLD

But Samuel said: "Does the Lord delight in burnt offerings and sacrifices as much as in obedience to the Lord's command? Obedience is better than sacrifice, to listen, better than the fat of rams
(1 Samuel 15:22).

Saul attacked and defeated the army, but instead of listening to God's command, Saul brought back the king with his best animals. Saul disobeyed God and then tried to justify his actions. It's imperative to listen to God's orders instead of anything we can do on our own. Like Saul, we might think we know a better way, but we should not depend on our own understanding. We need to do as the Lord instructs. It pleases God each time we listen to him and carry out his task the way he wants it done.

When my daughter was a college freshman, I asked her to study in the library instead of her room, where there were distractions. Some kids living in the dorms party the night away and act surprised when they receive poor grades. It can be maddening to watch your teenager make mistakes.

REFLECT

How do you feel when your teenager doesn't listen to you and does something his own way? It can be frustrating when your kids disregard your guidance. How do you think God feels when we disregard his guidance? Will you raise your teenager God's way or your own way?

✠ PRAY ✠

Dear Heavenly Father,

Open my ears, sweet Lord, so I hear your words of wisdom. Teach me how to discern between your way and my way, and help me to always do the right thing. I am open to your messages, Lord. Speak and I will respond according to your will. Amen.

june 14

FLAG DAY

Grant what is in your heart, fulfill your every plan. May we shout for joy at your victory, raise the banners in the name of our God (Psalm 20:5–6).

This psalm is David's prayer for the kings of Israel. Even men in high positions encounter troubles in one form or another. The prayer assures that God would enable him to go on in his endeavors for the good of the community. The prayer demonstrates confidence in God, with assurance of victory. To honor God, they will unfurl their flag victoriously.

We may not be in the same position as David; however, we can depend on God, just as David did, to be victorious raising teenagers. The battles David encountered were probably more ferocious, with swords, but many parents encounter clashes with their teenagers with words that cut like swords. Have you had brash conflicts or long drawn-out fights with your teen? A popular mantra of the 1960s was, "Make love not war." Try to adhere to that slogan now with your son. A fight could mar your relationship and change it forever. Is it worth it?

REFLECT

If a conversation with your teenager takes a turn for the worse, stop and pray. Ask God to get your discussion back on the right track. Give it to him to resolve his way, the right way, the only way. Sometimes you have to wave a white flag of surrender to the Lord before you can unfurl the victory flag.

✠ PRAY ✠

Dear Heavenly Father,

How glorious is your name, sweet and merciful God on high. Hear my prayer. Listen to my cries of desperation. Lead me to the dwelling place where I can bask in all of your grandeur. Amen.

june 15

FATHER'S DAY

As a father has compassion on his children, so the LORD has compassion on those who fear him. For he knows how we are formed, remembers that we are dust (Psalm 103:13–14).

God frequently compares himself with a father. Our idea of parenthood forms our best conceptions of God. We can relate to the natural affection and tender love of a parent for his child, the desire to care for her needs, and the ability to forgive. God's mercy is woven throughout holy Scripture; it's something we have all experienced at some point in our lives. God the Father teaches his children who have limited knowledge. He comforts them when they're sick and lifts them up when they've fallen. The Lord knows how frail our bodies are and how strained our endurance is. In those moments of weakness, we see and feel God's compassion. The Lord pities those who fear him with reverence.

Do you remember the first time you held your infant, how tiny and precious she was in your arms? That is a snippet of the way God feels about you. Do you remember how you fed your baby and attended to her cries in the middle of the night? That is a fragment of God's love for you. Do you remember how proud you were at your child's first accomplishment? That is similar to how God feels about you when you achieve something worthwhile. Do you remember the time when your teenager forgot to call you and you worried yourself sick? That's a smidgen of the apprehension God felt waiting for you to call out to him. Do you remember how much you missed your daughter when she spent the weekend with a friend? That's a hint of the disparity God felt when you stopped praying because you didn't have time. God loves you.

REFLECT

Close your eyes for a few moments to think about how much you love your child. That is a morsel of the love God has for you.

✠ PRAY ✠

Dear Heavenly Father,

Thank you for being such a kind and merciful Father to me. Thank you for your unwavering love and devotion to me, even when I don't deserve it. I love you, Lord. Amen.

june 16

GOD'S GIFTS

Hallelujah! I will praise the LORD with all my heart in the assembled congregation of the upright. Great are the works of the LORD, studied by all who delight in them. Majestic and glorious is his work, his righteousness endures forever. He won renown for his wondrous deeds; gracious and merciful is the LORD (Psalm 111:1–4).

God reveals himself to us in the pages of the Bible, through creation, and through his glorious works. God's majesty is all around us; all we have to do is open our eyes. Do you ever feel as if you are living with your eyes closed, not paying attention to the miracles of life that God sprinkles through each day? Did you notice the bird's nest full of chicks? Did you notice the wave of the postal carrier or the smile on the neighbor's face? Sometimes we have to take a step back to see God's hand guiding us through the minefield with our teenagers, careful to avoid explosions or outbursts.

If you feel that God is lacking, open the Bible and draw near to him through the stories and truths of his miraculous deeds. Talk to the Lord like you would a friend sitting beside you. Ask him to help you see him working through your life raising your family in his endless stream of affection.

REFLECT

Ponder how God has guided you through this school year with your teenager's class projects, sports, musical, or theatrical endeavors. Where is God in your child's life?

✠ PRAY ✠

Dear Heavenly Father,

Let me feel your presence, Lord, in my tumultuous life.
Wash over me a calmness that is lacking in my life.
Hold me in the hollow of your hand, Lord,
and breathe life back into my weary, dried-up bones.
I need you, Lord, now more than ever before.
I ask this in Jesus' name. Amen.

june 17

LEAD WITH GRACE

Moses, however, said to the LORD, "If you please, my Lord, I have never been eloquent, neither in the past nor now that you have spoken to your servant; but I am slow of speech and tongue." The LORD said to him: Who gives one person speech? Who makes another mute or deaf, seeing or blind? Is it not I, the LORD? Now go, I will assist you in speaking and teach you what you are to say (Exodus 4:10–12).

My daughter's ashen face cracked a nervous smile before she addressed her graduating class in high school. Her left hand slid casually into her pants pocket where she kept her rosary beads. She spoke with eloquence and grace because she remembered today's passage and had faith that God would help her speak. Have you ever asked God to help you speak? Perhaps you needed to talk intelligently to a school official, a therapist, or a counselor. Maybe you needed to address your son's abhorrent behaviors and didn't know how to begin the conversation. Remember that Moses exhibited difficulties speaking, but the Lord assisted him, teaching him what to say.

Moses was a glorious commander, but he didn't possess any leadership qualities. He could have been like you or an unassuming friend. And yet he led the Israelites out of slavery, then served proficiently as a priestly leader. He communicated God's will and prayed for his people. Moses said he wasn't a talented speaker, claiming he was slow of speech and tongue. Nevertheless, God told him he would assist him and teach him what to say. The Lord worked through him hugely on myriad occasions.

REFLECT

Think back to a time God has worked through you. How is God calling you to act right now?

✠ PRAY ✠

Dear Heavenly Father,

Move through me, using me as your earthly vessel to do the work you created me to do. Even if I don't understand it or think I'm capable, I know you will guide and assist me to be successful. You are my Savior and I love you. Amen.

june 18

BAD DECISIONS

Whoever answers before listening, theirs is folly and shame
(Proverbs 18:13).

Have you ever seen a game show on TV where the contestant buzzes in hastily to answer a question before he hears it entirely only to answer incorrectly? He was in such a hurry to win that he ended up losing. Hopefully, the contestant will learn from that bad decision to listen completely or more intently the next time. Is your daughter like that contestant, rushing to decisions without taking time to really hear the problem?

As a parent, it's difficult to stand by and watch your teenager make one bad mistake after another. Sometimes you might be tempted to jump in and fix it because you have the financial means or the knowhow. When you bail your teenager out, what lessons does she learn? Your teen might have much going for her, but she may be just throwing it all away. Why does she make terrible choices with her life when she has so much potential?

Your responsibility is to guide her to a better place. You have the power to influence your teenager's decisions by taking control of yourself, not your teen. You can't make your teenager do something she doesn't want to do. Let your teenager know that you're on her side and that you love and care about her. However, it's also important to tell her you don't like the choices she's making, you won't support those poor decisions, and you will take measures not to enable them. Establish strong, clear boundaries around what you will and won't do for your adolescent. Ask for strength and courage as you hand the situation to God to resolve on his terms.

REFLECT

What do you do when your kid makes a bad choice? Have you found the right balance between love and discipline? The next time your teen makes a bad call, pray for the Holy Spirit to guide your reaction.

✠ PRAY ✠

Dear Heavenly Father,

Please, Lord, help me through this difficult time. Empower me with the ability to think, say, and do the right thing. Help me to steer (name) in the right direction. Light the path and guide each step we take on the journey you planned for us. I trust your marvelous ways, even though I do not understand them. Amen.

june 19

READ YOUR BIBLE

Then we turned and proceeded into the wilderness on the Red Sea road, as the LORD had told me, and circled around the highlands of Seir for a long time. Finally the LORD said to me, you have wandered round these highlands long enough; turn and go north (Deuteronomy 2:1–3).

I don't know how I ever traveled without a GPS. Maps are difficult to interpret, and night driving makes navigating even more challenging. Hearing a pleasant voice say, "turn here" ensures I reach my final destination. If I make a mistake by taking a wrong detour, the GPS "recalculates" and helps me get back on track.

While the GPS supports my driving, holy Scripture encourages and inspires my everyday life. I don't know how I lived without my Bible! When I was a teenager, I didn't depend on the written word, the way I do now. I misinterpreted signs, felt lost in episodes of darkness, derailed by whirls of din and discombobulation. Reading the word of God lifts the veil of confusion from life and empowers me to reach my final destination: heaven.

REFLECT

Have you drifted off course while raising your family? Maybe your teenager has gone astray, and dealing with the pain of that situation has left you in a fog. Whatever is ailing you, start reading your Bible today. Open it randomly and let God direct you to the passages he wants you to discover. In the silence of your heart, listen to the message God wants you to hear. He will never lead you astray.

✠ PRAY ✠

Dear Heavenly Father,

Thank you for being there for me in my darkest hour.
Thank you for comforting me, loving me, and safeguarding me.
I love you. Amen.

june 20

HAVE A HAPPY HEART

The discerning heart seeks knowledge, but the mouth of fools feeds on folly. All the days of the poor are evil, but a good heart is a continual feast (Proverbs 15:14–16).

There are many TV commercials boasting merchandise and goods to ensure a healthy heart. There are food items, diet programs, exercise CDs, and weight-loss books. To be a wise consumer, you have to do research prior to purchasing. Not every product is worth having. Not every promise can be believed. Who and what do you believe makes your heart true, happy, content, and loving?

The simpleton believes whatever, but the wise gives thought to each step she takes. People validate the state of their heart by their attitude toward the divine laws of the kingdom of God. Those who desire righteousness will be content and enlightened with spiritual understanding and wisdom. Therefore, don't be consumed by outer appearances, the latest and greatest products, or things that won't please God. Only concern yourself with matters of the heart because that is what affects the Lord.

How do you maintain a happy heart? It isn't always easy to do, especially with boisterous teenagers coming and going, making demands, and eating you out of house and home. How do you overlook those irritants and manage to be cheerful? Try taking positive measures to obey God's laws because when you do, you'll experience his seal of approval and your heart will feel happy and light, even through tough times.

REFLECT

What challenges are you facing with your teenager today? Give them to God and ask him to replace your fears and worries with love and happiness.

✠ PRAY ✠

Dear Heavenly Father,

Take my weary heart into your mighty hands and mold it into the shape you want it to be: one as light as air, full of smiles and laughter, or somber and serious. Whatever you ask of me today, I am listening to you, Lord. I am here to answer and obey because I love you with every ounce of my being. Amen.

june 21

FIRST DAY OF SUMMER

Learn a lesson from the fig tree. When its branch becomes tender and sprouts leaves, you know that summer is near (Matthew 24:32).

Jesus used the budding fig tree to personify his Second Coming. When it's springtime and the trees sprout new leaves, those signal that summer is near. Jesus says we will have a "guesstimate" of his return. Therefore, we should strive to be prepared as if he will come tomorrow. The first thing we should do is watch for him. Instead of being consumed with accumulating more stuff to complicate our lives, we might want to focus on the pursuit of God's kingdom. If Jesus knocked on your door, would he find your home welcoming or would certain rooms be off limits? If Christ asked you to follow him, would you go? Are you anxious for Jesus' arrival? Watching for his reappearance will allow us to prepare our lives, homes, and families.

Having a Christ-centered home can be challenging with teenagers as they spread their wings seeking freedom and autonomy. Some teenagers have to have the last word when tempers flare, creating an environment of constant agitation. Teens become argumentative and easily riled because they lack control over the new feelings they experience. Some bizarre decisions they make could be due to their brains developing slower than their bodies. The last area of the brain to develop is that which controls impulses, judgment, and decision-making. It's not easy living with uncooperative teenagers, but try to be understanding and supportive as they grow and mature. Keep the lines of communication open even when they are being difficult. Be there to provide sage advice under God's guidance as your teen's identity flourishes.

REFLECT

If Jesus came to your home today, what would he find?

✠ PRAY ✠

Dear Heavenly Father,

Empower me to embrace the encumbrances involved in raising (name). My patience is worn thin as we bicker instead of loving one another. I've made so many sacrifices for this child, Lord, please don't let them be in vain. As you died on the cross for me, Lord, let me learn, compromise, and tolerate so I can be a better parent. I ask this in Jesus' name. Amen.

june 22

BACK TO BASICS

When you sit down to dine with a ruler, mark well the one who is before you; Stick the knife in your gullet if you have a ravenous appetite. Do not desire his delicacies; it is food that deceives. Do not wear yourself out to gain wealth, cease to be worried about it; When your glance flits to it, it is gone! For assuredly it grows wings, like the eagle that flies toward heaven (Proverbs 23:1–6).

The love of money is the root of all evil. Some people hunger more for money than they do for a place in heaven. Paul admonishes this greedy money-craving, equating it to dining with royalty: If we are controlled by our appetite, stick a knife to our throat. Paul implies gluttony leads to greed. He advises not to wear yourself out trying to become rich because wealth doesn't last. Only God lasts. We need to get our priorities in line by remembering that what we do on earth has to help us get to heaven. Buying fancy cars, taking lavish vacations, dining in expensive restaurants, and adorning ourselves in the finest jewelry and clothes will not help us gain favor with the Lord. These things lead to greediness. Everything on this earth is temporary. Our true reward is not here; it's in heaven.

What kind of example are you setting for your teenager? Are you teaching your daughter to be materialistic? If so, change directions now. Consider sorting through your closets and donating clothes to charity, encouraging your teenager to do the same. Take your teen grocery shopping and buy extra canned goods to donate to your local food pantry. Take your teenager to a shelter and serve meals to the less fortunate. These activities will broaden your child's horizons while working purposefully against the flow of greediness en route to heaven.

REFLECT

Is your focus really storing up riches in heaven? Or are you more focused on making sure you live in luxury here on earth? Take a step back and think of what you can do without to clear your way to heaven.

✠ PRAY ✠

Dear Heavenly Father,

Fan the fire of love that burns in my heart for you, dear Lord. Remind me to put my phone down and embrace you in the people I meet at the food pantry. Remind me to feed and comfort them. Remove the greediness from my life and raise (name) to hunger for you in heaven. Amen.

june 23

GOD'S IMMEASURABLE GIFTS

This God who girded me with might, kept my way unerring,
Who made my feet like a deer's, and set me on the heights
(Psalm 18:33–34).

Last spring a doe moseyed in our back yard and gave birth to a fawn. We watched the tiny spotted creature learn to walk and maneuver through our gardens under the watchful eyes of its mother. Instinct drives deer to guide their offspring to ensure their survival in nature. As a mother, I understand this and want to do the same for my own daughters. What I teach them is equivalent to the deer watching her fawn leap quickly from danger.

God gave David unusual swiftness, like a deer's. It was obtained as a gift through the goodness of God, not from anything David had done on his own. Consider how God instructed you to keep your children safe. Maybe you talk repeatedly about the dangers of drugs and alcohol. Maybe you insist on family dinnertime where there is an open forum to discuss topics like feeling secure saying no to premarital sex. As difficult as it is to have such conversations with your kids, it is imperative to arm your teens with as much information as possible, hoping they'll remember your advice if they find themselves in precarious situations.

Not only will God enable you to have the swiftness of a deer, his bounty is limitless when you do his work. Teaching your youngsters right from wrong, ensuring they make it into heaven, and raising moral kids: That's doing God's work. Ask God to provide the tools you need.

REFLECT

The next time you find yourself struggling with the right words to put your teenager at ease and lead him in the right direction, call out to God. He will give you the exact words to say.

✠ PRAY ✠

Dear Heavenly Father,

Fill me up with your kindness, generosity, and love while I raise (name) to honor and cherish you and your miraculous ways. You are the light in my world that shows me the way. Amen.

june 24

ON GOD'S AUTHORITY

But the LORD *answered me, do not say, "I am too young." To whomever I send you, you shall go; whatever I command you, you shall speak. Do not be afraid of them, for I am with you to deliver you—oracle of the* LORD (Jeremiah 1:7–8).

In order for my daughter, Juliana, to be considered to attend Cornell University, the program director required an on-campus interview. I was invited to watch a panel of professors grill her on a variety of topics. She looked so young, and I was afraid for her, but she did very well. That was a lot to ask of a teenager.

I can't imagine how difficult it would have been if Juliana was called to proclaim the coming of God's judgment upon Judah, like Jeremiah was asked to do. This was a new experience for Jeremiah, an inexperienced youth. God assured him that he would be with him. Jeremiah was called to speak on God's ability.

What might God be calling your son to do? Each of us has been called to do something special with our life by playing a particular role as a follower of Jesus Christ. It can be intimidating for us to consider the responsibility we have to other family members of our faith. You will not have to rely on your own abilities when God calls you. He will empower you to achieve whatever his will is, just as he enabled Jeremiah to speak eloquently. What has God called you to do?

REFLECT

Have you adequately presented the option of living a religious life to your son? Regardless of what stage of life he is currently in, if this is God's will, help your teenager to process it and embrace it.

✠ PRAY ✠

Dear Heavenly Father,

You are truly amazing and I feel blessed to be chosen
to do something extraordinary for you.
You are my saving Lord, filling me with empowerment.
I love you, Lord. Amen.

june 25

BE STILL WITH GOD

"Be still and know that I am God!
I am exalted among the nations, exalted on the earth" (Psalm 46:11).

When was the last time you saw your teenager be still during the day? My kids were always going somewhere: band practice, track, friends' homes, movies, or youth group functions at church. Use this time off during the summer to remind your family to slow down and spend time being still emotionally, mentally, and spiritually.

Summertime is a great time to relax. Begin with a new morning ritual, one that includes being still and meditating on the Lord. Establish a quiet corner in your home or get up earlier than usual to read the Bible and contemplate the words you just read. Devote time to saying the rosary or light a candle and talk to Jesus as you might speak with a friend. If you are struggling to pray, ask God to help you with it. The Lord wants to spend time with you; he wants to hear from you. Ask God and he will help you unwind in his presence and open your mind enough to absorb his divine glory.

REFLECT

In the quiet of your heart, you can listen for God to whisper a message to you. Even if you can only spend ten minutes alone with God, don't wait. Do it now! "Be still and know that I am God."

✠ PRAY ✠

Dear Heavenly Father,

Help me to carve out a portion of my day and give it to you in prayer. Help me to relax in your presence and visualize your loving face and kind eyes that I long to gaze into. Be with me, Lord, as I brace for a summer with (name). Let us do your work together. Amen.

june 26

OBEDIENCE

Children, obey your parents [in the Lord], for this is right. "Honor your father and mother." This is the first commandment with a promise, "that it may go well with you and that you may have a long life on earth." Fathers, do not provoke your children to anger, but bring them up with the training and instruction of the Lord (Ephesians 6:1–4).

Just because the Bible tells children to obey their parents doesn't mean teenagers will. There are several different passages that all voice the same message: honor your parents. Yet teenagers butt heads with their parents over almost everything. Teens can develop a Godly relationship with their parents by spending time together. While you might think it's best to give your kid space to grow and mature, this is when your child needs positive role models in her life—that means you!

Plan dinners so everyone participates by making one dish, or have a themed mealtime each Sunday night. Maybe one night could be cowboy night where bandanas are used for napkins. You could cook hot dogs on sticks over a bonfire in your back yard. Bonfires provide a great platform for exchanging stories about your week. It's easier for kids to open up about things that have been bothering them when they're making s'mores in the back yard. Instead of telling ghost stories around the bonfire, could you tell stories from the Bible? You could make all Sunday night meals this way during the summer. It can be fun to get the entire family involved in planning and preparations. And it doesn't cost much besides creativity and time.

REFLECT

Spending quality time with your teenager is an investment in her future. How will you make time for your teen today?

✠ PRAY ✠

Dear Heavenly Father,

Quell the fears that run through my home, sweet and merciful Lord. Turn my house from one filled with tension to one filled with tranquility and fun times. Put ideas in my head that will pique their interest so we can enjoy the time we have left together. Thank you, Lord, for your comfort and love during this difficult stage of transitions. Amen.

june 27

COME OUT OF THE DARKNESS

I kept faith, even when I said, "I am greatly afflicted!" (Psalm 116:10).

My mother taught me to call out to God in times of trouble. She said, "In every dark situation, Jesus always provides a way out; keep searching for it." Maybe a door closed in my face and that shock prevented me from realizing I could escape by climbing out a window. Or maybe God wants me to spend a little time in that darkness talking to him in the quiet of my heart. The key is to trust in the Lord and his ways. We have to do whatever God desires even if we don't like it. God knows what's best!

Do you feel trapped in a dark situation with your teenager and you can't see a way out? Sometimes when you are lost, you should stop and stand still. God knows where you are. Call out to him and he will rescue you. Especially when you are troubled, keep your faith and tell God what is causing you pain. Maybe your teenager failed a class or had a poor report card and you are worried that he will not be accepted into college. Give that problem to God. Worrying about it will not do you any good. However, calling out to God, knowing he will help you, will be good.

REFLECT

Think about all your son has on his plate right now, trying to decide who he is and who he wants to be. Most adults ask kids what they want to be when they grow up; most kids don't have a clue. That uncertainty must drive them crazy. Consider talking to your teen about what is causing his discouragement and then pray as a family. Become united on one front under God.

✠ PRAY ✠

Dear Heavenly Father,

Lift the darkness that has shrouded (name).
Bring our family into your brilliant light
and guide us all to the place you mean for us to be.
Please Lord, guide our steps as we take a new path,
trusting in you during each phase of our life journey. Amen.

june 28

OVERCOMING DISCOURAGEMENT

I went away full, but the Lord has brought me back empty. Why should you call me 'Sweet,' since the Lord has brought me to trial, and the Almighty has pronounced evil sentence on me" (Ruth 1:21).

Have you ever felt like Naomi? God brought great loss into her life. She blames God for her difficulties, even though she acknowledges that he is behind all of the events of her life. If God deals terribly with you, what can you do about it? If God has tormented you, will you turn to him for healing? If God has shut the door, will you call out to him to open it?

Don't live in fear that God will make your life miserable. We all go through times of extreme sorrow and suffering. What eases the fear is believing in God's benevolent plan. Some people believe God has to whip us into shape in order for us to get into heaven. God can bring good out of even the worst suffering, but we have to be willing to accept what he gives us and allow him to restore us to a better state.

When my daughter was very ill, I blamed God for it. After mourning the loss of her health, I turned back to God, pleading with him to make my child well. He not only restored her health but he also restored my faith tenfold.

REFLECT

When something unfortunate happens to your teen, it's natural to ask God, "Why?" Don't let that be the end of your conversation with God, call out to God for help and ask him to restore your faith and hope in him. God will not abandon you in your time of need.

✠ PRAY ✠

Dear Heavenly Father,

I come to you grieving over my sins and flaws.
Heal me, Lord. I am empty, Lord, and long for you
to nourish me with your word, love, and mercy. Amen.

june 29

MISBEHAVE

For the fool speaks folly, his heart plans evil: Godless actions, perverse speech against the LORD, letting the hungry go empty and the thirsty without drink. The deceits of the deceiver are evil, he plans devious schemes: To ruin the poor with lies, and the needy when they plead their case (Isaiah 32:6–7).

Mom always said, "A misbehaving child is a discouraged child." If one of my daughters misbehaved, I looked for her discouragement and attempted to help. Whenever they misbehaved, our family bond crumbled. To fortify ties and reestablish a feeling of connectedness, remind your kids that they are loved unconditionally. Their actions might be appalling, but parental love will endure. When kids feel better, they have a tendency to do better.

Listen to your son and validate his feelings. Perhaps you could say something like, "It must hurt terribly to have classmates who shun you." Talk to your teenager about the consequences of his actions and discuss the lessons he learned from it. You might say, "Now that you spent your lunch money on new shoes, how will you eat this week?" Perhaps you could say, "I'm wondering how you feel about it or what you hoped to accomplish" to springboard your conversation into a teaching moment without being condescending, hurtful, or accusatory.

If you are upset, take time to cool off. Go for a walk and talk to God. Ask the Holy Spirit to enlighten you. Ask your guardian angel to uplift you. By taking a break, you are less likely to say something you'll regret.

REFLECT

You might need to reaffirm your love for your teenager, regardless of what he did. Maybe your teen caused unjustified attention, was guilty of a mistaken influence, or supposed incompetence. Think back to when you were a teenager and you disappointed your parents. Didn't it hurt to know you were a disappointment to them?

✠ PRAY ✠

Dear Heavenly Father,

Help me, Lord, to be the best possible parent I can be today. Amen.

june 30

UNFATHOMABLE BLESSINGS

For this reason I kneel before the Father, from whom every family in heaven and on earth is named, that he may grant you in accord with the riches of his glory to be strengthened with power through his Spirit in the inner self, and that Christ may dwell in your hearts through faith; that you, rooted and grounded in love, may have strength to comprehend with all the holy ones what is the breadth and length and height and depth, and to know the love of Christ that surpasses knowledge, so that you may be filled with all the fullness of God (Ephesians 3:14–19).

This lovely prayer inspires us to pray similarly because the word is spread in vain unless God renders it productive, prolific, and dynamic. Everything we do on earth will be for naught except those actions the Lord blesses. Paul asks God to provide us with the power of the Holy Spirit to be strong within. Paul prays that Jesus resides in us through our faith and with our foundation in his rich and abundant love, even though it cannot be fully known. If Christ's laws are written on our hearts, then Christ dwells there, because where his spirit dwells, he dwells also.

As you begin a new summer routine with your teenager, whether it is around a day camp, part-time jobs, or summer school, guide her with God in your heart. Maybe you have trepidations about your daughter accepting the responsibilities that go hand in hand with these activities, but know that, with God's blessings, you can bask in the glory of his goodness even though you won't be able to comprehend it all. Trust in God.

REFLECT

What constant worries do you have about your teen? Offer that worry up to God today and pray that he finds a way to bless your teen's actions.

✠ PRAY ✠

Dear Heavenly Father,

Thank you for filling me with your limitless love.
With you in my heart, I can do your work, whatever it is.
Guide me, Lord, as I steer (name) through the summer months.
Let her work be fruitful and according to your plan.
I love you, Lord, with my heart and soul. Amen.

july 1

WE'RE SPECIAL

For we are his handiwork, created in Christ Jesus for the good works that God has prepared in advance, that we should live in them (Ephesians 2:10).

My dad took up painting later in life. We enjoyed watching the ideas that formed in his mind come to life on canvas. He was inspired by nature: the dew on early-morning grass, the rustling foliage on the trees, flowers that have birds and bees buzzing around them, and awesome sunrises and sunsets. Even though Dad says he's just an ordinary guy, his talents make him exceptional.

This passage reminds us that we are God's handiwork; we are dearly loved children of God. The creator of heaven and earth sees us as someone special; someone to be cherished. God doesn't think we are ordinary or boring. Contemplate all that God has given you: a family to take care of, a job, talents and skills, time to grow or reevaluate your life dreams. God has given you the endurance and fortitude to raise a teenager! When your son leaves your home to begin the next stage of life, God has something better in store for you, too. In time he will reveal that plan to you. Trust that he loves you, and there is no one else like you who can do what God calls you to do. You are special, God's chosen one.

REFLECT

Do you have talents that make you stand out as someone special, or do you feel like every other guy? Maybe the dull errands of your day make you feel stale or boring, comparing yourself to people who appear to have a more exciting life. Maybe you are unhappy with the person you are becoming or miss the personality you had before becoming a parent. Do you feel lost in the shuffle of the daily grind?

✠ PRAY ✠

Dear Heavenly Father,

Thank you for making me unique and giving me a purpose. Help me to feel useful when I'm caught up in the day-to-day and let me rejoice in your love and plan for my life. I trust you, Lord. Amen.

july 2

PRAISE

While he was still speaking, behold, a bright cloud cast a shadow over them, then from the cloud came a voice that said, "This is my beloved Son, with whom I am well pleased; listen to him" (Matthew 17:6).

As kids grow and develop their interests and ideas, they must learn how to express them without offending people. And they have to do this with an underdeveloped brain with an adult body image. This is the time when some teenagers think they know it all.

In the midst of all this turmoil, when was the last time you called your daughter beloved. When was the last time you told your teen you were pleased with her? People like to be praised; try complimenting your kid even when it's hard. Maybe your teenager has been acting out recently and you find it challenging to flatter her. Consider what Jesus would say to her now. Jesus might say, "I love you" or "I like your smile." Find something positive to say even if it might seem silly. It might mean the world to your kid.

REFLECT

Imagine your boss bringing you in front of your coworkers and informing everyone that you are the favorite worker, that the boss is thrilled with your abilities, and that everyone should listen to you. How would that make you feel? Try to do that very thing for your teenager today.

✠ PRAY ✠

Dear Heavenly Father,

Thank you for providing pleasing examples for me to follow.
Thank you for enabling me to search (name)'s soul to praise.
Thank you for the reminders to tell (name) how much I love her, and thank you, Lord, for bringing this child into my life.
Help me to raise her into a mature, respectable adult. Amen.

july 3

NIX IMMORALITY

I wrote you in my letter not to associate with immoral people, not at all referring to the immoral of this world or the greedy and robbers or idolaters; for you would then have to leave the world. But I now write to you not to associate with anyone named a brother, if he is immoral, greedy, an idolater, a slanderer, a drunkard, or a robber, not even to eat with such a person (1 Corinthians 5:9–11).

When my daughter ran cross-country in high school, she would finish her workouts covered in mud. I lined the car seats with a plastic shower curtain so dirt wouldn't contaminate the car. Like today's passage denotes, it's important to have a good barrier between you and filth. It's easy to keep the dirt and grime out of our lives, but it's not as easy to build a barrier between our families and the contamination of immorality, greediness, drunkenness, and any number of other sinful behaviors.

Paul was struggling with this issue at Corinth. Similarly, we might fear that our desire to be Christlike might wane if we associate with immoral unbelievers. Would their immorality rub off on us or could we "catch it" like a cold? On my daughter's school bus, a girl was bullied by an upperclassman. It didn't take long for other kids to join in. Instead of helping this girl, classmates turned against her. In some cases, we can be controlled by the fear of being considered weak, different, or uncool. When this happens, we need to remember to be a good example for those around us. My daughter told the bus driver about the bad behavior and the driver immediately intervened.

REFLECT

We need to be a shining light on an otherwise darkened path. We can do this by acting like Jesus even when it isn't popular to do so. Let the barrier between you and filth be your Christlike behavior.

✠ PRAY ✠

Dear Heavenly Father,

Empower me with fortitude to stand up against the bullies of the world, especially for those who cannot do it themselves. Shield me from harm as I walk the path you have chosen for me. I trust you, Lord. You are the Savior of the world. Amen.

july 4

GOD WILL REDEEM YOU

Therefore, say to the Israelites: I am the LORD. I will free you from the burdens of the Egyptians and will deliver you from heir slavery. I will redeem you by my outstretched arm and with mighty acts of judgment (Exodus 6:6).

The Israelites' work was physically exhausting. Just as God promised to bring the Israelites out from the burdens of the Egyptians, Jesus promises to provide rest from the mental and emotional encumbrances of life.

Like God promised to the Israelites, he will liberate you with an outstretched and judicial arm; he will save you. What unfair act have you had to endure recently? Maybe your teen failed her road test or was denied a job. Maybe she is experiencing an unfair boss and navigating the work place. Or is your teen's perspective on life unrealistic? Perhaps your daughter is holding on to the feeling of injustice a lot lately, feeling like a victim more frequently. Is she using it to manipulate people to get what she wants? Let your teen know that you support her to resolve her difficulties. Being victimized won't define them. Sometimes life isn't fair, but it's still good. Help your teen to move on while trusting in God. Whatever the problems are, have faith that God is reaching out to you; take his hand, hold on, and never let go.

REFLECT

What have been your most troubling afflictions raising your teenager? Maybe you both can't come to an agreement on a particular topic. It doesn't have to be all or nothing. Try to compromise with your teenager. Draft a list of possible scenarios and rate their feasibility on a scale of one to ten. Compare your list to your daughter's to try to resolve your differences a different way.

✠ PRAY ✠

Dear Heavenly Father,

Help me through this difficulty, Lord.
I'm swamped with problems that have been coming at me,
one right after another and I feel like I am drowning.
Reach out to me, Lord, and pluck me from the
raging waters that have been carrying me away.
Let me rest in your loving embrace today and always. Amen.

july 5

GRATITUDE PERPETUATES GENEROSITY

At that, the servant fell down, did him homage, and said, 'Be patient with me, and I will pay you back in full.' Moved with compassion the master of that servant let him go and forgave him the loan. When that servant had left, he found one of his fellow servants who owed him a much smaller amount. He seized him and started to choke him, demanding, 'Pay back what you owe' (Matthew 18:26–28).

Stories can work on a deeper level if we let them, which is true in this example. I appreciated this parable when I was raising teenagers because kids have a tendency to be ungrateful. In this case, the servant was shown mercy and an enormous debt was excused. However, when the servant was owed a small amount by a friend, he showed no mercy whatsoever. Sometimes teenagers, like the servant, just don't get it.

Whenever I buy lottery tickets, I remind friends that I'll share the winnings because gratitude perpetuates generosity. I would be extremely grateful to win and want to spread the joy around. Joy is better when it's shared. If someone owed me a few dollars but I already had a million, I would let the debt go. When there is ingratitude, stinginess often follows, like the servant who wanted to choke his friend for a few bucks.

God's way is to be all-giving and merciful, like the king who forgave his servant's huge debt. But we can reset that pristine standard by living ungraciously despite the gifts God bestows on us, and the new standard of ungraciousness might not work in our favor.

REFLECT

If your teenager demonstrates signs of thanklessness, remind him that his standard of living can be reset, which might not be to his liking. It might take a while before he gets it, but be patient. Kids learn at a different pace, and remember that love is patient and kind.

✠ PRAY ✠

Dear Heavenly Father,

Help (name) to appreciate your bounty and blessings. Enable me to teach mercy and sympathy. Parenting is a difficult job; help me to do it in your divine grace. I ask this in Jesus' name. Amen.

july 6

GOD MAKES THE RULES

And on receiving it they grumbled against the landowner, saying, 'These last ones worked only one hour, and you have made them equal to us, who bore the day's burden and the heat.'..."Am I not free to do as I wish with my own money? Are you envious because I am generous? Thus, the last will be first, and the first will be last" (Matthew 20:11–12, 15–16).

Do you give your kids an allowance? If so, how do you determine how much is allotted for the chores you want done? It's not easy to be fair and equitable. Perhaps you are more like the landowner in this parable: You are the boss, therefore you make the rules and what you say goes. It's challenging to teach your kids responsibility, taking ownership of problems and resolving them in the face of adversity and injustice. But sometimes it's necessary to simply trust.

This parable used to upset me when I considered working more than my neighbor but reaping the same benefits: getting into heaven. God is the supreme ruler and what he says goes regardless of what I may think about his generosity and rules. This reading is more reasonable when I stop cogitating about doing more grueling work in the heat of the day than my neighbor and shift my focus. I imagine a long line of people aching to enter the best party of the century. Everyone is dressed in their finest; all can hear the music and roar of laughter inside. I am one of the first ones inside! I am able to spend the most time indulging in the best food and the finest libations. I am having the time of my life at this party because I am with God in heaven. Wouldn't you want all people to experience that kind of joy, no matter how long they'd been waiting in line?

REFLECT

The chores we do on earth are actually done for our master in heaven, so they should bring us immense pleasure. When I hand a homeless man a granola bar, I am really handing it to Jesus. When I share my linens and towels with refugee families, I am sharing them with Jesus. What chores do you do for your master?

✠ PRAY ✠

Dear Heavenly Father,

When something gives me grief, enable me to see it differently so I understand it more clearly. Let me see you in everything I do. Amen.

july 7

BE PERSISTENT

And he said to them, "Suppose one of you has a friend to whom he goes at midnight and says, 'Friend, lend me three loaves of bread, for a friend of mine has arrived at my house from a journey and I have nothing to offer him,' and he says in reply from within, 'Do not bother me; the door has already been locked and my children and I are already in bed. I cannot get up to give you anything.' I tell you, if he does not get up to give him the loaves because of their friendship, he will get up to give him whatever he needs because of his persistence (Luke 11:5–8).

I have exceptionally nice neighbors. I could wake them at any hour and they would give me what I need. However, in life we sometimes have to make several requests in order to get what we want, especially if we are asking our teenager for something. How many times do I have to ask for their rooms to be straightened? How many times do I have to remind them to vacuum before company comes? How many times do you need to ask your teen to do something before it gets done? For some, persistence pays.

Some believe that God doesn't have to be asked for blessings. God is generous, therefore he will provide. Others believe that the best blessings are reserved for those who ask persistently. God is aware of our needs and wants because he knows everything about us. He knows every word we are going to say before it comes out of our mouths! The reason we ask is because asking is an affirmation of our trust in God.

REFLECT

Is there something you've been hoping God would do in the life of your teen? Pray about it today, and then again tomorrow, and then again after that....

✠ PRAY ✠

Dear Heavenly Father,

Thank you for always listening to me and for considering my constant requests. If it is your will, dear Lord, please grant them. If it is not good for me, give me the strength to carry this burden until the time is right for me to let it go. Keep me strong and bless me as I wait. I love you. Amen.

july 8

WHO IS YOUR IDOL?

He does not think clearly; he lacks the wit and knowledge to say, "Half the wood I burned in the fire, on its embers I baked bread, I roasted meat and ate. Shall I turn the rest into an abomination? Shall I worship a block of wood?" (Isaiah 44:19).

When I was a teenager, I hung posters on my bedroom wall of my favorite singers: David Cassidy, Bobby Sherman, and Donny Osmond. I played their records so many times I nearly wore them out. I wrote fan letters, read everything about them, and hoped to see them live in concert. I didn't spend that much time getting to know Jesus. In fact, I never opened the Bible. I belonged to a youth group at church and attended Mass with my family each Sunday, and I believed that was enough.

In today's passage, ludicrous worship is clear from God's standpoint. It's crazy that one side of a log is holy and the other side is not. Teen idols find their way into our homes through television, newspapers, magazines, friends, and school. They slip easily into every culture. View your daughter's heroes from another vantage point. Do you want her adoring athletes or performers? Try this. Encourage God's point of view that the Scripture sanctions. These idols are nothing compared to God.

REFLECT

What do you do to cultivate and enrich your teenager's spirituality? Could you encourage your family to do more to get to know Christ and truly experience his kindness, mercy, love? What if your family listened to Christian music, religious hymns, and chanting? Consider hanging religious paintings, artwork, or statuary in your home. Watch religious television stations, read religious books and the Bible, and watch movies about saints. Do service projects together and pray as a family.

✠ PRAY ✠

Dear Heavenly Father,

You are my light and my salvation.
You are the lift in my step, the smile on my face,
the beating of my heart. Help me to convey your magnificence
to (name) so she might bask in your glory. Amen.

july 9

BE AT PEACE

Finally, brothers, rejoice. Mend your ways, encourage one another, agree with one another, live in peace, and the God of love and peace will be with you. Greet one another with a holy kiss. All the holy ones greet you. The grace of the Lord Jesus Christ and the love of God and the fellowship of the Holy Spirit be with all of you (2 Corinthians 13:11–13).

While kids love vacation away from school, parents get worn down from their bickering. Perhaps you have been away on a vacation and too much time together in close proximity has been stressful. Summers offer kids time to get into trouble while they try to overcome boredom by getting into mischief with friends. Sometimes kids get on each other's nerves over the summer. Do your teenagers act out over the summer months more than at any other time of year?

In today's passage, Paul's message is one of harmony. He says to mend your ways. How will you seek self-improvement and see eye to eye with your teenager? How can you be a better parent? Consider hugging your kid more often. Say, "I love you," frequently. Smile and tell him what you love about him. Pray over him. Tell your kid when you make a mistake, apologize, and make a plan not to repeat it. Tell your kid you are not perfect and are trying to improve. Give your kid room to grow and blossom into the adult God intends him to be, not a clone of you.

REFLECT

Work to exterminate contention and strife in your heart and home life. Choose to follow and pursue peace because when you do, God will be with you. Cultivate a peaceful disposition and avoid saying or doing anything you know will be exasperating. When your family loves each other, you can expect that the God of love will be with you. God delights in the love his people show each other.

✠ PRAY ✠

Dear Heavenly Father,

Break down the walls I have been building around myself throughout the summer. Remind me that the Holy Spirit dwells within (name), and when I speak to him, I am speaking to you. Let me show reverence, kindness, and love to my teenager, even though he drives me crazy sometimes. Give me strength, Lord. I ask this in Jesus' name. Amen.

july 10

CHILDREN OF GOD

When I was a child, I used to talk as a child, think as a child, reason as a child; when I became a man, I put aside childish things (1 Corinthians 13:11).

Raising teenagers can be wearisome because we sometimes still think of them as helpless children. Yet they are like miniature adults with a body that is constantly changing, growing, and maturing. Their façade resembles an adult, but their brain is underdeveloped and affected with wild hormonal surges. Teenagers can feel perplexed by unpredictable and unstable behaviors, emotions that strike like lightning from out of nowhere.

Today's passage reminds us that even though we are adults, with well-balanced brains and mature emotions, the knowledge we have now compared to what we will have in heaven is like comparing our knowledge of the world with our teen's. The future state of sanctity is as far beyond the semblance of perfection that can be attained in this world, as our adult state of Christianity is above our infancy.

We are all children of God trying to do our best while we are on earth. Therefore, it's wise to cut some slack to our teenagers when they misbehave or are out of line. Try to be merciful to them as God is to us. After practicing forgiveness, strive to have your teen learn from it, then let it go and move on.

REFLECT

Consider all that your teenager is going through at this point in her life. As demanding as it is to parent a teen, it is equally bewildering to be a teenager. The next time you consider speaking condescendingly or treating your daughter contemptuously, remember that compared to the intelligence of heaven, your earthly abilities leave much to be desired.

✠ PRAY ✠

Dear Heavenly Father,

Surround me with your infinite stream of wisdom to enlighten me while I raise (name). Give me the grace to carry on through rough patches. Shine your brilliant light into the dark corners of my life and enable me to do your work, even if it is something I don't think I have the capabilities to do. With you, I can do anything. Amen.

july 11

FILL YOUR HEART WITH LOVE

Also from arrogant ones restrain your servant; let them never control me. Then shall I be blameless, innocent of grave sin (Psalm 19:14).

Nutritionists believe you are what you eat. If you constantly fill up with junk food, your health will suffer. Similarly, when you put poor-quality fuel in your car, it might not drive the way you want it to. If you surround yourself with sin, corruption, and immorality, negativity will seep from your heart, permeating everything else in your life. As a parent, I wanted my kids to eat right, be well-rested, hydrated, get exercise, and incorporate prayer into everyday life. Not only do teenagers need to be physically fit, they need to be spiritually strong, too.

If your teenager sees you gossiping with neighbors and friends, using foul language, or treating service workers rudely, he will mimic those undesirable behaviors. Change your ways now. Meditate on the Lord; fill your heart with peacefulness and love for everyone, not just a select few. If you find yourself dwelling on unkind thoughts toward others, ask God to replace them with goodness. Remember today's verse throughout the week if your thoughts and actions are unsatisfactory to God.

REFLECT

The psalmist declares that what you say originates from your heart. Therefore, make an effort to surround your kids with all that is good, pure, and just. Fill their hearts with prayers, songs of praise, and quiet meditations for the Lord. Keep them away from influences who cut class, speak disrespectfully to teachers, use bad language, or bully unpopular kids at school.

✠ PRAY ✠

Dear Heavenly Father,

If the words that form in my head and heart are not from you,
remove them from me. Fill me with loving thoughts of you.
Guide me on the right path and safeguard my every step.
Father, I only want to walk in your light. Amen.

july 12

CALL OUT TO GOD

But the Lord sent a great fish to swallow Jonah, and he remained in the belly of the fish three days and three nights. Jonah prayed to the Lord, his God, from the belly of the fish: Out of my distress I called to the Lord, and he answered me; From the womb of Sheol I cried for help, and you heard my voice (Jonah 2:1–3).

Do you have a teenager who never listens to you or refuses to take your advice? Then, when she's in a hot mess, she calls you for help. When the phone rings, do you think, "What is it now?" It's not that you don't like helping people, but it's problematic when your kids constantly make poor decisions. When your teenager brings a problem onto herself, do you bail her out, hoping eventually she will wise up, or do you let her resolve it? Do you feel resentful when your teenager's mistakes impact your quality of life?

Jonah cried out to God in a distress that he caused himself. If Jonah had done what God asked of him, he wouldn't have gotten stuck in the belly of a large fish. Instead of God allowing Jonah to work out his problem, after God heard the man's plea, he answered. God bailed him out! Isn't it marvelous that God will answer our prayers regardless of how badly we've behaved? If God can forgive your kid's mistakes, can you be more like God in your own reaction?

REFLECT

When was the last time you messed up? God is never too angry to answer your prayers, pardon your sins, and point you in the right direction. God always makes room for you. When he hears your cries, he will come. You might not like his response, but he will give one, so be open to it.

✠ PRAY ✠

Dear Heavenly Father,

Thank you, Lord, for your infinite stream of graciousness in answering my prayers. Thank you for hearing my cries, scooping me up in the hollow of your hand, and safekeeping me night and day. Thank you for your steadfast love and affection, even when I don't deserve it. I love you, Lord, my Savior and my way. Amen.

july 13

MORAL COMPASS

Blessed is the man who does not walk in the counsel of the wicked, nor stand in the way of sinners, nor sit in company with scoffers (Psalm 1:1).

My daughters told me that a "friend" jumped lines at Disney World, believing it wasn't a big deal. He didn't have a moral compass and without it he could do whatever he wanted without worry or concern for others' feelings. Shortly thereafter, they avoided this boy. It isn't easy to take a stand and watch "friends" go astray as you dodge the counsel of the wicked. Has your son questioned the morals of friends? Has something happened recently that has you concerned about your kid's friends' scruples? These are the people David warns us about in Psalm 1:1.

Our spiritual life can be fluid and ever-changing, flowing in and out, back and forth, figuratively and literally. The key is making God the focal point of life, with everything revolving around the criticality of God's word, making it the core of life. There are two ways we can live. God wants us to live in a state of blessedness, happiness, and fruitfulness. The other way brings damnation, unhappiness, and judgment. God allows us to choose which way we want to live. While blessedness is the optimal choice, it requires obeying the conditions of faith.

REFLECT

Encourage your teen not to idolize those with questionable morals because they can be influenced by those they look up to. Instead of looking up to immoral athletes and singers, urge your kid to admire saints and those who adore the Lord.

✠ PRAY ✠

Dear Father in Heaven,

Let me rejoice and sing sweet praises to you,
Lord God almighty. You alone I adore and look up to.
Grant with favor on my family your blessings of goodness.
Thank you from the bottom of my heart for loving me. Amen.

july 14

GOOD SHEPHERD

Amen, amen, I say to you, whoever does not enter a sheepfold through the gate but climbs over elsewhere is a thief and a robber. But whoever enters through the gate is the shepherd of the sheep. The gatekeeper opens it for him, and the sheep hear his voice, as he calls his own sheep by name and leads them out. When he has driven out all his own, he walks ahead of them, and the sheep follow him, because they recognize his voice (John 10:1–4).

The shepherd in this passage put his life on the line for the flock he safeguarded, especially at night where he would corral the skittish creatures in a crude pen with only one way in or out. The shepherd called each sheep by name, and they entered through the gate and settled down securely for the night. No one could bypass the shepherd because he slept at the gate, and the sheep wouldn't follow a thief because they didn't know his voice. Jesus is our shepherd and we, the sheep, are the true believers who belong to him. We know him, we recognize his voice, and we follow only him when he calls our name. He knows our name!

Read these verses again, substituting your name for the shepherd watching over your teenager, calling her by name. Don't you safeguard your children in a similar fashion, leading them, guiding them, protecting them from harm? Think about the places you have led your kids, the things you have taught them, how they identify you by the sound of your voice. Remember that Jesus does the same for you and your daughter. He watches over you and your teenager and wouldn't allow harm to fall upon either of you. Rest assured that Jesus is the good shepherd watching over his flock night and day.

REFLECT

If Jesus called you, would you know his voice and follow him, or do you need to spend some time getting to know your shepherd again?

✠ PRAY ✠

Dear Heavenly Father,

Thank you for safeguarding my family and me.
Thank you for the intimacy we share.
Thank you for making me feel special
and for the closeness you provide each day.
You are my saving Lord and I adore you. Amen.

july 15

REJOICE IN PERSEVERANCE

Now Jesus loved Martha and her sister and Lazarus. So when he heard that he was ill, he remained for two days in the place where he was. Then after this he said to his disciples, "Let us go back to Judea" (John 11:5–7).

Why would Jesus wait two days before responding to Lazarus? Maybe to teach Martha and Mary that he will respond, just not in the way they were expecting. Sometimes we get frustrated when we cry out to God and then have to wait for him to answer our prayers. Martha and Mary only had to wait two days, but it must have felt like an eternity to them. When we wait for God to respond to us, he is not just twiddling his thumbs; he is teaching us patience and perseverance and strengthening our faith in him.

The next time you find yourself in a waiting phase, cleanse yourself of negativity and dwell only on the goodness of the Lord. Fill your heart with all that is good, positive, and loving. Remember that God will always answer you, even though you might not like the time you have to wait or you might not like the answer he gives. It's vital to remember that God knows what is best for us. Focus on living your life God's way. God will never lead you astray, just as you would never lead your son astray.

REFLECT

Think about the last time you were exasperated waiting for a doctor to return your phone call, or perhaps you were waiting for your teenager to call you to say he arrived someplace safely. Perhaps you called out to God and were impatient waiting for him to help you through a particular difficulty. What did God teach you in those situations?

✠ PRAY ✠

Dear Heavenly Father,

Thank you for the reminder to be patient while I wait for you, just as Mary and Martha waited. And what a glorious miracle you gave them! Thank you, sweet Jesus, for helping me cope and teaching me to wait to receive your grandeur. I truly love you! Amen.

july 16

CALL ON GOD

In danger I called on the LORD; the LORD answered me and set me free. The LORD is with me; I am not afraid; what can mortals do against me? The LORD is with me as my helper; I shall look in triumph on my foes. Better to take refuge in the LORD than to put one's trust in mortals (Psalm 118:5–8).

After spending an exhausting day walking the streets of New York City, I inadvertently guided my daughters onto the wrong bus. It was late at night and we were lost in a strange section of town. We got off the wrong bus and began to pray that the right one would show up quickly so we would get back to the security of our hotel. After bombarding heaven with prayer, God immediately rescued us by sending the right bus to ensure our safety.

What distressing situation have you recently found yourself in? Perhaps your teenager attended a party with drugs and alcohol. Did she experiment with them and are you beside yourself because of it? Did your daughter have an accident of some sort and you are struggling to sort it out? Whatever grief you are grappling with, give it to God and trust that he will send help. God's ears are always in tune with the sound of your voice; he'll hear your cries and answer. His watchful eyes are always on you. Trust in God; he will rescue you.

The Lord is bigger than any problem you could possibly give to him. He is mightier than any fear you could have. God is smarter than any person working against you. God is larger than life; he is the perfect one to seek in your time of need.

REFLECT

Think back to other situations God helped you through. Use that for impetus to continuing to lean on him with each problem that weighs you down.

✠ PRAY ✠

Dear Heavenly Father,

Thank you for being there for me when times become too difficult. Thank you for helping me with the new problem (name) has brought into my life. Help keep us grounded through this difficulty so we can resolve it in your tender mercy and love. I ask this in Jesus' name. Amen.

july 17

A GIFT OF PEACE

Peace I leave with you; my peace I give to you.
Not as the world gives do I give it to you.
Do not let your hearts be troubled or afraid (John 14:27).

As Jesus was preparing to return to his Father in heaven, he said these words to remind us that he filled our hearts with peace. What a marvelous gift! Our world is filled with disparity at every turn, including terrorism, deadly diseases, drugs, violence in schools, and gangs. When our world is rocked by such things, it disturbs our harmony as anxiety seeps in. Jesus gave us a tool to help us through it: peace, the healing balm for life's discord.

Jesus told us that we will encounter trials and tribulations on earth, and he will walk beside us as we plod through. Sometimes when your child acts out, it causes tension between you and your spouse. If this should happen, remember not to let the discontentment with your son spoil the love you have with your partner. Safeguard your marriage by getting on the same team as your spouse to combat the troubles with your teenager. Two heads are better than one. Work prayerfully and consciously to devise sound strategies that will bring tranquility back into your home. When you feel stressed, join hands with your spouse and pray together to restore the love and harmony you once shared and enjoyed.

REFLECT

What is disturbing the peace in your home? Do you and your spouse agree on the best methods to raise your teenager, or do you have different philosophies that create conflict between you?

✠ PRAY ✠

Dear Heavenly Father,

Permeate me with your peacefulness to keep my family on track. Peel away the layers of worry, discontentment, and stress so I can focus on what's really important: you. Let me exemplify your kindness and compassion as I raise (name) in a loving, stable home. Keep me strong, Lord. This job is difficult and at times I feel so frail. Build me up, Lord, so I can spend every day of my life doing all that is right and good according to your plan. Amen.

july 18

WORK FOR THE LORD

I want you to insist on these points, that those who have believed in God be careful to devote themselves to good works; these are excellent and beneficial to others (Titus 3:8).

My first job as a teenager was working part time in the candy department of a high-end department store. I loved being surrounded by sweets because I frequently sampled them. Your job doesn't have to define you, but your life's employment should be enjoyable because you spend so much time doing it. How might this apply to your teenager who doesn't know what to do and might possibly take any job offered in a poor economy regardless of whether it is enjoyable? What job could your teenager do?

Many teens start out earning money by babysitting, doing yard work, caring for pets, or other odd jobs. A job teaches kids how to develop a solid work ethic while learning to budget their money. Consider how your teenager could seek opportunities for doing good works influenced by love and gratitude. Maybe your adolescent could hold a garage sale by selling items from your home or organize a neighborhood garage sale and donate a portion of the profits to worthy charities. Perhaps your teen could clean out the closets and donate duplicate or superfluous items to the needy. Could you ask your teenager to clean out the garage or basement of an elderly neighbor or her grandparents?

REFLECT

Whether your teen works for intrinsic rewards or cash, try to ensure her heart is in each project. A local Catholic Charities might have opportunities for your teenager to teach refugees how to read and write, or perhaps she could read stories to underprivileged children at libraries. Doing good deeds by participating in activities like those held by Habitat for Humanity to build houses or Big Brother/Big Sister programs are worthwhile. Encourage your kid to send packages to American soldiers serving overseas.

✠ PRAY ✠

Dear Heavenly Father,

Help (name) to find a worthwhile activity this summer. Open your eyes to the right project, the one you are guiding her toward. Amen.

july 19

OVERCOMING BOREDOM

I said in my heart, "Come, now, let me try you with pleasure and the enjoyment of good things." See, this too was vanity. Of laughter I said: "Mad!" and of mirth: "What good does this do?" Guided by wisdom, I probed with my mind how to beguile my senses with wine and take up folly, until I should understand what is good for human beings to do under the heavens during the limited days of their lives (Ecclesiastes 2:1–3).

For adolescents, summer is the best time of the year. Most don't have any responsibilities, they can sleep until noon, play video games, and have a kitchen full of food. Without the structure of classes and adult supervision, the summer can lead teens to fall into a bad crowd, experiment with drugs or alcohol, or get into all kinds of mischief. Tempt your son to explore opportunities like donating blood at the American Red Cross. Offering this lifesaving gift only takes about an hour of his time, but it can leave him feeling good about himself.

What are your teen's talents? Maybe the summer is the perfect time to discover newly emerging talents or improve existing ones. Perhaps he could learn to play a musical instrument, learn a foreign language, take a dance class, or try a new hobby. Some local colleges might offer low-cost programs especially for teenagers. Keeping his mind busy learning enables him to have a dynamic and safe summer vacation.

REFLECT

Consider doing good deeds as a family. When my daughters were teenagers, we painted the inside of our local food pantry. They were proud of their accomplishment and ended up volunteering at the pantry several days a week that summer. Would your son be interested in volunteer work? There are animal shelters, nursing homes, churches, and soup kitchens that can keep your teenager engaged while developing his self-confidence and accountability (and it looks fantastic on college applications).

✠ PRAY ✠

Dear Heavenly Father,

What is your will for (name)? Help us to see your hand guiding him to the tasks that you have presented in his life. Amen.

july 20

BETRAYAL

When he had said this, Jesus was deeply troubled and testified, "Amen, amen, I say to you, one of you will betray me" (John 13:21).

It's hard to imagine that after the apostles spent much quality time with Jesus, experiencing miracles, and listening to him preach, that one of them would actually betray him for a bag of measly coins. Betrayals rock our world. It's painful picking up the pieces of a broken relationship with your teenager and trying to put it back together, especially when you're feeling disappointment, anger, and embarrassment. Has your teenager messed up her life so badly that you doubt you'll ever be able to trust her again?

When your teen abuses privileges or responsibilities that you extended, don't take it personally because it's not a reflection of your parenting abilities. It's vital to take away the privileges from your adolescent. If your teenager smashed the car, take away the keys. If she flunked out of college because of partying, don't send her back. It's harsh—but necessary. Ask the Holy Spirit to keep you calm so you don't overreact to what your child did. When you stay calm, you can turn the incident into a teaching moment instead of a power struggle.

REFLECT

If something like this has happened in your teen's life, ask her to write about the areas that went awry and what was learned from those events. After you read it, you can discuss it calmly, hearing her out. If your daughter is now in trouble, don't enable her by blaming others, making excuses, or minimizing the problem; make her take responsibility.

✠ PRAY ✠

Dear Heavenly Father,

Help me through this difficult time with (name) while I deal with my own feelings of hurt and betrayal. Pour your healing love on my wounds and raise me up so I am not bitter, but better in your divine care and tender mercy. I love you, Lord God almighty. Amen.

july 21

GOD'S LIGHT

How sweet to my tongue is your promise, sweeter than honey to my mouth! Through your precepts I gain understanding; therefore I hate all false ways. Your word is a lamp for my feet, a light for my path. I make a solemn vow to observe your righteous judgments
(Psalm 119:103–106).

God provides a light for every step you take on your life journey. He can shine his dazzling light into every nook and cranny, every dark corner or uneven pavement that could throw us off course. God is with us through every aspect of our lives, including raising teenagers, which can sometimes feel like riding a roller coaster. God is there beside us! God's amazing light guides us to realize and appreciate his mighty plan. He guides us through raging waters and through fires and storms as the darkness of the world closes in on us; he won't allow a hair on our head to be harmed.

We don't have a crystal ball or the ability to know our future, but we have something better: God and his brilliant shining light. He leads us to the places we need to be and helps us to make sound decisions while we continue moving forward. Sometimes we make mistakes with our peculiar parenting styles, but God is there to get us back on track. Have you made a mistake raising your teenager?

REFLECT

Have you ever allowed your emotions to get in the way of raising your teen, or have you overreacted to a situation because you were fed up with problems? Have you ever said something hurtful to your child during an argument without even thinking about it? Instead of trying to justify your actions, simply apologize and try to right the wrong. Then, move on prayerfully and respectfully.

✠ PRAY ✠

Dear Heavenly Father,

Forgive me, Lord, for allowing my emotions to get the best of me.
Light up my life and show me the way from here.
I want to be the best parent I can possibly be.
Help me, Lord. I ask this in Jesus' name. Amen.

july 22

GOD IS THERE

I pray not only for them, but also for those who will believe in me through their word, so that they may all be one, as you, Father, are in me and I in you, that they also may be in us, that the world may believe that you sent me (John 17:20–21).

Is your teenager going to a sleep-away camp this summer or traveling with a family on a minivacation without you? It's not easy watching your kid leave the security of your home, even though you know she will be perfectly fine. It's natural for all parents to worry a little. God watches over your kid no matter where she is or what she is doing.

When my daughters were thirteen and fourteen, they went to a sleep-away camp begrudgingly. Not only did they survive, but they had fun. They came home with mosquito bites and a few scrapes and bruises, but they were glad they went. During the week I was child-free, I pampered myself by doing things I had put off. I got my hair done, browsed antique shops, served food they didn't like, and read a book in one sitting because I could.

After the girls returned from camp, I made time for myself each day. That brief ritual made me a better person and a better mom. I designated a comfy chair as a prayer chair. Whenever I sat to pray, the girls didn't disturb me. If they wanted to talk to me, there was a stool they could sit on while they waited. Then I'd read from prayer cards or the Bible aloud to draw them into the prayer time. What began with trepidations over camp turned into tranquility with God.

REFLECT

Is there something you haven't had time for in a while because you've been devoting so much time to your children? Find a way this summer to establish a routine that gives you time for yourself.

✢ PRAY ✢

Dear Heavenly Father,

Thank you for watching over my family when we are apart.
Thank you for protecting my loved ones.
You fill me with peacefulness as I rest in your tender care.
I love you, Lord. Amen.

july 23

SPEAKING WITH LOVE

Pleasing words are a honeycomb, sweet to the taste and invigorating to the bones (Proverbs 16:24).

When I left home to attend college, my mother said I was smart and I could do anything. Each time I struggled with homework, I remembered my mother's kind and empowering words propelling me through my assignments, studies, and exams. What messages have you given to your teen recently? Make your words encouraging.

Words carry such incredible power. They can be loving and healing, building up your teenager, or destructive and negative, tearing him down. If your teenager debates or questions you, try to be patient by offering reassurance and promising words with a lighthearted tone. Teenagers will be more receptive to your suggestions or plans when they understand how something will benefit them. How do you motivate your teen? How do you encourage your teen to have a more balanced life?

Your teenager will do well when he feels better about himself. If he only hears criticism and complaints, chances are good he will not be receptive. Hearing compliments will greatly impact his motivation because he will feel worthy.

REFLECT

Start each morning with a positive phrase, notice a bright smile, or how quickly he gets ready for work. Give your son a hug and say how much you love him. Providing encouragement will motivate your youngster even when he feels down because of mistakes. Everyone makes mistakes.

✠ PRAY ✠

Dear Heavenly Father,

Fill my head and heart with positive words to inspire (name).
Teach me how to be a source of encouragement to him.
You are my source of inspiration and blessings
and I thank you, Lord, for always keeping my chin up
through the difficulties of life. Amen.

july 24

MAKING SOUND CHOICES

Are not two sparrows sold for a small coin? Yet not one of them falls to the ground without your Father's knowledge. Even all the hairs of your head are counted. So do not be afraid; you are worth more than many sparrows (Matthew 10:29–31).

I enjoyed watching a robin build a nest, warm her eggs, and feed the two chicks once they hatched. Within two weeks the fledglings outgrew their nest and began flapping their immature wings. One left successfully, but the other struggled terribly. For several weeks that hatchling continued flying up against my house and crying for its mother, who stayed a fair distance away. For the longest time this bird did nothing to help itself. Do you have a child who isn't doing much to help herself? Don't be afraid to let your kid fail. It's nerve-racking to stand on the sidelines and watch kids struggle, but sometimes that's the only way they learn.

It's tempting to rush in and fix everything for our teens or be a helicopter parent, pointing out every possible pitfall. Sometimes we have to step back and pray they make the right choices. Overprotecting young people can have an adverse effect. Teens need to be able to take some calculated risks and then be held accountable for them; it enables them to mature into responsible adults. Risk-taking behavior peeks during adolescence. Normal risk-taking during the teenage years prepares them for leaving home and beginning life on their own.

REFLECT

Next time you find yourself wanting to hover over your teen, step back and pray instead. You won't be able to make every life decision for her, and she'll have to leave the nest eventually.

✠ PRAY ✠

Dear Heavenly Father,

It's hard for me to allow (name) to make one poor decision after another. Bolster me to stay on the sidelines and love unconditionally as you do. Remind me that you walk with my child, with a protective stance and guiding light. You know everything, Lord. I trust in you. Amen.

july 25

HAVE NO FEAR

Do not fear: I am with you; do not be anxious: I am your God. I will strengthen you, I will help you, I will uphold you with my victorious right hand (Isaiah 41:10).

When my daughter took her road test to get her drivers license, she was a nervous wreck. Being that nervous could've caused her to fail. Even though I reminded her that God was with her, she was still afraid. It's easy to tell someone not to be scared or nervous, but it's another thing to take our own advice. Have you ever told your son not to worry about something but then you worry? We have so much to worry about: natural disasters, rampant shootings in schools, terrorism, and a poor economy. How can we not worry about those things?

The Almighty is all-powerful and all-knowing. God means what he says; if he tells us not to fear, we need to obey him. He will never leave us in our time of need. His presence in our life promises fortitude to withstand every difficulty. God will enable us to endure all sufferings with courage. When we feel weak, God will revitalize us. When we stumble and fall, God will lift us up. When we feel spent, God will fill us up.

REFLECT

Whatever problem has you worried, remember that you are not alone in your suffering; God is with you. Throughout your day, when overwhelming problems arise, take a deep breath and relax because you have the Almighty king of heaven with you.

✠ PRAY ✠

Dear Heavenly Father,

Thank you for always being with me through the difficulties of life. Each time I struggle with (name), I am comforted knowing I am not alone. I surrender unto you, Lord, knowing you will safeguard me. There isn't anything that you and I can't do together.
I love you, Lord. Amen.

july 26

ONLY GOD JUDGES

Rather, "if your enemy is hungry, feed him; if he is thirsty, give him something to drink; for by so doing you will heap burning coals upon his head." Do not be conquered by evil but conquer evil with good (Romans 12:20–21).

My daughter was bullied by a mean girl who lived in our neighborhood. It took enormous courage for my daughter to be nice to her because she saw her often in Girl Scouts, classes, and on the bus. Worse, she attended the same college and even had the same major. They lived in the same dorm and took the same classes. When this girl needed help, my daughter gave it gladly, treating this girl as if she were Jesus. This is exactly what Christ wants all of us to do. It isn't necessary for us to take justice into our own hands by taking vengeance when a wrong has been done to us. Ultimately, God will deal justly with all, including those who inflict injury.

Have you been judgmental of a neighbor or friend? Did your neighbors have a party and not invite you? Maybe you judge the way other people in your social circle are raising their teens. Perhaps you are judgmental of your teenager. If so, be kind. It's not her fault she's grumpy; growing up drains her energy. Your teenager is learning how to express her own ideas; therefore, there will be occasions when you don't agree. Achieving independence is a part of growing up. Changes in the developing brain can sometimes cause oversensitivity, moodiness, or a bad attitude. This is all a normal part of her growth and development. Invoke God's help as you overcome life with an uncouth teen.

REFLECT

How have you taught your teen to respond when confronted by someone she doesn't like or who treats her poorly? Have you been following your own advice?

✠ PRAY ✠

Dear Heavenly Father,

Grant me patience as I learn to balance smothering (name)
with kindness while offering leeway to develop her own identity.
This process is long and at times hurtful.
You are my saving Lord and I love you. Amen.

july 27

GOD-LOVING FAMILY

Blessed are all who fear the LORD, and who walk in his ways. What your hands provide you will enjoy; you will be blessed and prosper: your wife will be like a fruitful vine within your home, your children like young olive plants around your table (Psalm 128:1–3).

What a glorious image of a God-loving family, living by his laws, protected and unified by his love. There is a sense of hopefulness for their future. When families flourish with tranquility, love, and joyfulness, that peace emanates to others.

Think about how peaceful your home is right now. Does the TV blare shows with guns and violence into your living room each day, or do you watch shows that promote learning, nature, inspiration, or religion? Do your teenagers spend countless hours playing video games and perusing the internet, or do you encourage reading religious books or playing games that support togetherness?

To prevent the disintegration of your family, gather your kids around the dinner table and eat together. Pray before meals. Take turns speaking about the wonderful events that God blessed you with today and then thank God for them. If your day was exceptionally bad, talk about that, too. It will give your family members a platform to reveal problematic topics or discuss subjects they might have avoided otherwise. One of the best things you can do to strengthen your family bond is to pray together as a family. Maybe you could all put your heads together and say a quick prayer. For example, "Help us, Lord, to do our very best today. Bless our work; we do it all for you."

REFLECT

God is the answer to all of your family concerns. God desires us to submerge ourselves in his pure love while enjoying the fruits of our labors and obeying God's laws. Be a God-loving family.

✠ PRAY ✠

Dear Heavenly Father,

Bless our family. Teach us to stop living for ourselves and instead follow your ways more dearly. Open our eyes to the wonders of your glory today and always. Amen.

july 28

ELIMINATE EVIL FROM YOUR LIFE

For while your obedience is known to all, so that I rejoice over you, I want you to be wise as to what is good, and simple as to what is evil; then the God of peace will quickly crush Satan under your feet. The grace of our Lord Jesus be with you (Romans 16:19–20).

We can thank Adam and Eve for eating the forbidden fruit that opened their eyes to good and evil. In today's passage, Paul provides a key to a moral life. He recommends that we know what is good by living wisely and avoiding sinfulness by being innocent. Do you live your life out of the convictions of your heart? Does what you do and say come from the beliefs and values ingrained in your heart and thought process? If you believe stealing is wrong, you won't be tempted to take office supplies from work or shoplift from stores, and you will instill those values in your teenagers.

My dad once said, "Don't go looking for trouble; what you don't know can't hurt you." We can't be tempted by things we don't know about. Don't think about evil things or go looking for trouble. If a bad thought enters your head, tell Satan to get out! If you worry about your teenager driving home late at night, say a prayer instead of thinking through every possible worst-case scenario. Nothing good can come from worry, but much good comes from prayer.

REFLECT

Paul reminds us to be innocent with our thoughts and actions. Focus on all that is good, pure, and honest. Dwell on Christ accompanying your teenager as she drives home safely. Ask your teen's guardian angel to be extra vigilant if the worry persists.

✠ PRAY ✠

Dear Heavenly Father,

If the questionable thoughts in my head are not from you,
take them away! Fill my head and heart with lovely thoughts of you.
Let me dwell on your exquisiteness so that it spills over into my
everyday life. Thank you for creating me with innocence.
I love you, Lord. Amen.

july 29

THE FRUIT OF THE SPIRIT

In contrast, the fruit of the Spirit is love, joy, peace, patience, kindness, generosity, faithfulness, gentleness, self-control. Against such there is no law (Galatians 5:22–23).

This is typically the time of year when my next-door neighbor gets inundated with tomatoes and zucchini from her garden. She cooks, cans, and freezes them but still has baskets left over. She gives us plenty, sharing with other neighbors until we all have had our fill. Isn't that precisely what Christian life should be like? We are so overflowing with love, joy, peace, patience, kindness, generosity, faithfulness, and gentleness that we have to spread it around. The fruit of the Spirit that Paul talks about in Galatians ought to be more than we need, so we have to share it.

Sometimes teenagers can be downright moody for no reason, and that can bring down the general tone of your entire family. If you have an irritable teen, stop his negative disposition before it infects everyone around him. The best cure for this type of grumpiness is to sing praises to the Lord. It might initially seem corny, but it works every time. Even if you make up the tune, create your own words, or sing off-key, when you live in the promise of God, your joy will be contagious.

REFLECT

Praising God is music to his ears no matter what form you use. If your teenager plays a musical instrument or sings, invite him to join in or choose a tune of his own.

✠ PRAY ✠

Dear Heavenly Father,

We sing your praises on this glorious day! Thank you, Lord, for (name) and all of his wonderful and challenging attributes. I feel so special that I want to shout it from the rooftops! Thank you, Lord, for giving me the strength to lift him up when moodiness strikes. By focusing all of our energy on you, the misgivings of life fall by the wayside, and we are left standing in your glorious light. You are the answer to everything on earth. Amen.

july 30

I WANT NOT

The Lord *is my shepherd; there is nothing I lack* (Psalm 23:1).

This is the time of year when almost every teenager in America wants something in preparation for the beginning of the new school year. Some want school supplies like backpacks, notebooks, binders, and folders. Some kids want locker accessories. The top of the shopping list is usually new clothes, jeans, tops, hoodies, and shoes. They want the latest and greatest so they fit in with what everyone else is wearing. Some kids become greedy as they page through newspaper fliers deciding what they want. How many pairs of jeans does one kid need?

Pope Francis warned of the dangers of the idolization of money and commended sharing wealth with the poor. He said, "Our consciences thus need to be converted to justice, equality, simplicity and sharing" (from the pope's 2014 *Lenten Message)*. Each summer I encourage my daughters to clean out their closets and give half of their stuff to the indigent in our community. They have so much that they don't need any more. Perhaps there is a refugee resettlement program, a Salvation Army, or a St. Vincent De Paul in your area where you could donate items. Consider volunteering your time at these organizations with your teenager. You never know if it might spawn a future career or a desire to continue giving to these charities in the future.

REFLECT

Stuff can weigh you down, and you certainly can't take any of it to heaven. Teach your teen that God is all she needs. His grace will suffice. With the good Lord as your shepherd, he will provide everything so there is nothing you will lack. Those who seek the Lord shall not want.

✠ PRAY ✠

Dear Heavenly Father,

Let me rest in your love and the satisfaction knowing that you provide everything I need. Thank you, kind and generous Lord, for filling me with your grace and divinity. Amen.

july 31

BUILD YOUR LIFE ON GOD

Unless the LORD builds the house, they labor in vain who build.
Unless the LORD guards the city, in vain does the guard keep watch
(Psalm 127:1).

Years ago, my dad and I built a playhouse for my daughters. We started it in early spring and spent the entire summer constructing it. Dad said the most important thing was having a solid foundation, so we put the most work into that. It was backbreaking effort and seemed to take forever, but we wanted it done right so it would last.

Our lives are built on foundations, too. To make a truly strong base for our lives, we should construct it on and around the Lord. Jesus says in today's parable that if we build our lives on our own foundation of desires and self-fulfillment, it will disintegrate when misfortunes strike. When our foundation is not centered on God, it is built in vain.

REFLECT

Did you initially start building your life on God but then did you get sidetracked with your own agendas, the business of raising teenagers, and their constant wants and needs? Be optimistic that you can start over with Christ as your foundation today. By doing this, you are teaching your kids that it's OK to start over. When God creates your foundation, he creates your life direction. When storms hit, you will survive them by focusing on God.

✠ PRAY ✠

Dear Heavenly Father,

Help me to do my foundation over and create one on you.
Enable me to trust completely in your will, not my own.
Encourage me to teach these skills to my teenagers so they can have a strong foundation built on your love and tender mercy.
I ask this in Jesus' name. Amen.

august 1

REPENT

Or do you hold his priceless kindness, forbearance, and patience in low esteem, unaware that the kindness of God would lead you to repentance? (Romans 2:4).

The moment my daughter's drivers license arrived, she wanted to be like all of the other kids at her school and drive there. When I didn't succumb to that pressure, there were other requests. Many of her friends were having co-ed sleepovers, parties without parental control, shopping sprees with parental credit cards. It's disturbing that many teenagers' parents cave in to such requests. The parents' generosity toward their teenager isn't helping the kid. In fact, it's not kindness. It hurts the teen.

Many people expect God to act like these parents who give in to their kids' demands and give them whatever they want. These people see the heartache in their communities or catastrophic world events and wonder where God is. They might claim that God isn't all-loving, all-good, all-powerful, all-merciful when these devastating events occur. Even if good fortune comes their way, they are successful with their employment, they achieved good health, and all is going well for them, they don't change their life to repent for their wrongdoings or give back some of the blessings they have received. It is like a one-way street where everything is about getting what they want from life—always taking. Today's verse reminds us that God's kindness and blessings should compel us to repent and turn over a new leaf.

REFLECT

If you believe that God provides to you and your family, do you try to live the kind of life that is pleasing to him or just pleasing to you? Contemplate past kindnesses that God bestowed on you and decide if they led you to atonement.

✠ PRAY ✠

Dear Heavenly Father,

When bad things happen, I turn to you.
Help me to examine my life each day in your merciful light,
celebrate it, and repent for any sinfulness, hidden or exposed.
Thank you, Lord, for all you give me: good and bad.
I thank you for it all. Amen.

august 2

MAKE A JESUS FOUNDATION

I will show you what someone is like who comes to me, listens to my words, and acts on them. That one is like a person building a house, who dug deeply and laid the foundation on rock; when the flood came, the river burst against that house but could not shake it because it had been well built. But the one who listens and does not act is like a person who built a house on the ground without a foundation. When the river burst against it, it collapsed at once and was completely destroyed"
(Luke 6:47–49).

People either like summer storms or they don't. I love the soft sound of rain with a rumble of thunder and flash of lightning. This inevitable part of life is easier to endure from the confines of a sturdy home. One particular rainstorm was wearisome because I was camping in a pup tent. I worried that I might wash away.

This parable emphasizes the sturdy foundation constructed on the rock; the person obeys God and his house stays up. He must still endure the storm but is unharmed because his foundation is strong. Both men go through the storm, but the one with the weak foundation is destroyed. We will weather storms in life and must ensure we do so with Jesus as our secure basis. Without God as our foundation, we will get washed away the minute a storm hits. Jesus never said we would live trouble-free lives, but with him as our foundation, we will not be destroyed.

REFLECT

What storms are you weathering with (or because of) your teenager? Have you ensured Jesus is your foundation?

✠ PRAY ✠

Dear Heavenly Father,

Teach me to focus on you each day so that when the rains come, I will be secure in your love to endure it. Help me to fortify my life foundation around you through prayer, fasting, service, and meditation. I truly love you, Lord. Amen.

august 3

GLORY OF GOD

Therefore, since we have such hope, we act very boldly and not like Moses, who put a veil over his face so that the Israelites could not look intently at the cessation of what was fading (2 Corinthians 3:12–13).

On my wedding day I wore a veil over my face as I walked down the aisle. Family and friends said I was radiant, but I didn't see it until I looked at my wedding album. My face was glowing. Imagine speaking with God face to face like Moses did. You would glow, too! Whenever Moses conversed with God, his face would shine. After he conveyed God's message to the Israelites, he covered his face because eventually the shine disappeared. Who would want the glory of God to fade from his face?

Moses was lucky to have such encounters with God. Being followers of Christ, we could also have glowing faces. But first you need to pull yourself away from the TV, turn off the computer, put away your cell phone, and go out and find the Lord. Consider the places you can find him: at the homeless shelter, the soup kitchen, the food pantry, or the refugee resettlement house. Get your teenagers involved in helping out in some way, maybe by making sandwiches for the poor. Through that humbleness you and your teens will see the face of God. Then you might see a glow on your teenagers' faces. Let the glory of God shine forth from all aspects of your life.

REFLECT

When your kids tell you they are bored or that you never do anything "fun" over the summer, tell them you are going to experience the glory of God. Go out and look for him today.

✠ PRAY ✠

Dear Heavenly Father,

Inspire (name) to help others.

Tell me what to say to her so she can experience your true glory.

Move through me to get her involved and to stay focused on your work. I live for you, dear Lord, and so does she. Amen.

august 4

READ THE BIBLE

*With all prayer and supplication, pray at every opportunity in the Spirit. To that end, be watchful with all perseverance and supplication for all the holy ones and also for me, that speech may be given me to open my mouth, to make known with boldness the mystery of the gospel for which I am an ambassador in chains, so that I may have the courage to speak as I must (*Ephesians 6:18–20).

Our world is full of distractions. The thoughts of food and online shopping distract me. Checking email distracts some, while the phone could be the biggest distraction of all time. Who leaves home today without his phone, and how many times will it be used throughout the day? Is your teenager always on his phone? How many hours each day does your son spend on it? Is he obsessed with apps, games, or texting friends? Now consider how much time your teenager spends doing chores and reading holy Scripture. Does your kid even know where his Bible is?

Many schools provide a reading list to students as a head start on the next year's curriculum to be completed over the summer. Add reading the Bible to that list. Perhaps you can read passages together each morning, think about them all day, and discuss them over dinner. If you simply tell your kid to start reading the Bible, that might fall on deaf ears. However, if you decide as a family to all expand your faith by reading, learning, and understanding the Bible one passage at a time, it might be easier to digest. The Bible is our arsenal in truth, faith, hope, and love. We cannot put God's words to good use without reading it, accepting it, and living it.

REFLECT

Are you just as bad as your teen when it comes to reading your Bible? Take this opportunity to get your own faith life back on track alongside your teen.

✠ PRAY ✠

Dear Heavenly Father,

Help me to interpret the Holy Bible as our family reads it. Help me to engage each member so we are blessed with the wisdom inscribed on the pages. We welcome your message into our hearts, our minds, and our lives. Amen.

august 5

WHAT DO YOU GIVE?

Give and gifts will be given to you; a good measure, packed together, shaken down, and overflowing, will be poured into your lap. For the measure with which you measure will in return be measured out to you" (Luke 6:38).

One summer vacation was spent driving across the country with teenagers, singing as we drove. We were laughing and talking more, bickering less. We brought CDs and regretted not having an iPod. At a rest stop we found one on the ground; the thing we desperately wanted. But someone else's music was downloaded on it. Even though we wanted it, rationalizing that it would be better off with us, we brought it to a "lost and found." We felt good doing the right thing. The remainder of our vacation overflowed with goodness and we stopped thinking about it. That Christmas my eighty-year-old dad couldn't forget what we did and bought us iPods.

That summer's valuable lesson has come back to us many times over the years: You reap what you sow literally and figuratively. Jesus wants us to love those who are difficult to tolerate, do good deeds even if we don't feel like it, and give, hoping for nothing in return. In the end our reward will be tremendous when we are welcomed into heaven. God asks us to be merciful and nonjudgmental. We are reminded that if we don't condemn others, we won't be condemned. If we forgive others, we will be forgiven. If we give, it will be given back to us. If you are a gracious and forgiving person, God will bless you likewise.

REFLECT

What do you give back to God?

✠ PRAY ✠

Dear Heavenly Father,

Help me to be more Christlike with my teenager.
Let me be kinder, gentler, more merciful, and loving.
Keep me strong, Lord, during these difficult years.
With you, I can do anything. Amen.

august 6

THE TRANSFIGURATION

After six days Jesus took Peter, James, and John his brother, and led them up a high mountain by themselves. And he was transfigured before them; his face shone like the sun and his clothes became white as light (Matthew 17:1–2).

God selects us as his special ones, the way he chose Peter, James, and John to go up a mountain as close as they could get to heaven to give them a glimpse of who he really was. While this transfiguration unfolded before their eyes, it was frightening and they couldn't comprehend all that was happening.

In this day and age it might be necessary for God to appear like that again in order for people to heed his call. Some can connect the dots in their lives and do what God has been preparing them to do. But it isn't always easy to hear to God calling.

I listen with my heart, mind, and soul. When there was a shortage of religion teachers, I found myself volunteering without a shred of teaching experience. It would've been much easier to tune out the request. God gave me the resources, the words, and stories so I could overcome my fears and stand in front of a classroom full of teenagers and enlighten them about the word of God. In the end, that teaching experience was one of the best gifts anyone could have given me. And it gave me a chance to get to know my daughter's classmates. God has given each of us unique gifts and talents, then he calls us to use those gifts to serve.

REFLECT

What talents has God given your teen? Can you show him how to use those talents for himself and the glory of God?

✠ PRAY ✠

Dear Heavenly Father,

Calm my fears while I try to do what you are asking of me.
I trust in you. Amen.

august 7

ANSWER THE CALL

As he was walking by the Sea of Galilee, he saw two brothers, Simon who is called Peter, and his brother Andrew, casting a net into the sea; they were fishermen. He said to them, "Come after me, and I will make you fishers of men." At once they left their nets and followed him (Matthew 4:18–20).

Would you leave your job to follow Jesus? When God calls, we should respond, even if it means leaving work and the comfort of home. In the 1990s, I watched heartbreaking television reports showing abandoned children in Romanian orphanages. I felt God calling me there to adopt. I didn't have a clue how to do it, but I believed that God would help me if I answered his call.

Jesus called fishermen to follow him. They dropped their nets and obediently set out to proclaim the gospel of the kingdom and healing people as they traveled. Answering God's call isn't easy, especially when he takes us from our jobs to foreign places and asks us to do things we're uncertain of. God reinforces us with courage when we need it. He strengthens our voice, rejuvenates our body and mind with inconceivable resilience, and fills our hearts with untold love and awe.

When I finally met God's unrelenting call with open arms by plotting an uncharted course, surrendering every last dime I owned and falling into total submission to his will, God showered me with blessings beyond my wildest imagination. I wasn't expecting any gifts. I was hoping to bring a child home, but God gave so much more. He opened my eyes to things I normally wouldn't see. He opened my heart and gave me experiences that I thought I would never know.

REFLECT

When God calls, remember Peter, Andrew, James, and John, and respond the way they did. There really is no other way to go.

✠ PRAY ✠

Dear Heavenly Father,

I don't always know what you are calling me to do. Help me to be the very best parent while I wait for you to tell me what my next job will be. I am here, Lord, ready to do your will. Amen.

august 8

DON'T QUIT

After recalling the apostles, they had them flogged, ordered them to stop speaking in the name of Jesus, and dismissed them. So they left the presence of the Sanhedrin, rejoicing that they had been found worthy to suffer dishonor for the sake of the name. And all day long, both at the temple and in their homes, they did not stop teaching and proclaiming the Messiah, Jesus (Acts 5:40–42).

I was mocked by neighborhood children for wearing a uniform to attend a Catholic grammar school. I wept in my mother's lap. That was the closest I came to being humiliated for my faith. Have you tried to do something for God but became discouraged when things went awry? That happened with the apostles when they relied on faith to perform miracles in Jesus' name. Instead of being praised for them, they were flogged. The apostles' reaction astounds us: they rejoiced and continued teaching and proclaiming the good news that Jesus is the Messiah.

When we become discouraged, it's essential to continue onward. When your kids don't want to attend Mass, it might be easier to leave them home, but God doesn't want us to give up on them. He wants us to keep teaching them. If you are ridiculed for standing up for your beliefs as a Catholic, don't become discouraged. Rejoice that you are worthy to suffer for the Lord.

REFLECT

Continue proclaiming what Christ has done because when you do, that is pleasing to God. Genuine fulfillment is derived from living for Christ, no matter what the price.

✠ PRAY ✠

Dear Heavenly Father,

Help me to overcome the discouragement from others
that surrounds me when I speak your name.
Empower me to keep going, for I have so much more to say.
You are my saving Lord. Amen.

august 9

HOW GREAT IS GOD?

For my thoughts are not your thoughts, nor are your ways my ways—oracle of the LORD. For as the heavens are higher than the earth, so are my ways higher than your ways, my thoughts higher than your thoughts (Isaiah 55:8–9).

On a blustery winter day, my husband and I bundled up and went for a walk where we found a sobbing woman crumpled in a snow bank, not wearing a coat or shoes. We immediately ran to comfort her with words and actions that were not our own. When we first spotted her, I said, "Help me, Lord," and he did. I had no idea what to say or do, but God in his greatness did, and he worked through us.

God is magnificent and flawless. We are not. He is omnipotent and everlasting, while we fumble our way through life day by day living a few meager years on this earth. God is gargantuan; he created the entire universe. We are like tiny ants. We can never truly fathom God, yet we long to know him. However, God can work through us if we let him.

When it comes to parenting, there are no guidelines for us to follow. We just try to do our very best with what we have. Luckily, we have God! We can raise our kids through prayer, relying on God's infinite wisdom to guide us. When you are in a precarious situation with your teen or are unsure of what to do, invoke the Holy Spirit within you for reassurance.

REFLECT

God is beyond us in every imaginable way, which is humbling when you consider our teenagers' lives depend largely on us. When we trust God and ask for his guidance, he will draw us remarkably close to him. In his greatness and wisdom he will help you be the parent your teen needs.

✠ PRAY ✠

Dear Heavenly Father,

You can reach down and fix what is broken, but you send me instead.
You can speak words of comfort, but you use my voice.
You can guide the weary traveler, but you use me.
Thank you for choosing me. Amen.

august 10

GOD'S PERFECT TAPESTRY

Do not conform yourselves to this age but be transformed by the renewal of your mind, that you may discern what is the will of God, what is good and pleasing and perfect (Romans 12:2).

When I read Corrie ten Boom's poem "Life Is But a Weaving," I knew the tapestry she was describing resembled my life. Because I enjoy needlepoint, I know how bad the straggly underside can look with its mismatched threads and random knots strewn without rhyme or reason. But when you flip the fabric over, the embroidered picture is beautiful. God sees that big picture from above; we only see the underside. We don't appreciate that the dark threads of our life are necessary until we see the completed tapestry. God is the master weaver; he knows exactly what he's doing.

In your everyday life, all you may have is raising your offspring, feeding them, grocery shopping, your job, errands, projects, and chores. Give it all to God as an offering. Invoke the Holy Spirit to transform your thoughts and attitudes toward God and away from the sinful ways of the world. It can be tricky living in an unbelieving world, which can influence your mind and the decisions you make. Don't conform to this world but the next.

Be satisfied with what you have and what you're doing, even if it doesn't feel like much. In whatever you do, make it the best and ensure that it's for the Lord. Be kind in all circumstances, even if you don't feel like it; even after a long day of work when you come home to find your house a total wreck. Consider it one of those straggly threads that's necessary to make your tapestry beautiful.

REFLECT

Reading the Bible fills you with the knowledge of God, while prayer strengthens your spirit and renews your thoughts. Find time to refresh amid chaos. You'll be a better parent and a more God-centered person for it.

✠ PRAY ✠

Dear Heavenly Father,

Even though I don't understand, I trust your plan for me. Amen.

august 11

LOVE OVERLOOKS FAULTS

Above all, let your love for one another be intense, because love covers a multitude of sins (1 Peter 4:8).

One afternoon, my daughters and I baked a cake from scratch. The lovely idea turned into quite an ordeal. The kitchen looked like a disaster area and the cake was a massive pile of crumbs. Not wanting to crush their spirits, I told them, "Don't worry, frosting covers a multitude of sins." With enough frosting we hid every imperfection. The girls were proud of their efforts, the dessert was delicious, and it was a win-win for us.

Like frosting, love enables us to cover, or overlook, the faults of others. Today's passage teaches us to act charitably toward each other; that our love enables us to ignore someone's transgressions. Perhaps love enables you to overlook your teenager's weaknesses or negative behavior and instead you're able to focus on her positive attributes.

Love is much more than affection. It's the divine ability to sacrifice yourself for others. This kind of love allows parents to run into burning buildings to save their children. It allows parents to lift cars when their children are trapped underneath them. It allows parents to walk away from their careers to stay home and raise kids. It allows parents to empty their savings accounts to buy them things they need or desperately want. This kind of love drives parents to the ends of the earth to build up their children into caring adults.

REFLECT

Ponder the many sacrifices you have made for your kids, and then contemplate the ultimate sacrifice God made for us by sending his only Son to be crucified on a cross for our sins. That is true love!

✠ PRAY ✠

Dear Heavenly father,

Thank you for filling my heart with pure and genuine love. I will spread it to people I meet today, whether or not I like them or whether or not they deserve it. My love could transform their hearts and make them kinder, more amicable human beings.
Amen.

august 12

IN ALL THINGS, PRAY

Give ear to my words, O Lord; understand my sighing.
Attend to the sound of my cry, my king and my God!
For to you I will pray, Lord; in the morning you will hear my voice;
in the morning I will plead before you and wait (Psalm 5:2–4).

Prayer builds on our weaknesses and frailties. God reminds us from time to time just how much we need him. When you can't change something on your own, surrender to the Lord; then in God's care, on his terms, things will change for you. Consider times where you were in trouble and forgot to pray. How might things have changed if you'd focused on prayer instead of your trouble?

Prayer is good for you and it delights God. We are unified with our spirit, and prayer is a remarkable tool to communicate with God. Prayer promotes self-esteem when you appreciate how much God cares for you and loves you the way you are. Remember to be patient. Things don't always change on your timetable but on God's. Be patient. Consider how long it takes a tree to grow to provide you with shade or fruit. God is not an instant fix, but what he does for you will be everlasting.

REFLECT

If you are struggling with the best way to parent your teen, give it to God through prayer.

✠ PRAY ✠

Dear Heavenly Father,

Shine your warm heavenly light down upon us gently,
guiding us to find peace, happiness, and contentment in our lives.
Let my heart rejoice as I call out to you, dear Lord,
knowing you will hear and answer me. Amen.

august 13

GOD'S CREATIONS

God made every kind of wild animal, every kind of tame animal, and every kind of thing that crawls on the ground. God saw that it was good (Genesis 1:26).

After our fourteen-year-old dog passed away, my daughters pestered me relentlessly for another pet. I wasn't keen to get another dog because I walked, fed, and cleaned up after Sparky. Even though the girls had promised to help, I knew the jobs would ultimately fall on me. Has this ever happened to you? Animals can bring so much joy to families, they're adorable and hard to resist. Maybe your teenager only asked for a pet turtle, which sounds easy enough—until you actually get one. The decision to get a pet is not one to take lightly.

After I initially told my daughters we could not get another pet, I remembered Jesus was born in a stable surrounded by animals. God created animals to give us pleasure. He created the birds in the air and the fish in the sea. In the Bible it says that the wolf and the lamb shall graze together; the lion shall eat straw like the ox. Animals are mentioned numerous times throughout the Bible. Noah built an ark and filled it with animals to preserve their lives from the Flood.

There are numerous benefits to being a pet owner. Pets can empathize with human suffering. Sparky knew when I was sad; she never left my side when I was sick or feeling down. Some dogs can actually sense medical problems: detecting cancer, spikes in glucose levels, or seizures before they happen. Pets reduce stress in our lives, while dogs can keep us more physically fit and more social by walking them each day. (Yes, we got another pet—fish.)

REFLECT

Whether your teens are pestering you for a pet, a new device, or an unplanned vacation this summer, ask God to help you with your decision.

✠ PRAY ✠

Dear Heavenly Father,

Thank you for making the creatures that roam the earth. They bring me great pleasure. If it is your will for me to own a pet, I accept it. Help me, Lord, with this decision. Amen.

august 14

FITTING INTO HEAVEN

Come to him, a living stone, rejected by human beings but chosen and precious in the sight of God, and, like living stones, let yourselves be built into a spiritual house to be a holy priesthood to offer spiritual sacrifices acceptable to God through Jesus Christ (1 Peter 2:4–6).

My dad helped me build a shrine to Mary holding the Baby Jesus in my back yard. I had been going through an especially difficult time with recent unemployment and health problems. I hoped seeing Mary in a stone grotto would inspire me. The process was cathartic, building it up slowly, one layer of rock at a time. To construct the arch, my dad chiseled a triangular stone to fit perfectly high up in the corner. It was then that I realized God was chiseling me on earth to fit perfectly into heaven.

You don't necessarily have to build a huge stone grotto in your back yard; however, perhaps you could buy a small statue and make a minishrine inside your home. That way, each time you see it you can say a prayer and ask God for patience, mercy, or special grace. Welcome God into your life on earth so you will fit into heaven perfectly!

REFLECT

Consider what difficulties you may be experiencing on earth as a process of reforming to ensure that you will fit perfectly into heaven. Maybe you need to learn to be humble or accept a disability that you would rather not have. Whatever the struggle is, God will help you to carry it and live peacefully with it.

✠ PRAY ✠

Dear Heavenly Father,

Enable me to withstand being chiseled into the shape you need me to be in. It hurts, Lord. Take this pain from me or help me to endure it. I feel so weak and powerless at times. Pick me up and bolster me with your enduring love. With you, I can do anything. Amen.

august 15

THE ASSUMPTION OF MARY

A great sign appeared in the sky, a woman clothed with the sun, with the moon under her feet, and on her head a crown of twelve stars. She was with child and wailed aloud in pain as she labored to give birth (Revelation 12:1–2).

On the solemnity of Mary it's important to pause and give reverence to our Blessed Lady. She didn't have to think about it when she was asked to be the Mother of God. Instead of thinking only of herself, she thought about pleasing God. Without hesitation she agreed to deal with ridicule from the villagers she lived among. She accepted her parents' disappointment and her new husband's disparity as they struggled to accept the news of her pregnancy. Mary quickly and happily obeyed every request asked of her in order to bring salvation to the world through the Son of God.

Contrast Mary's humility and complete submission to God with Eve, who put her own desires above the request of the Lord. Even though God had given everything to her, Eve was unwilling to comply with the only demand he made of her. Eve's selfishness led to sickness. Through Mary came healing. Eve brought sorrow. Mary brought joy. Death came through Eve. Life flowed through Mary. Eve bargained with the devil. Mary fought Satan off when she gave birth to Jesus.

REFLECT

What type of parent would you most like to resemble: Eve or Mary? Are you making decisions that are best suited for your daughter or for yourself? When you are faced with making a hard choice at great expense, remember the Blessed Mother of God and all she did to bring Jesus into the world. Choose to be like Mary.

✠ PRAY ✠

Dear Heavenly Father,

Thank you for enabling me to make difficult decisions.
I want to be strong like Mary. Bless me with the courage to make
sacrifices for (name)'s sake because I want to do what is right.
Let me dwell on your loveliness, dear Lord. Amen.

august 16

ABANDONED SHEEP

At the sight of the crowds, his heart was moved with pity for them because they were troubled and abandoned, like sheep without a shepherd (Matthew 9:36).

Orthopedic surgeons didn't know what to make of a rare bone tumor in my daughter's foot. Not one doctor in my hometown knew how to help. I felt deeply troubled and abandoned by the medical community. But when I traveled to a Shriner's hospital in Massachusetts, I was welcomed with open arms by a diverse group of surgeons. They knew exactly what to do. The relief was palpable.

In today's verse I imagine the pity Jesus felt for those troubled and abandoned, the same way I felt about my daughter's medical problem. I was like a lost sheep, elated to discover my shepherd in the Shriner's hospital. In everyday life we are surrounded by lost sheep: self-centered coworkers or neighbors whose only priority is themselves. They don't live for God; they only live for themselves. They're inflexible and obstinate, making interactions with them challenging and oftentimes unpleasant. Do you know anyone like this?

Feeling helpless, that a situation is out of your control, or feeling abandoned is dreadful. Jesus took pity on those who didn't follow him because that's what they were experiencing. It's hardly surprising that they only care about themselves when they barely have confidence and stability to their lives. This passage shows us what Jesus felt for them: compassion.

REFLECT

Try to see those in your midst the way Jesus did. Be an example to your teen and show compassion to the lost.

✠ PRAY ✠

Dear Heavenly Father,

Fill me with sympathy for the selfish people I encounter today because I don't understand their behaviors. Let me love them the way you would: with kindness, tenderness, and humility. You are my saving Lord and I will sing your praises every day of my life. Amen.

august 17

MAINTAIN YOUR FAITH

Faith is the realization of what is hoped for and evidence of things not seen....But without faith it is impossible to please him, for anyone who approaches God must believe that he exists and that he rewards those who seek him (Hebrews 11:1, 6).

How strong is your faith? Hebrews 11 reminds you to maintain faith regardless of your situation. By faith Abraham, when put to the test, offered up Isaac (Hebrews 11:17–19). By faith Moses, when he had grown up, refused to be known as the son of Pharaoh's daughter; he chose to be ill-treated along with the people of God rather than enjoy the fleeting pleasure of sin (Hebrews 11:24–25). These people had exemplary faith. If you were in their situation, what would you have done?

What in your current situation requires faithfulness? When I adopted children with medical issues, I had to keep the faith that God would walk with me and help me. I maintained faith that God would resolve the problems. It wasn't easy, and I often slipped a bit when times were excruciatingly painful. In your disparity, keep your faith strong because that's what God wants of you. God works through people: doctors, nurses, therapists, social workers, counselors, teachers, and caregivers. God works through strangers, neighbors, friends, and relatives. You have to trust in God and his ways. Have faith that all things work through him. Without faith it's impossible to please God.

REFLECT

This week, try connecting everything you do to your faith in God. Pray with the faith that God will answer your prayers. He might not answer them exactly the way you desire. You just have to trust in him, believe, and keep your faith.

✠ PRAY ✠

Dear Heavenly Father,

I believe and trust in you and your miraculous ways.
I love you, Lord. Amen.

august 18

EMBRACE THE NEWS

The child's father and mother were amazed at what was said about him; and Simeon blessed them and said to Mary his mother, "Behold, this child is destined for the fall and rise of many in Israel, and to be a sign that will be contradicted (and you yourself a sword will pierce) so that the thoughts of many hearts may be revealed" (Luke 2:33–36).

Imagine taking your newborn infant to the pediatrician where he announces your child is destined for the fall and rise of many, that you'll experience great pain, possibly breaking your heart, so that the hearts of many will be revealed. Would the doctor's words cause you to raise your child any differently? Most parents accept that over the course of the child's life there will be scraped knees, bumps, bruises, and even a little heartache. But Mary and Joseph were told something quite different.

Have you heard news about your adolescent that was difficult to accept? Whatever it is, remember how Mary and Joseph felt when Simeon spoke to them about Jesus: They were amazed. Embrace your teenager's news, make peace with it, and God will enable you to accept it and live with it.

REFLECT

Remember that God doesn't give us more than we can bear. He helps us through our difficulties and never leaves our side throughout it all. With God, anything is possible, so keep trusting in the Lord.

✠ PRAY ✠

Dear Heavenly Father,

Thank you for choosing me to parent (name).
You have enormous faith in me that I'll do a good job raising him.
Thank you for the gift of this child. Help me through the difficulties, Lord. Sometimes I doubt my abilities. Reinforce my fortitude with your unending stream of love and mercy. I love you, Lord. Amen.

august 19

CORRECTING GENTLY

Brothers, even if a person is caught in some transgression, you who are spiritual should correct that one in a gentle spirit, looking to yourself, so that you also may not be tempted (Galatians 6:1).

Newspapers are filled with reports of individuals stealing from churches, the sex scandals of the clergy, and more. Today's passage reminds us that we who are spiritual should correct in a gentle spirit, doing an introspection to ensure we don't sink into a quagmire of sin, too.

If you surmise your teens are experimenting with cigarettes or alcohol, your reactions could bring you to the brink of sin by telling your kids that you never tried it when you were underage, when in actuality you did. Later when you relax with a drink or two, remember that your kids are learning by watching what you do.

Do you overreact when you learn about your kid's transgressions? If you scream, rant, or yell, ask God to bring you to your senses. Take a deep breath and try to remain calm by remembering the Holy Spirit within you. Allow God to speak through you. Try to be spiritual so that your pride doesn't spill out. Then, confront your daughter in a way that will not disgrace her. Don't be obnoxious or rude to persuade her to see your side. Teach through love.

REFLECT

If you were caught doing something you shouldn't be doing, how would you want to be treated? Keep that in mind as you confront your teen.

✠ PRAY ✠

Dear Heavenly Father,

Wash sinfulness from me while I enlighten (name) and shelter her from the perils of the world. Help me to reinforce her arsenal of knowledge and prayer to make wise decisions for a sound future free from sin. Let us rest in your unending stream of mercy, love, and affection today and always. You are my saving Lord.
With you I can do anything. Amen.

august 20

FAMILY DIFFICULTIES

Joseph rose and took the child and his mother by night and departed for Egypt. He stayed there until the death of Herod, that what the Lord had said through the prophet might be fulfilled, "Out of Egypt I called my son" (Matthew 2:14–16).

Do you ever compare your family with your neighbors? Do the people next door appear to have an easier life than you? The Holy Family had a rocky start: Joseph finds his wife pregnant and wants to divorce her, he learns the baby is the Messiah, there's no room in the inn, Jesus is born in a cave, Herod wants to kill Jesus, so they flee to Egypt. It sounds wildly unbelievable, but we know it's true. Mary and Joseph obeyed God, and God protected them.

What is throwing your life off kilter? As the summer winds down, you might be ready to send your kids back to school. They could be showing signs of agitation, boredom, or discontentment. This would be an excellent opportunity to volunteer with them in community projects that help the less fortunate. Perhaps you could invite elderly neighbors to your house for a cookout or volunteer at a nearby nursing home. Spending time with the aging population could enable your teens to experience a special closeness.

REFLECT

How will you convert your family's restless energy during these last few days of summer?

✠ PRAY ✠

Dear Heavenly Father,

Fill our lives with the richness that comes from your divine grace.
Guide us to the projects that need our loving touch.
We are here to serve, Lord. Amen.

august 21

EMBRACE THE PLAN

As they were proceeding on their journey someone said to him, "I will follow you wherever you go." Jesus answered him, "Foxes have dens and birds of the sky have nests, but the Son of Man has nowhere to rest his head" (Luke 9:57–58).

After I graduated from college, I called several places "home." My mom said, "Home is wherever you hang your hat." I hoped some day I would find a rewarding job, buy a nice house, marry the man of my dreams, and have a few children. That was my dream, not realizing God's plan for me involved adopting orphans from Romania.

Whatever God's plan is for you, roll with it; let it unfold the way God desires. It's easier to adjust when you accept that you are living out God's plan, even if it's different from what you originally imagined. My life turned out better with adopted children. But if you'd asked me after college if I wanted to adopt kids from Romania, that wouldn't have been my first choice. Yet, listening to God and his ways brought more love, blessings, excitement, and happiness into my life.

It's possible that your plan is the same plan as God's. But there is a chance that he wants you to do something different. Maybe it wasn't your idea to raise children with a learning disorder or a personality disorder. Maybe you hoped your kids would be musically gifted or talented athletes, but they're not. Perhaps following Jesus means that you must let go of certain dreams. Decide to embrace the dreams God has in store for you regardless of what it is. What do you think God's plan for you is? What would you give up to follow Jesus and join his mission?

REFLECT

Embrace God's plan for you, even if it might seem unappealing initially. The first time I saw a chestnut in its prickly outer shell, that looked unappealing, too. But after I tasted it, I loved it! Give God's plan a chance.

✠ PRAY ✠

Dear Heavenly Father,

Speak and I will listen. Ask and I will answer. Lead and I will follow. I will rest in your love and lay my weary head on your sturdy shoulder after I do all it is you want of me. Amen.

august 22

DON'T WORRY

Do not worry about tomorrow; tomorrow will take care of itself. Sufficient for a day is its own evil (Matthew 6:34).

In September 1988, Bobby McFerrin released the song "Don't Worry, Be Happy." The corny lyrics drive home the first part of the message from this Bible passage: an optimistic outlook to live each day fully because tomorrow is uncertain. The second part of the message has a hint of pessimism, suggesting the evil of each day makes it hard enough to get through one day let alone worrying about two.

My mom used to say, "Don't worry about tomorrow, it may not come; just get through today." We can't assume that God will grant us another day, so it's wise to make today really count. The message Mom wanted me to hear: worrying is a waste of time, thought, and nervous energy. When my children were younger, I would worry for nothing because what I fretted about never happened.

Each time I handed my daughters the car keys, I worried. While I trusted their driving abilities, I was concerned about everything that could go wrong. The worry made me sick until I put it in God's hands and trusted that he would watch over them. Reality drives us to plan for the worst, even though it might not ever happen. We saved aggressively after we adopted our children, fearing financial ruin if my husband lost his job in the recession. Having a plan, ensuring there was a cushion, allowed us to sleep easier at night. What kind of action will you take to enable you to stop worrying?

REFLECT

What are you worrying about? Raising teenagers is a battle, and while there is plenty we can worry about, God wants us to trust him more, giving our problems to him, and pray unceasingly.

✠ PRAY ✠

Dear Heavenly Father,

Take care of us, Lord. I give you my worries and concerns. Put ideas in my mind to enable me to move past them. I take comfort knowing you are always with me in good times and bad. Thank you for this day and the promise of tomorrow. Amen.

august 23

A MOTHER'S INFLUENCE

When the wine ran short, the mother of Jesus said to him, "They have no wine." [And] Jesus said to her, "Woman, how does your concern affect me? My hour has not yet come." His mother said to the servers, "Do whatever he tells you" (John 2:3–6).

Sometimes a mother just knows when trouble is brewing. At Cana, Mary wanted to spare the bride and groom's embarrassment when the wine ran out, so she turned to Jesus for help. She knew Jesus would surely do something if she asked. Mary knew that her motherly influence could impact Jesus to do something great even though there were no miracles before this moment. Mary knew his potential. She believed in his capabilities. Sometimes a mother just knows.

Even though you don't have proof, is there something you just know about your daughter? Perhaps you are confident of her potential even though she doesn't see it or feel it. Like Mary, you might have to prod your child to do something you believe she is capable of. Maybe your daughter lacks the confidence to try out for a play or apply for a part-time job.

REFLECT

It isn't easy encouraging your teenager to step outside of her comfort zone to try something new. In Cana, Jesus performed his first miracle. You never know what your adolescent is capable of until she tries. Just be sure you're also there to help pick up the pieces if she fails.

✠ PRAY ✠

Dear Heavenly Father,

Enable me to motivate (name) to branch out and grow into the person you created her to be. I believe in your plan. Fill me with encouraging words to expand her horizons. Amen.

august 24

GOD'S LOVE NEVER CHANGES

Your years last through all generations. Of old you laid the earth's foundations; the heavens are the work of your hands. They perish, but you remain; they all wear out like a garment; Like clothing you change them and they are changed, but you are the same, your years have no end (Psalm 102:25–28).

I visited Banff National Park in Alberta, Canada, when I was a teenager. I was in awe of the beauty of the glaciers that formed the majestic mountain peaks and sparkling lakes. I hoped to revisit to marvel over its beauty again. As an adult I returned to find much of the glacier had melted; the landscape was transformed. It's hard to believe that mountains and lakes change, but they do with time, fluctuations in temperature, the flowing of streams, and blowing of the wind.

Consider how much your kids have changed over the years. They are taller and more self-sufficient now that they are teenagers. You can even see differences in their personalities. Humans change. We grow and mature; we wear out and, eventually, die. But God is eternal and truly unchangeable. The foundation of the earth is a reflection of his strength, which exists for his eternal glory. As we change, problems and judgments of Christ's Church shift. Our climate changes, our wealth fluctuates, our living and breathing world oscillates, but God exists forever.

REFLECT

Sometimes it's difficult to embrace the changes in our families, especially when our kids start dating. Cling to God's love because it never varies. God has always taken care of his people throughout generations. Take comfort knowing God will care for you, too. God will help you through the teenage years, the hormonal surges, the outbursts, and the drama. God will walk the bumpy road with you.

✠ PRAY ✠

Dear Heavenly Father,

Allow me to feel comforted by your unchanging presence and never-ending love. You alone are my rock and my salvation. With you I can do anything. Amen.

august 25

CHEW ON WORDS

You will eat until you are fully satisfied, then you will praise the name of the Lord, your God, who acts so wondrously on your behalf! (Joel 2:26).

Mealtime was interesting when my daughters were young. While we ate, we would take turns discussing the good and bad of our day. This practice allowed each person a platform to speak openly without interruption or judgment. This method gave my daughters a turn to celebrate their achievements, discuss disappointments, and share sorrows. This exercise was initially implemented to prevent one kid from monopolizing the dinner discussion. However, as time passed, we all anticipated our roundtable discussions more than the actual meal.

When my daughters were teenagers, topics for discussion evolved into lengthy debates over which colleges to apply to, which friends were hosting parties and who was going, who needed to use the car, or what would make a good part-time job. It's important to have a safe place to allow your teens to voice their concerns or opinions about the events of their day. Is what you are doing in your home working?

REFLECT

There may not be a perfect way to bring up delicate topics or to open discussions when kids clam up. The important thing is to let your kids know that they can feel safe to talk to you about any issues that concern them. My family incorporates food into discussions. Food keeps us grounded. This might not work for every family, but it's worth a try.

✠ PRAY ✠

Dear Heavenly Father,

Direct my family to an amicable way to open family discussions.
When our kids talk to us, we feel connected to them.
Strengthen our bonds. Empower us to be the best parents.
Amen.

august 26

WHERE THERE IS LIGHT

There the angel of the Lord *appeared to him as fire flaming out of a bush. When he looked, although the bush was on fire, it was not being consumed* (Exodus 3:2).

We have a small fire pit in our back yard. Throughout the summer months we have bonfires where we burn tree branches while we gather to talk or share stories. Some nights after the flames have died down, the last marshmallow has been roasted, and only hot coals remain, we linger to marvel over the fireflies or twinkling stars overhead. There is something magical about a bonfire. It attracts us like a moth to a flame, and even when it has died down, we hesitate to leave.

As a kid I used to gather around a bonfire with my cousins to tell ghost stories before going to bed. As a teenager, we listened to our parents talk about the days when they were kids. The fire was a place for us to gather and reflect or just relax with those we love. Bonfires brought us together. All of my childhood memories of bonfires are warm and encompassing.

Some schools have huge bonfires as a part of their homecoming pep rallies. Students gather to sing songs or use the fire as an ending spot to a parade. In Christian religious tradition, a fire is considered to be the "Seat of God," the symbol of the presence of God. The light eradicates darkness, which implies evil. In the Bible, God appears before Moses in the form of fire at the bush on Mount Sinai. The fire during the Christmas liturgy signifies the burning bush Moses witnessed, symbolically linking us to the glory of God.

REFLECT

Can you incorporate fire to unite your teens closer in your family life? Maybe you could build your own fire pit or involve your kids in storytelling around it.

✠ PRAY ✠

Dear Heavenly Father,

Let the fire of warmth that burns within me spread to my family members in such an affectionate way that it draws us closer to each other. Shine your love on all of us, Lord. Amen.

august 27

ASPIRATIONS TO SAINTHOOD

To the holy ones and faithful brothers in Christ in Colossae: grace to you and peace from God our Father (Colossians 1:2).

Saint Monica is venerated for her virtues, particularly her suffering with the adultery of her husband, and a prayerful life dedicated to reforming her son. She is considered the patron saint of mothers because she never lost hope in her rebellious son, Augustine. Saint Monica urged Augustine to change his life, and she prayed fastidiously for his conversion. Her example of devout faith and steadfast love finally convinced Augustine to reject his sinful life and he converted. He now is St. Augustine.

One of Timothy Cardinal Dolan's goals is to become a saint. Why can't we all do that? Like St. Monica, we can all pray for the conversion of our kids when they go astray. We can kill them with kindness, love them unconditionally, and be more accepting of their differences. Saints were just ordinary people, like you and me, who did extraordinary things. But really, how extraordinary is it to pray without ceasing? It's within our power to aspire to sainthood. When teenagers roll their eyes, it's hard to be nice to them, especially when we want to groan. When they break rules, it's difficult to be trusting and fair. We aren't expected to be a doormat and let our kids walk all over us. But we should be pleasant and kind, loving, and reasonable.

REFLECT

How mindful are you in nurturing your relationship with your daughter? Do you pay attention to your teenager on a conscious level, or could you be taking your kid for granted? How will you put your teenager on your priority list while being respectful, realistic, compassionate, credible, and prayerful?

✠ PRAY ✠

Dear Heavenly Father,

Help me to be more like St. Monica.
Teach me to be kinder and more generous with (name).
I am sorry that I haven't been as loving as I could be.
Enable me to be less judgmental and more accepting of the differences between us. Thank you, Lord, for giving me this child. Amen.

august 28

HOW BIG ARE YOUR PRAYERS?

Now to him who is able to accomplish far more than all we ask or imagine, by the power at work within us, to him be glory in the church and in Christ Jesus to all generations, forever and ever. Amen (Ephesians 3:20–21).

Several years ago, our quest was to find a suitable university for my older daughter to study. One campus had an enormous library building filled with more books than any one person could possibly read in a lifetime. Standing beside it like a tiny ant, I realized just how limited my knowledge was and how vast God's is. God's infinite wisdom has no boundaries because he is all-knowing, all-encompassing, and all-powerful.

Think for a moment about all that God created: the universe and everything in it. Think about everything he has done in the world and in your own life. Not only can God work miracles on a grand scale, but he can also touch your small life with the answers to trivial prayers, too. Your prayers are not too big, insignificant, or impossible for God. He can do anything.

REFLECT

Whatever is happening in your life with your teenagers, call out to God for help. He knows how to settle everything. All of your prayers are important to him. Maybe you are worried about the upcoming school year or your child behind the wheel of your car. If God can split the Red Sea, he can help your family, too.

✠ PRAY ✠

Dear Heavenly Father,

Sometimes I'm afraid I ask too much of you.
My hands are full raising teenagers. I am at the end of my rope.
Help me, Lord! Help me untangle the mess I am in.
Show me the light at the end of the tunnel.
Tell me that light is you shining the way for me.
Call me and I will follow. Amen.

august 29

MOVE ON THROUGH HOPE

The Lord, our God, said to us at Horeb, "You have stayed long enough at this mountain" (Deuteronomy 1:6).

As the summer ends and your kids are restless about returning to school, what can you do to help ease them through the process? The first thing we did in our home was establish a new bedtime. During the summer months our girls liked to stay up late and sleep in, but that schedule won't work once school starts, so we scaled back a week or two before Labor Day. What do you do differently once the new school year approaches?

Perhaps your kids are heading to high school or college for the first time. Many parents go "school shopping" for necessary supplies to springboard them into a new level of learning. This doesn't mean your wallet has to be assaulted getting them designer clothes so they'll be the coolest-looking kid on campus. Now that your teens are older, can they pay for a portion of their new school items? Teach them how to recycle or reuse last year's materials.

Changing from one learning environment to another isn't easy on you or your kids. But change is an important part of growth. Part of our job as parents is to let our kids go. You did this the first time your child climbed on the big yellow school bus when she entered kindergarten. You were probably filled with hope as you encouraged her to leave the security and love of home. God tells us when it's time to move on.

REFLECT

Consider what is changing in your own life and what coping techniques you can use to move through this new school year.

✠ PRAY ✠

Dear Heavenly Father,

Give me the courage to free (name) as she begins a new school year. Enable us all to move through the experience filled with hopefulness and optimism. Give us the insight to make intelligent decisions for the growth and development of our teens.
Amen.

august 30

WISE YOUTHFULNESS

Rejoice, O youth, while you are young and let your heart be glad in the days of your youth. Follow the ways of your heart, the vision of your eyes; yet understand regarding all this that God will bring you to judgment. Banish misery from your heart and remove pain from your body, for youth and black hair are fleeting (Ecclesiastes 11:9–10).

Have you seen your high school yearbook photograph recently and thought how young you looked back then? You might have a different hairstyle or glasses. Do you remember your hopes and dreams back then? Today's Bible passage reminds us to enjoy our youth before it's gone. It beckons you to follow your dreams remembering that God judges you for what you do. Don't let your worries weigh you down. However, remember that youth, with a whole life before it, still faces the threat of meaninglessness.

You were a teenager once. Consider if you are trying to form your kids into a clone of yourself or if you are allowing them to grow individually into their own skin. There is a fine line distinguishing guiding them purposefully in love and respect to march to the beat of their own drum or funneling them to fit your mold. Just because something worked for you doesn't mean it will work for your teenagers.

REFLECT

Does your parish have an active youth program that your teenagers would enjoy being a part of? Maybe you could start one to ensure your kids have a safe environment to enjoy being young while learning more about God and living his word.

✠ PRAY ✠

Dear Heavenly Father,

Thank you for my youthfulness, for it allows me to act favorably, honoring you while I raise my family. Fill my mind with invigorating ideas to pique (name)'s curiosity about you;
to love, honor, and be respectful of you always.
Amen.

august 31

SAGE ADVICE

Hear, my son, your father's instruction, and reject not your mother's teaching; A graceful diadem will they be for your head; a pendant for your neck. My son, should sinners entice you, do not go if they say, "Come along with us!" (Proverbs 1:8–11).

I still ask my parents for advice. They have profound wisdom and experience; maybe because they have been around the block a few more times than I have. They have seen it all with a house full of children, grandchildren, and great-grandchildren. However, I'm sure that when I was a teen I didn't think their advice was so sage. My folks were concerned about preventing me from making the same mistakes that they made. Isn't that what we want for our kids, too?

When my daughter was overspending, I encouraged her to save. I didn't want her to go into debt and incur high interest fees. But she went into debt, and all I could do was pray that she would come to her senses. When your advice gets ignored, hand the problem to God and trust that he knows what to do. Ponder if you have ever disregarded the Lord's words for you. Maybe you thought God was calling you to do something you didn't want to do, so you chose not to hear. After acknowledging my daughter's spending problem, I felt God calling me to bring her a bag of groceries, but I was so angry at her that I didn't want to do it. Paying attention to Christ's words will guide the oblivious into the saving knowledge of the truth. Where there is a sympathetic heart and an inclination to accept the truth in love, wisdom is the best prize.

REFLECT

What advice have you been trying to give to your teenager?

✠ PRAY ✠

Dear Heavenly Father,

Fill my head and heart with your inexhaustible love.
Tell me what to say to (name) and guide me because I don't know what to do. Take this problem, Lord, for you know how to handle it. Please, Lord, turn it into something wonderful. I trust in you, Lord.
Amen.

ACKNOWLEDGMENTS

I am profoundly indebted to Patrick Canale, my soul mate and best friend. Thank you from the bottom of my heart for journeying through our convoluted life with a calm demeanor, eloquence, and fortitude. You are a wonderful father to our daughters, with an endless reservoir of love and devotion. Your ability to sift through the gravel to find the diamonds in our daughters makes you a true gem. Sharing the parenting responsibility with you has been a gift. I truly appreciate your remarkable ideas and heartfelt stories to share with other parents who read this book. Your unwavering love and devotion moved me through many roadblocks.

To Juliana and Andrea, thank you for allowing me to bring stories about you to life in order to encourage parents everywhere to seek the silver lining that parenting teenagers is worth the extra effort. You are a joy, and I thank God for bringing you both into my life.

This book wouldn't be complete without acknowledging my friend and pastor, Reverend Monsignor J. Robert Yeazel, for his friendship, his spiritual guidance, and his immeasurable words of inspiration.

I am sincerely grateful to my editor, Theresa Nienaber, who believed in this project and worked diligently on it to see it through to completion. You transformed it into something quite magnificent! Thank you to you and the entire Liguori staff for making it possible to enrich the lives of the parents of teenagers.

To my loving Lord, who gives me everything and keeps my life on track, I thank you for it all.

Barbara Canale
Jamesville, NY
June 2015

Other Devotional Books by Barbara Canale...

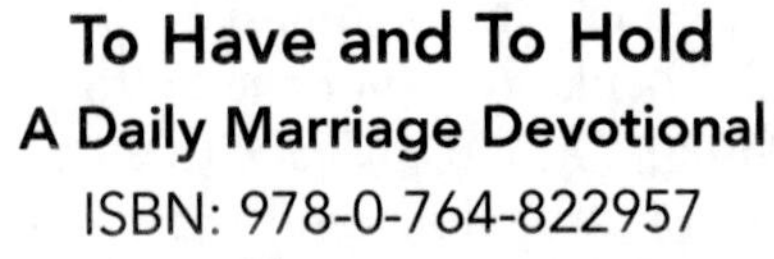

To Have and To Hold

A Daily Marriage Devotional

ISBN: 978-0-764-822957

Prayer is integral in building strong marriages. By combining Scripture with heartfelt and thought-provoking reflections, this 366-day devotional (leap year included!) will help couples keep their marriages sacred and strong—with the awareness that all relationships journey through peaks and valleys. Use this book to develop holy habits for your marriage and family.

Prayers, Papers, and Play

Devotions for Every College Student

ISBN: 978-0-764-821547

Barbara Canale encourages college students to continue to embrace their faith while away from home. Taking only a few minutes each day, each devotion begins with a Scripture quote accompanied by a short reflection and a prayer. The themes follow the academic year and center on the unique experiences of college life.

CPSIA information can be obtained at www.ICGtesting.com
Printed in the USA
LVOW06s0404310815

452064LV00005B/9/P